wild water WEST VIRGINIA

A PADDLER'S GUIDE TO THE
WHITE WATER RIVERS
OF THE MOUNTAIN STATE

BOB BURRELL
and
PAUL DAVIDSON

FIRST EDITION 1972
REPRINTED 1973
SECOND EDITION 1975
REPRINTED 1977
REPRINTED 1980

THOMAS PRESS

PO Box 2210, Ann Arbor, MI 48106

Standard Book Number 87012-123-5
Library of Congress Card Number 72-77291
Printed in the United States of America

Printed in West Virginia
By McClain Printing Company
Parsons

TABLE OF CONTENTS

Preface vii

Introduction ix

Glossary xv

White Water Difficulty Rating System xix

River Gauges xxi

Finding Your Way in West Virginia xxiii

Chapter I—George Washington's River and Its Tributaries—The Potomac Drainage 1

Introduction 1
Abram Creek 6
Stony River—2 sections 7
North Branch—3 sections 9
Seneca Creek 13
North Fork—4 sections 14
Moorefield River—2 sections 18
South Branch—6 sections 20
Lost River 26
Cacapon—3 sections 27
Shenandoah 30
The Main Stem of the Potomac 32
Other Streams in the Potomac Basin—Back Creek, North River, Patterson Creek, New Creek, Lunice Creek, Thorn Creek, Tearcoat Creek, Sleepy Creek, Little Cacapon River 33

Chapter II—The Big Mountain River—The Mighty Cheat 35

Introduction 35
Otter Creek 38
Shavers Fork—5 sections 39
Glady Fork 45
Laurel Fork—2 sections 46
Gandy 49

Red Creek 50
Dry Fork—3 sections 51
Blackwater—2 sections 54
Black Fork of Cheat 57
Buffalo Creek 57
Saltlick Creek 58
Muddy Creek 58
Horseshoe Run 59
Cheat—4 sections 60
Big Sandy—4 sections 66

Chapter III—Fastest Water to the North—The Tygart Sub-Basin 69

Introduction 69
Middle Fork—2 sections 71
Buckhannon—3 sections 73
Tygart—7 sections 76
Three Fork Creek 84

Chapter IV—Miscellaneous Streams In the Ohio Drainage 86

Introduction 86
Miscellaneous Accounts of Dunkard, Hughes, Middle Island, Wheeling, and Little Wheeling Creeks 86
Decker's Creek—2 sections 88
Little Kanawha 90
Whiteday Creek 91

Chapter V—The Beautiful Valley River—The Greenbrier 92

Introduction 92
Greenbrier—10 sections 95
Anthony Creek 100
Miscellaneous Greenbrier Tributaries 101

Chapter VI—Wildest Water From the Central Heartland 102

Introduction 102
Williams—3 sections 105
Cranberry—3 sections 107
North Fork of Cherry 110
Laurel Creek 110
South Fork of Cherry 111
Cherry 112
Meadow River—3 sections 113
Gauley—7 sections 116

Left Fork of Holly 124
Back Fork of Elk 125
Elk—3 sections 126

**Chapter VII—Big Water From the South—
The New and Bluestone 129**
Introduction 129
Bluestone 132
New—6 sections 135
Piney Creek 142

**Chapter VIII—Troubled Waters
Draining the West 143**
Introduction 143
Armstrong Creek 145
Coal 146
Little Coal 147
Guyandotte 148
Paint Creek 149
Tug 150

**Chapter IX—And a Couple From
Neighboring States 151**
Introduction 151
Youghiogheny—3 sections 152
Savage 157
Casselman 159

Index 161

COVER: Lower Keeney Creek Rapids in the New River Gorge. Arnout Hyde, Jr., photo. Reprinted from WONDERFUL WEST VIRGINIA Magazine, West Virginia Department of Natural Resources.

PREFACE TO THE SECOND EDITION

The first edition of this book was the outgrowth of three years of data accumulation and experience on West Virginia white water following our original book, *A Canoeist's Guide to the Whitewater Rivers of West Virginia.* Another three years have been associated with more change and experience necessitating another revision of our book in an attempt to keep it a current and meaningful guide.

White water paddling sport is expanding to an ever increasing rate. Ten years ago no one knew what it was. Five years ago we could not find anyone to paddle with. Now it is getting crowded at the popular sites. Our attitude toward guidebooks is ambivalent. Do we want to advertise the sport into an undesirable state of urbanization? Or does this guide serve to dilute out the congestion by pointing out new runs? Hopefully the growth of the sport will level off before saturation destroys the wilderness experience quality. West Virginia is to eastern white water as Vermont was to skiing twenty years ago. We think with wise planning, white water can become a major tourist activity in this mountain state.

This edition features a number of new runs, some of which were too tough for our state of the art in 1972, some of which are difficult to catch and were only "discovered" since 1972, some of which changed because of new access points, and some of which we reexperienced and decided our earlier impressions were significantly enough wrong to warrant a rewrite. We have paddled over 2,000 more miles of West Virginia white water since the first edition. We have tried to keep from becoming too sophisticated and have tried to approach each new run in the same wide-eyed state of an intermediate paddler. The guidebook is intended to introduce the intermediate paddler to some different white water runs so we want to be cautious lest we lead him into a poor experience either because a run is overrated or because it is broadcast as easier than found.

A guidebook by definition can not be entirely complete. If the descriptions were so detailed that the paddler could vicariously experience every aspect of a trip there would be little reason to personally explore a river. The most we can do is give the paddler some evenings of planning, some water levels we have experienced and how to compare with other trips, some timesaving hints on how to get on and off the water, a rough guide to help avoid getting on water that is not suited to the reader's experience, and a few points to dispute. We welcome comments and criticisms and will catalog them carefully for consideration during future revisions of Wildwater West Virginia.

Finally, we wish to dedicate this guide to the late Randy Carter, the man from whom we first learned about white water paddling and the wealth of such water in the Mountain State. We have tried to follow the high standards Randy set in his guidebooks and we hope we have done more than simply borrow his graphic format. We hope also that paddlers using this book will have the same regard for clean, free flowing streams that Randy maintained throughout his life.

B. B.
P. D.

INTRODUCTION

This guide is a collective effort of members of the West Virginia Wildwater Association who since 1965 have been paddling and exploring the creeks, streams, and rivers in almost every nook and cranny in the state by means of white water boats and techniques. Their efforts have been hampered by sparse numbers, poor roads, long drives, faulty maps, and vagaries of the weather, so it is with an exceeding sense of pride that these collected experiences are offered to the white water paddler at large and those interested in the West Virginia out of doors in general. It is more than an encyclopedia of mountain rivers and hydrologic data. It is also a collection of experiences and memories, an introduction to some of the amazing geography that constitutes the Mountain State, and it is a plea for its preservation in an era when so many vested interests are unwisely abusing these treasures.

This is really a second edition of an earlier homemade effort burdened with the cumbersome appellation *A Canoeist's Guide to the Whitewater Rivers of West Virginia.* Most of the descriptions appearing in it have been rewritten and all of the known errors have been corrected. Hundreds of miles of additional experience and exploration have enabled us to be more precise and thorough in this edition. The present guide is an attempt to be as comprehensive for the entire state as possible, perhaps an overly ambitious goal. No one will ever run all of the white water in our state, but we feel that all of the significant water and a good deal of the insignificant have been dealt with here.

This book is aimed at the intermediate to advanced paddler who possesses the basic skills and judgement to paddle moving water. It is not for the flatwater boater who fancies himself ready for anything because he managed to cross a lake in a high wind once without tipping over or the self-styled expert who boasts that he is so good that he has never had to kneel in a canoe. Such people will kill themselves with this book. For those novices or beginning intermediates who are seriously interested in white water technique, let this guide be a challenge for them to improve their skills to meet the river, but not a challenge to tackle a river beyond their ability.

Similarly, the guide is not for the real expert who considers the Cheat Canyon "a good winter river," who runs the North Branch at 7′, or who runs the entire Gauley without scouting. Such people of exceptional ability, stamina, and courage do not need books, only maps. These folks might belittle this effort and think we have overstated the case. Rather, this book is for the majority of paddlers who are interested in action, yes, but not to the exclusion of everything else. We are aiming this book at the person who gets turned on as much by Class 2 as Class 4 water.

The guide includes a few explanatory sections which both the seasoned paddler and the curious non-paddler should read first. Usually one finds a glossary at the end of a book, but ours is placed first to sort of set the tone for the descriptions, give you an idea of what to expect, and to get the housekeeping chores out of the way. We suggest you read the entire glossary first so that you will know how we use the specialized terms. Similarly, since the subject of river classification is so controversial, we have gone to great lengths to explain our values of river rating. This likewise should be read first. Each system of rivers has been provided with a regional introduction and each is accompanied by a short bibliography concerning further information about that region. At the end of the book, there is a general bibliography to the technical aspects of white water sport and other informative guides.

Our river ratings and descriptions contain certain biases which should be pointed out. Our ratings will seem conservative by experts' eyes, but as we have stated above, the ratings are not for the experts. The ratings are not as conservative as our earlier effort and we feel that most will agree with our conclusions. Most of the information was written from the point of view of the C-1 paddler so that when we say the waves are chest high, the C-2 bowman and the K-1 paddler will have to realize that such will be up to his ears. Paddlers in open boats are considered on some of the gentler rivers, but are on their own for the others. Also, we have not given much consideration to C-2s. If we say the maneuvering is intense, then your C-2 partner had better be awfully good and the two of you work extremely well as a team. In general we believe neither age nor sex need be any limitation in white water sport, but if we (who are in reasonably good shape for our late 30s) say that paddling is strenuous or hard work, make your own allowances.

In general we have tried to be honest in our descriptions and we have tried very hard not to let our familiarity with certain rivers breed contempt. The response from the first edition seemed to indicate that we have succeeded. If we have not run a river personally, we have said so either by stating that such is a scouting report or else by presenting the river as a general description without any statistics. Paddlers of such streams should therefore be prepared for surprises. The book was not written from the topo maps or from the car except in those few places so indicated. The reason for including them at all was to make the guide comprehensive for the entire state and also serve as an inspiration to those who are still looking for unrun, untried rivers.

We are aware that running a river a few times increases your familiarity and decreases your apprehension or respect. As paddling skills and techniques improve, what once was considered difficult, now becomes commonplace. When Walter Burmeister and Erich Seidel first ran the New below Hinton in 1959 in decked foldboats, they were apprehensive about running all of the big ledges and were filled with a sense of accomplishment at successfully running Brooks Falls. Today we consider it a good family run in open boats—wives, kiddies, pets, the works. When John Berry first led an exploratory trip into the Cheat Canyon in 1957 using half-decked Grummans, it took him two days. Today, using equipment that John helped design and knowing techniques and skills he pioneered, we breeze through in 3 hours if we are in a hurry. What this is leading up to is a plea for future readers to respect the time and the level of skills during which this guide was written. In a few more years when running the Gauley is commonplace and that kid of yours in the Cub Scout uniform breezes through the Blackwater Canyon on a Sunday afternoon, don't pooh-pooh this guide. As far we we know we are with it in paddling circles as of 1972.

This book in addition to describing the rivers in as much informative detail as practical, provides explicit shuttle directions. Finding your way around this state is very difficult and even the major attractions are poorly marked. We have included reproductions of maps from the West Virginia Department of Highways and the forest service as well as some homemade jobs for those regions where access points are especially hard to find. Hence this book should be carried in the car to help locate the put ins and take outs. (You should also have an additional copy in your pack and since it is likely to get wet, you should have a third copy at home.) Most of these sites are reachable by ordinary car providing there is no snow. A few are usable only by high-clearance, 4-wheel drive vehicles. Some roads are privately owned and permission must be obtained first, while no roads of any kind even exist to the access points of a few rivers.

Each description gives the river miles traversed between put in and take out. We have given very conservative paddling times for each which do not allow any extra for lunch, scouting, playing, or slothful behavior. Wind, flips, river speed, and your ability will greatly alter these times. In general, figure on 3 mph. Right and left refer to directions as you look downstream unless otherwise specified. The river classification is based on that system devised by the American Whitewater Affiliation although we prefer Arabic to Roman numerals. More of this later. We have defined gradient as the average drop of the river in feet per mile (fpm). If parts of the river drop at a value significantly different
40
than the average, we have given that information as 3@60 which means that although the average is 40 fpm, 3 miles of it drop at 60 fpm. Such figures are meaningful only to one who has tried to paddle down such a gradient.

Merely knowing the gradient isn't enough. One must compare this figure with the volume. A 2′ wave on a small stream simply cannot be compared with the force behind a similar wave on a large powerful river. Similarly, a Class 4 small river is something quite different from a Class 4 of larger volume. We have used as an index of volume the annual mean discharge in cfs where 400 is the division between small and medium and 1500 between medium and large. As a rule of thumb, rivers are runnable when the flow equals or exceeds this value. They should be avoided during seasons when they are below this figure as well as when they exceed a value three times their average discharge. The small rivers are early spring and very late fall runs. The larger rivers have a fall-winter-spring season, but with dangerous mid-season high levels. The largest river, the New, is safe only in the summer and early fall. Often the government bureaus can give you the cfs flow of a particular river and knowing the mean annual discharge of a river you are familiar with will help you in comparing it with a river new to you.

Each river has its own personality when it comes to "too high" and "too low" and must be learned by experience. What might be too low for an aluminum canoe with two passengers may still be runnable by a C-1 white water canoe. The first figure given under level is the lowest it has been run and the second figure is the highest (in our experience). In general, our zeros are rather liberal as we do not enjoy scraping over too low rivers. Measuring the discharge of a river consists of measuring the cross sectional area and flow velocity of the river over the full range of its levels at the gauging site. Since the most readily measurable of these related variables is the surface level, tables are compiled relating the discharge in cubic feet of water per second (cfs) to depth measured in hundredths of feet. Where these gauges are convenient, we have used them to indicate runnable levels on each river section. At other places there are gauges painted on bridges and rocks by various paddlers. These boating gauges are done in the style of Randy Carter where zero is the minimal paddling level in the maker's estimation. One advantage of the more exact government gauges is that the information is collected and recorded daily. One can determine the level of the rivers over a wide area by making a few key phone calls. Some of the more pertinent follow:

Potomac Basin	(301) 899-3210
Monongahela Basin	(412) 644-2890
Kanawha Basin	(304) 529-2318 Ext. 604

The continuity of rapids must also be taken into account, but this is difficult to give a value. In the lower Smoke Hole there is only one Class 4ish rapids. If you get through this, you may not necessarily be ready to run the North Branch of the Potomac where there is one Class 3 or 4 rapids after the other in almost continuous succession. The New, Cacapon, Greenbrier, and middle Yough are rivers that have widely spaced rapids, while Glady Fork, Seneca Creek, Meadow, and Savage are rivers practically containing one long continuous rapids each. Paddlers who are comfortable on the Cacapon will find the lower Glady Fork much more exciting although the difficulty of the individual rapids is no greater.

Scenery is ranked on an A to D scale with A being considered remote, wilderness areas and little sign of civilization; B would be more settled, but still beautiful pastoral countryside; C ratings include a lot of development, either cities or industry or nothing special about the setting; while D is reserved for acid pollution, strip mines, tipples, slag-heaps, povertyvilles, gross pollution, and other ultimate forms of land-scape abuse. The quality of such scenery can be changed quickly. The Elk River below Sutton is usually considered B, even A at times, but immediately becomes D when it passes through Clay. Cities and man-made settings need not be detracting. Parsons, Philippi, Petersburg, and especially Harpers Ferry are towns that look pretty when paddled through. Morgantown, Richwood, and Webster Springs do not.

So much for the technical aspects of this guide, but let it serve a purpose for other types of readers as well. To the person interested in the out of doors or the geography of West Virginia, let it serve as a way to show you the state as very few people see it and to point out places of wonder that you didn't even know existed. To the person that is fascinated by the sight and sound of moving water, let it be a lesson in applied hydrology. To shutterbugs everywhere, let it be a lure to provide you with subject matter for your film whether you are interested in action, natural beauty, or novel backgrounds for your nudes. To the occasional chicken thief, let it serve as a source of ideas for novel ways out of town. Finally, to federal and state legislators, the U.S. Army Corps of Engineers, the purveyors of electric power, and anyone else who believes that our public rivers are their own personal property just waiting for exploitation for private profit, let it serve as a warning of the treasures that they would destroy. Above all, let this book be a catalog of descriptions of some of our best natural resources that have not been described anywhere from such a continuous, river level viewpoint. Let this guide awaken in all citizens a quest for knowledge and an appreciation of West Virginia's magnificent rivers, so that they can help us repulse such river rapers. If this book piques the curiosity of just one non-paddler enough to cause that person to see what some of these treasures are and what is happening to them, it will be considered a success.

See you on the river!

GLOSSARY

White water paddling, like most everything else, has its own lexicon of cant expressions used to describe itself. The following glossary was felt necessary for three reasons: (1) to explain to the white water paddler precisely what we mean by these terms as usage tends to vary from region to region; (2) to explain to the non-paddler the lingo of applied hydrology; and (3) to explain some of these words or meanings which may not be found elsewhere or even exist.

DESCRIPTIVE ADJECTIVES:

Juicy—a particularly heavy, aerated turbulence in which the C-1 boater gets hit in the chest and a K-1 in his face.

Good—depends on who is talking; refers to anything from Class 1 to 5. An expert considers Class 5 as good and 1 as bad, but with a novice it's vice versa.

Bad—see good.

Bodacious—a particularly expressive adjective borrowed from one of Appalachia's most celebrated heroes, Snuffy Smith. Used to describe anything in a truly superlative way.

Horrendous—a Langdale-Smithian adjective reserved for the most ferocious rapids. A cultured variant of "bodacious."

HYDROLOGY AND HAZARDS:

Rapids—collective noun referring to either a singular or plural set of waves, turbulences, etc., on a river. Like our pants and scissors, we do not use the word without a final "s."

Riffle—a shallow rapids with very small waves.

Pillow—see "padded boulder."

Rock Garden—a rapids of Class 2 or 3 complexity characterized by many small exposed or partially covered boulders that necessitate care in maneuvering.

Boulder Garden—a bodacious rock garden.

Haystack—caused by deceleration of current due to underwater resistance. A high standing wave. Height of waves is measured from the trough to the crest. Only evident when on the water. To get an idea of what the paddler experiences when getting ready to paddle a 7′ wave, sit or kneel in front of a door and look up at the top of the jamb.

Curler—a wave that curls or falls back on itself (upstream).

Surfing Wave—a very wide wave that is fairly steep. Used for playing around on. A good paddler can slide into it and either stay balanced on its upstream face or else travel back and forth across it much in the same manner as a surfer in the ocean.

Stopper—any very heavy wave or turbulence that quickly impedes the downriver progress of a fastly paddled boat.

Keeper—a bodacious stopper. A dangerous situation found in very heavy water which would be extremely difficult if not impossible to get out of if accidentally entered. A bad trip and to be avoided.

Hole or Souse Hole—the condition resulting from the turbulence created when fast water pours over a boulder which creates a depression of aerated turbulence immediately downstream of the boulder. Will impede progress of boat and vigorous paddling is required to free boat from the back current.

Hydraulic—similar to a souse hole only caused by water moving quickly over a low ledge or dam. Hydrologically, the two are very similar. The violent, downward hydraulic action of the water over the boulder often forces the stern downwards with equal violence while the bow is forced upwards on the turbulence thus cracking the stern smartly.

Slide Rapids—an elongated ledge that descends or slopes gently rather than abruptly and is covered usually with only shallow water. Terminates in stopper-type waves.

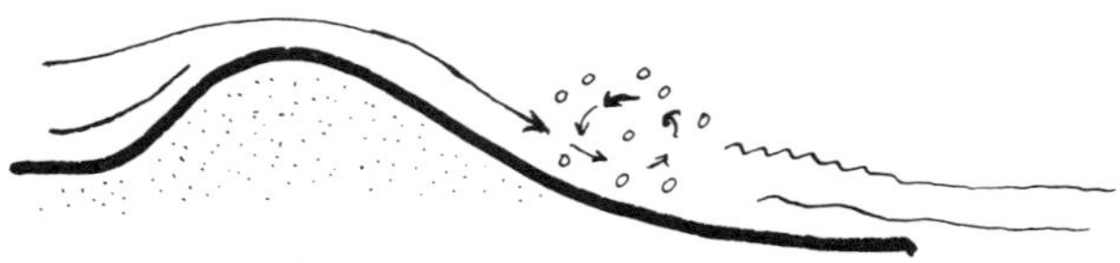

SOUSE HOLE

HAYSTACKS

SLIDE RAPIDS WITH A CURLER AND HAYSTACKS AT BOTTOM

Drop—an abrupt descent in the middle of a rapids.

Falls—a bodacious drop although not necessarily straight down (a localism).

Pool—flatwater; no rapids.

Eddy—any area of reversed flow, usually downstream of an obstruction. Last name of a famous singer. In eastern West Virginia, used by locals to mean a pool.

Undercut Rock—a potentially dangerous situation where a large boulder on the outside of a bend has been eroded or undercut by centuries of water flow and which could trap a paddler if accidentally swept under it and pinned.

Low Water Bridge—a cheap bridge across the river that barely clears the surface of the water or may even be awash. Very dangerous for the paddler if in a fast current.

Padded Boulder—see "pillow."

CFS—cubic feet per second; an accurate method of expressing river flow in terms of function of flow and volume.

Gradient—the geographical drop of the river expressed in feet per mile (fpm).

PERSONNEL:

Locals—natives indigenous to the area being paddled who often have interesting ideas about the kind of people who are white water paddlers.

Skillful Paddlers—ourselves paddling a bodacious river.

Stupid Paddlers—others running a bodacious river without us.

U.S. Army Corps of Engineers—people who obtain drinking water from a full bathtub because they cannot stand the sight and sound of running water.

APPARATUS:

C-1—In this book it means a specialized, completely *and* integrally decked white water canoe which looks like a kayak to the uninitiated.

K-1—a white water kayak that looks like a kayak even to the initiated.

C-2—same as C-1, but seating two persons. Such esoteric varieties as "slalom" or "downriver" are beyond the scope of this book.

Open Boat—Loosely used by us to refer to any conventional canoe whether literally open or decked with canvas. This was not done to denigrate people who prefer to paddle complicated water in such boats. We simply do not know many people who are good at it and such will have to translate the descriptions to their own situations.

Deck—that part of the boat which covers the hull to prevent water from entering. Contains one or two cockpit openings for occupant(s).

Skirt—literally that; worn by paddler and fits snugly around waist at the top and around cockpit flange at the bottom to keep water from entering cockpit.

TECHNIQUE:

Flip—upset; wipe out; turn over; bottom up.

Roll—saving face after a flip by using a well-practiced paddle stroke when upside down that enables boat to be returned right side up with occupant still in place. Can only be done reliably with specialized white water craft and not with conventional canoes.

Shuttle—since it is impractical to paddle back up the river you have just descended, most paddling parties arrange to have a car(s) or other means of transportation at the take out point and then drive other cars to the put in. Often takes hours and is referred to as "setting up the shuttle." Shuttling is an art frequently foiled by lost car keys, flat tires, missed road signs, knocked out oil pans, and inept shuttlers.

Broach—to be turned broadside to the current; a no-no.

Blort—used in frisbee to denote when the wrimpleplatt falls short of the sprovit. Has no use in white water parlance.

Pinned—helplessly snagged or caught in a rapids by a forceful current pressing the paddler against an immovable object made worse if pinned between the boat and the object. A very dangerous situation.

Scout—to carefully examine a rapids before running it. The way to run a complex rapids may not be readily obvious.

Paddling by the Seat of Your Pants—paddling a river without any prior knowledge of it and without scouting.

Draw—basic paddling technique of moving boat sideways towards the paddle.

Pry—same, but away from the paddle.

Brace—basic paddling technique used most often to prevent boat from flipping in unstable situations. Exists in several varieties.

Snuck—past tense of sneak.

Sneak—to take a less formidable route around a difficult spot.

Take the Girl Scout Route—see sneak.

Eddy Out—one of the few ways a paddler has to stop in the middle of a rapids. Enter an eddy or area of differential current by turning 180° and pointing upstream. Very spectacular even if attempted and failed.

MISCELLANEOUS EXPRESSIONS:

Y'er crazier 'en hell!—frequent expression of locals observing white water paddler splash by.

Heave Ho!—what you do when you get seasick and you have eaten too much ho.

See you on the river—traditional sign-off used by white water paddlers in place of such trite expressions as good-bye, so long, be seein' you, toodle-oo.

WHITE WATER DIFFICULTY RATING SYSTEM

This seems to be a very controversial subject and the debates over what class a particular rapids is goes on and on. The most dangerous river ratings are from the truly expert paddler who either forgets what it was like to be ordinary or perhaps never even knew. Such folk tend to underrate everything. The inexperienced paddler goes too far the other way and tends to overrate everything. What seems horrendous to him (and rightly so) may only be a Class 3.

To settle such arguments, two solutions come to mind: one is to have a standard paddler run all of the rivers. Using ourselves as the standard this is what we have attempted to do. The other is to use an objective point system and let the chips fall where they may. This we have tried to do by following the guidelines set by the American Whitewater Affiliation (admittedly in need of revision). Certain key characteristics which shouldn't lead to any argument are assigned point values and all of these are totaled up. The final score determines the class.

We have tried to strictly define each class and stick to these definitions in rating each river. Like any system of classification, it is a human attempt to sort out disorder and, being a human activity, is subject to human foibles.

A. Standing or slow flowing water, not more than 2.5 mph.

B. Current between 2.5 and 4.5 mph, but backpaddling can effectively neutralize the speed.

C. Current more than 4.5 mph and backpaddling cannot neutralize the speed of the current. Simple obstacles may occur that require a certain amount of boat control.

1. Easy. Occasional small riffles consisting of low, regular wave patterns. About what you might encounter on a lake on a mildly windy day. Most of the Elk River below Sutton or the Cheat River between Parsons and Rowlesburg.
2. Medium difficulty. Rapids occur more frequently, usually retaining a regular wave pattern as on a lake with a fairly vigorous wind (enough to cause "whitecaps"). Although there may be more than one route, the most practical one is easily determined. There may be simple, uncomplicated chutes over ledges up to 3′ high. Almost all of Shavers Fork north of U.S. 33.
3. Difficult. Numerous rapids, with higher, irregular standing waves, hydraulics, and eddies. The main thing about Class 3 is that you

are forced to maneuver in the rapids. The most practical route is not always obvious and you will find that you start having to work a little. Ledges up to 4′, waves to 3′, overhanging branches, and deeper water characterize this class. The Cruiser Course of the North Fork at medium to high water levels and the Quinnimont Rapids of the New River.

4. Very difficult. Long, extensive stretches of rapids with high, irregular standing waves and difficult hydraulics, holes, eddies, and crosscurrents. Decks are a necessity as is a very high degree of boat control. Not only are you working, but you are working very hard. Class 4 requires a good deal of instant decisions as the most practical route is not obvious. Difficult ledges with irregular passages, "stopper" waves, or souse holes in the way. This class includes most of the really difficult water in the state and covers a lot of ground technically. The Cheat Canyon at medium levels, the North Branch of the Potomac at low to medium, and a lot of the Tygart River are solidly in this class.
5. Exceedingly difficult. This is a hard Class to define and to tell where 4 ends and 5 begins. There is very little Class 5 in the state at normal levels although many rivers can take on this character in high water including many of the rivers already named. The rapids are not only difficult, but they are long and continuous. Irregular stoppers and souse holes are unavoidable, partially submerged boulders and ledges are everywhere; very complex eddies and crosscurrents, etc., are not only present, but also occur in long dazzling combinations. Common practice also refers to any single, dangerous rapids that requires a lot of skill and courage to run as Class 5, even if a short one. The Gauley River below Summersville Reservoir contains a good deal of this kind of water, the Double Z and certain others in the New River Gorge, and a few on the Tygart are legitimate 5s.
6. Utmost difficulty. This isn't a hard class to define, but in recent years there has been a tendency to ignore the definition. It is supposed to mean the utmost limit of navigability and its chief, distinguishing characteristic is *risk of life*. There has been a tendency to degrade any Class 6 rapids to a 5 once it has been run, but such practice is not followed in this guide. Flooded rivers often get up into this category. A mistake can be costly and no one should ever be urged or taunted into running a 6 (or anything else for that matter).

When the difficulty of a river falls between two grades, two numbers are used, i.e., Class 2-3. If most of the river is of one classification except for one or two spots, it is referred to as Class 3_4. Ratings used in this manual are for normal water levels. It should be kept in mind that these ratings might change drastically in high water. Similarly, if you run one of our Class 4s in very low water, don't think you are a 4 paddler. Ratings usually drop at least a class under such conditions.

RIVER GAUGES

The water flow on most rivers in this country is quantified at frequent intervals by the Water Resources Division of the Geological Service, Department of Interior. The data are recorded as discharge in cubic feet per second (cfs) and available to everyone. The principle is based on the velocity of flow past a point of known cross sectional area in the river. Discharge is readily related to a single variable the height of the river at a fixed point. Gauge houses are situated on most rivers. They consist of a well at the river's edge with a float attached to a recording clock. The gauge reading is in hundredths of feet. Rating tables are constructed for each gauge relating these readings to discharge. The recorded gauge heights are collected regularly.

Some key geological survey gauges are reported to the Corps of Engineers and the National Weather Service offices very frequently for flood control and river navigational regulation. Power companies also need this information in operating hydroelectric dams. Some of these gauges are read by observers who call central offices at regular intervals. Some are attached to a telephone and can be read by a sound code. A few are read by radio signal. Some have data collected by messengers only at infrequent intervals.

The paddler can plan trips using this information. Most key gauge results can be obtained from offices dealing with an entire river basin as cited on p. xii. The Pittsburgh and Washington offices can be contacted at anytime and an efficient recorded message gives a series of gauge readings. However the Kanawha Basin office only gives river gauge information during business hours. Since most river trip planning occurs during evening hours and on weekends we are publishing a list of gauge telephone numbers for this area. *As of 1975 these numbers take priority over all numbers appearing elsewhere in the book.* Since some of these phones and gauges are so remote that they are battery operated unnecessary use of them is discouraged to the extent that the number will be changed as use increases. We have decided to publish these unlisted numbers because of their importance to our sport and in hopes that the usage of the numbers will not be abused. It is also hoped that the Huntington office will provide a recorded daily gauge reading message if the direct telephone gauge reading traffic becomes too heavy. Eventually this information should be made available daily as a news release comparable to skiing condition reports.

Telephone gauge signals are a series of buzzes for tens, units, tenths and hundreths with an interval following each digit. Zeroes are a long buzz. An example for a 4.32′ reading would be as follows: ——— (0) - - - - (4) - - - (3) - - (2).

River	*Distance*	*Class*	*Gradient*	*Level*	*Gauge*	*Phone**
Black Fork	4	2-3	25	4-6	Parsons	412-644-2890
Bluestone	25	2-4	31(16)	5-9	Pipestem	304-466-1234
Buckhannon	13	3-5	53(4)	7-10	Buckhannon	412-644-2890
Cacapon	12	1-3	14	1-3	Capon Bridge	304-856-2750
Casselman	11	1-3	25	2-4	Markleton	412-644-2890
Cheat Narrows	4	3-4	20	2.3-5.4	Parsons	412-644-2890
Cheat Canyon	11	3-4	25	0-4	Albright	304-329-1748
Cherry	9	2-3	30	11-13	Craigsville	304-742-3227
Cranberry	7	2-4	40	11-13	Craigsville	304-742-3227
Dry Fork	12	3	25	4-8	Parsons	412-644-2890
Elk	8	3	30	4.8-6	Webster Springs	304-847-5532
Gauley	24	3-5	28	3-4.5	Belva	304-632-2071
Glady	8	1-3	46	5-6	Parsons	412-644-2890
Hopeville	5	3-4	33	2.4-5	Petersburg	301-899-3210
Laurel	13	1-4	72(7)	5-8	Parsons	412-644-2890
Lost	6	2-4	40	1.5-	Capon Bridge	304-856-2750
Meadow	5	2-4	39	4.6-6	Mt. Lookout	304-872-1133
Middle Fork	6	4-5	79(2)	4-5.5	Belington	412-644-2890
Moorefield	10	2-4	25	4.5-6	Springfield	301-899-3210
New	41	2-3	10	2-3	Hinton	304-466-4896
New Gorge	14	3-5	19(6)	2-3.3	Hinton	304-466-4896
North Branch	13	3-4	51	4.6-6	Kitzmiller	301-899-3210
North Fork	10	2-3	22	2.4-5	Petersburg	301-899-3210
Potomac		1-2		2-5.5	Hancock	301-899-3210
Red Creek	6	3-4	75	5-9	Parsons	412-644-2890
Seneca	6	4	80	4-8	Petersburg	301-899-3210
Shavers						
Bemis	9	2-4	65(3)	4-8	Parsons	412-644-2890
Parsons	22	1-2	19	4-8	Parsons	412-644-2890
Shenandoah	7	1-2	10	2-4	Millville	301-899-3210
Smoke Hole	5	1-3	35	3.6-8	Petersburg	301-899-3210
Stony	13	3-5	76	4.5-7	Kitzmiller	301-899-3210
Trough	11	1-2	5	1.6-3.6	Springfield	301-899-3210
Tygart Loop	5	3-5	25	4-5	Belington	412-644-2890
Tygart Gorge	11	3-5	37	3-5.5	Belington	412-644-2890
Tygart, Arden	8	3-5	27	2.5-4.5	Philippi	412-644-2890
Williams	11	3-5	53	11-13	Craigsville	304-742-3227
Yough, Upper	11	4-5	116(3)	3-4	Friendsville	412-644-2890
Yough, Middle	10	1-2	10	2-5	Confluence	412-644-2890
Yough, Lower	7	2-4	20	1.8-4	Confluence	412-644-2890

*Verified June 1979.

FINDING YOUR WAY IN WEST VIRGINIA

Trying to find take outs and put ins in white water country can be difficult unless you are native to the immediate area. Often topographical maps are quite helpful especially for geographical features. However, a good deal of West Virginia has not been surveyed for over 60 years (particularly those portions with the best white water) and landmarks such as railroads, bridges, and secondary roads have changed a good deal since those days. Usually, however, they are helpful and in most cases, our river write-ups contain the quadrangle name for pertinent maps of the area. Unless stated otherwise, the quadrangle name is for the 7½′ size. These maps may be obtained for 50¢ each from the West Virginia Geological and Economic Survey, Mineral Industries Building, West Virginia University Campus, Morgantown 26506.

A very good map to have is the Monongahela National Forest Map (MNF). This map contains the best features of road maps and topo maps. It is very good and up-to-date for finding the remoter put ins for rivers in the forest or in lands contiguous with it. It is also quite helpful for places of natural interest, hiking, trails, and camping sites. It is too bad we do not have ready access to a map such as this for the entire state. National forest maps are free and obtainable from any district ranger's office or by writing the Superintendent's Office, Box 1231, Elkins 26241.

The Official State Road Map is practically worthless in that secondary roads are not numbered and many important shuttle roads are not even on it. It is good for finding locations of state parks and major highways.

County road maps are excellent, especially in finding secondary roads, however private and forest service roads are not always on them. Under SHUTTLE directions for each river, a federal highway is prefixed with U.S. as in U.S. 220, a major state highway with W.V. as in W.V. 39, forest service roads with F.S. as in F.S. 92, while state secondary and tertiary roads (county roads in most states) appear in quotes as in "6". Strangers may have a hard time finding road signs with this number. At most intersections you will find a green sign (often with bullet holes) pointing to the direction of a village and followed by an encircled number, e.g., Arden 6. This doesn't mean that it is 6 miles to Arden. Six is the number of the secondary road. Prices of the county road maps vary from 20¢ to 70¢ plus mailing charges. To get these maps, write for a free price list from the West Virginia Department of Highways, Advanced Planning Division, Charleston 25311.

CHAPTER I

GEORGE WASHINGTON'S RIVER AND ITS TRIBUTARIES—THE POTOMAC DRAINAGE

Of all the rivers in the state, the mighty Potomac and its tributaries are by far the most historic. Sometimes referred to as George Washington's River or the Nation's River, the Potomac has witnessed and has been a part of our country's birth and growth. Much of the upper drainage remains nearly the same as it was in George's day, but much of it has changed greatly. It is a huge and fascinating watershed of outstanding beauty that offers an almost unlimited variety of white water adventure. This is truly canoe and kayak country at its best.

As will be pointed out frequently, most of the headwaters of the Potomac, especially the Cacapon and the South Branch tributaries, are characterized by immense cliffs and rock formations which provide some of the most breathtaking scenery. Caudy's Castle, Royal Glen or Petersburg Gap, Seneca, Eagle, and Champe Rocks are, of course, known well enough to have their own names, but there aren't enough names in the book to name all of such formations, many of which can only be seen by the white water paddler. The limestone sedimentary layers of the South Branch highlands have been eroded by underground rivers for centuries creating underground a spelunker's bonanza in caves with as much variety, beauty, and challenge as that which is offered to the paddlers and rock climbers above ground. Smoke Hole and Seneca Caverns are, of course, well known to the public, but Cave Mountain, Schoolhouse, Hell Hole, and the like are examples of caves known intimately only by the skilled spelunker. Few areas in the country can boast that they look as good underground as above.

The main stem of the Potomac is formed near Green Spring by its two major branches—the beautiful, bountiful waters of the South Branch, most of which arise in the mountains of Highland County, Va., and the ugly, polluted water of the North Branch which arises where the extreme southwestern tip of Maryland cuts down into West Virginia's Eastern Panhandle. Later, near Berkeley Springs, the Potomac picks up the Cacapon system and then a little farther merges with the Shenandoah to form West Virginia's easternmost tip, Harpers Ferry.

The North Branch never gets a chance to be beautiful. It starts right in the midst of some of the worst air pollution and strip mining in the country and really never sees anything much better. The water is laden with silt and mine acids, passes through the most depraved communities imaginable, where tossing garbage in the river is not only a habit, but a way of life, and continues on to receive the discharges from paper mills, factories, and municipal sewage plants. Some of the scenery is pretty and even quite striking, but too often it is pretty depressing, like Shallmar, Md.—a long row of unpainted houses in front of which is the river bank fouled continuously by garbage and refuse and behind which are the most devastating ravishes by strip mining anywhere. As Morrison writes, "Some scars of . . . early industrialization are still to be found along the North Branch. And today, the by-products of modern industry—air and water pollution and defacement of the land—are more evident along the North Branch than anywhere else in the valleys of the Potomac. But there is a danger in other parts of the Valley as well. Either we cherish this 'Cradle of the Republic' as Gutheim called it, or we let it become stifled by the refuse of unplanned and uncontrolled exploitation."

The South Branch can be thought of as the collection of three main tributaries—the South Branch proper, the North Fork, and the South Fork or Moorefield River. The distance separating the two streams farthest from each other at potential put ins (Circleville and Fort Seybert) is but 17 miles as the crow flies and all three rivers can be paddled in Pendleton County. Each of these rests in its own beautiful valley separated from its neighbor only by a single high mountain ridge. All of them begin as clear cold trout streams gradually drawing warmth from the fabulous South Branch Valley until below Petersburg and Moorefield, they mingle to form some of the finest warm water fishing in the eastern United States. Seneca Creek, Little Cacapon, Patterson's Creek, New Creek, and North River are significant minor tributaries in the magnificent basin.

All of the Potomac tributaries are laden with history as all of the early explorations followed the rivers. The early settlers traced these valleys in their quest for freedom and independence. The rivers were the main channels of transportation for people and goods from the beginning until very recent times. In addition, as elsewhere throughout the state, the railroads usually followed the river valleys. Finally, political boundaries were either drawn at the rivers themselves or at the edge of their watersheds. George Washington was the most celebrated of the early explorers of the Potomac valleys. His aim was to find a means to connect the Potomac and Ohio River basins by waterways. He did not succeed, but what he learned in his travels and recorded in his journals greatly influenced subsequent events in these lands.

Little of the French-Indian and Revolutionary wars actually penetrated the Potomac Highlands due to the transportation difficulties, but a few sites are memorable. Chief among these is Old Fields, just north of Moorefield near the head of the Trough. This site began as a place where the Indians burned away the forest to form grazing areas for game. Later one of the first white settlements was made here only to be annihilated in 1756 in an Indian battle. Old Fields later became an important stop on various transportation routes. It was situated on the South Branch, and also at the intersection of the Seneca Trail and McCullough's Path, two of West Virginia's earliest highways. Several defense forts of the West Virginia frontier were located in this area. In addition to Fort Pleasant at Old Fields, there were some 30 others, two of which, Fort Ashby and Fort Seybert, still exist in white water country. Scenes of terrible Indian massacres occurred within 24 hours of each other at this latter fort and Upper Tract led by Killbuck and his warriors.

The Potomac headwaters witnessed much of the Civil War although no major battle like that at Antietam Creek was fought here. Sectionalism literally tore the highlands apart politically as well as militarily. The Potomac Highlands escaped with only "minor" skirmishes, like Romney which changed hands some 56 times, wild chases through Franklin and at Old Fields, mining saltpetre in Cave Mountain in the Smoke Hole, and so on. Fort Mulligan, located high above the river just west of Petersburg was occupied by northern troops and the trenches and gun emplacements are still visible as is a water tank of more recent vintage squarely within the outline of the fort. Keyser, then called New Creek (they should have left it like that) was an important outpost as was Moorefield, but of course when one thinks of the Civil War, one thinks of Harpers Ferry where the whole shootin' match started. A National Park Service park now commemorates and displays some of the original buildings and fortifications of the latter near the mouth of the Shenandoah (try this for an interesting lunch stop). Moorefield also keeps some of this heritage alive when each year in late September, many of the antebellum homes in the area are opened for public display.

Several parks exist in the area for camping or touring, but few of these are on or near rivers. Suitable developed spots for camping in conjunction with paddling are the Forest Service campgrounds at Seneca Creek, Smoke Hole, and Big Bend, but there are no other suitable campgrounds on the rivers. All of the land is either privately owned or inaccessible. Some of the landowners will give camping permission (some for a small fee), but they are all undeveloped and without sanitary facilities. It remains a mystery why the state Department of Natural Resources has no campgrounds in the Eastern Panhandle. Possibly because they have been too busy investing in golf courses.

The eastern streams are known throughout the east for the fine bass and trout fishing that may be had. Suckers, muskie, and fall fish are very common as are bluegills and redeyes. The Shenandoah is well known for its different species of catfish. All of the lower Potomac and the Cacapon also produce eels. The forest communities and the prevalence of pulpwood production on family farms help contribute to the large populations of deer and wild turkey that exist. Hunter success is very high for these species as well as the large numbers of squirrels that live in the abundant oak forests. The black bear finds refuge in the very high, isolated areas such as North Fork Mountain, but it would be highly unlikely for a paddler to see one. Beaver and muskrats are common especially along the Moorefield and Cacapon rivers, but being close to the Atlantic flyway, it is the variety and numbers of waterfowl that are the most impressive. The shale barrens of the Panhandle are associated with some unusual plant communities perhaps the most unique member of which is the prickly pear cactus, a plant well adapted to the summer droughts common to this area having the least rainfall in the state. The Panhandle is well known for its apple orchards, grazing, and poultry production. The farms are very well kept, productive, and easy on the eye everywhere.

Few dams exist in the area which makes it a natural Corps of Engineers' target. Among the most interesting are those that are built below Cumberland on the Potomac for maintenance of the famous Chesapeake and Ohio Canal. Begun in 1828 and completed in 1850, the system consisted of 74 locks which had to lift or lower a mule drawn barge a collective total of 605 feet. The barges moved only about 2 mph or slower than a C-1 against the wind and was a very noncompetitive but leisurely form of transportation. Such traffic existed until 1924 and many of these dams still impound water. There are a few power company dams around—one on the Shenandoah above Millville, one on the Potomac below Williamsport, the one on the Stony River headwaters, and one on the Cacapon down near its mouth. There are a couple of dams in the vicinity of Cumberland, but nobody in his right mind paddles the North Branch near there. Pumped storage projects are becoming more popular and the kilowatt-hour people are vying with the Corps for the choice sites. The Corps' activities have been confined to promoting a dam on the North Branch below Shaw (now under initial construction) and pushing real hard to build one at lovely Royal Glen above Petersburg. If the local politicians would work as hard at clearing up land and water abuse tactics as they do at building dams, there would not be any arguments for dams. Other than for several low water bridges and dams and a few old millpond dam remains, that is about it in the way of man-made obstructions.

Petersburg of course is the capital of the Potomac white water being not only the host of the annual Petersburg White Water Weekend, but also admirably situated right in the middle of all of the Potomac Highlands' tributaries. It is a great town to use as a base of operations for a whole week of canoeing. What is remarkable about this is that white water sport has not been taken up by the natives of the area who must certainly be well acquainted by this time with cars bearing license plates from all over the country and racks of variegated white water boats hustling through town. Franklin, Harpers Ferry, Romney, and Mouth of Seneca are also conveniently located near good action. The interesting thing about the latter is to stop at one of its two restaurant-motels on a Sunday morning in the early spring and gawk at the nature freaks from all over who have come to paddle, rock climb, spelunk, trout fish, hike, or otherwise enjoy the outdoors in the immediate area.

Being so close to the metropolitan eastern coast, the Potomac tributaries are very well known to paddlers and most have been well described by Carter and Corbett and Matacia for some time. They are paddled often by Easterners, but not too often by West Virginia paddlers and it is hoped that the following pages offer some fresh insight for the former and whet the appetite of the latter.

BIBLIOGRAPHY

Cleland, H. 1955. *George Washington in the Ohio Valley*. Pittsburgh: University of Pittsburgh Press.

Judy, E. L. 1951. *History of Grant and Hardy Counties, West Virginia.* Privately printed.*

Moore, A. E. 1963. *History of Hardy County of the Borderland.* Privately printed.*

Morrison, C. 1970. *The Fairfax Line: A Profile in History and Geography.* Parsons, W.Va.: McClain Printing Co.

———. 1971. *Wappatomaka: A Survey of the History and Geography of the South Branch Valley*. Parsons, W.Va.: McClain Printing Co.

Morton, O. F. 1967. *A History of Pendleton County, West Virginia.* 2nd ed. Privately printed.*

Smith, J. L. 1968. *The Potomac Naturalist.* Parsons, W.Va.: McClain Printing Co.

*Available from The Hermitage, Petersburg, W.Va. 26847.

ABRAM CREEK

U.S. 50 to North Branch of the Potomac—8.5 Miles

CLASS	GRAD.	VOL.	SCENE	TIME	LEVEL
2-4	47 1@110	60	A-D	3	?-5.9′

MAPS: USGS—Kitzmiller and Mt. Storm
COUNTIES—Mineral and Grant

DESCRIPTION: This is an exciting little stream, but about which we have little information. It is difficult to catch up and when it is, so is everything else. It starts off with a big, big bang right below U.S. 50 and drops the 110 fpm. There are no big drops, but it is very bouldery for the first mile. It is steep and of course much maneuvering is required. Most of the middle section is just fun type riffles and open rapids of up to Class 3 difficulty which offers no particular difficulty. In fact, most of the river is that way. The last mile is like the Savage at 1000 cfs (at least at the 5.9′ level) in that although there is not much maneuvering around boulders and the like, there are big waves and complex currents. The scenery alternates from pleasant woods to coal mines, haul roads, RR tracks, and old houses.

DIFFICULTIES: The first mile is the hardest part and would compare with such streams as the Upper Yough and the Stony. The easy middle section contains a low water bridge which must be portaged, and since the bridge is in the middle of a rapids, it is best to carry the rapids. Towards the end watch for a coal mine on the left bank. A rapids or two below this there is a big sliding ledge. It is advisable to scout this for runnability.

SHUTTLE: Put in at the U.S. 50 bridge east of Mt. Storm. To allow preview of the creek and gauge on the way to put in go east on U.S. 50 for three miles, turn left to Emoryville, and follow the creek (the gauge in on the second bridge crossing) through Oakmont to a railroad fork at the mouth.

GAUGE: The 5.9′ refers to a government gauge located on the third bridge below the put in, but it is not conveniently located for inspection. The water at the 5.9′ run was at the top of the base of the concrete abutment at U.S. 50 and unlikely to happen more than once a year. Inspection here and at the mouth should be satisfactory.

STONY RIVER

A. VEPCO Dam to U.S. 50—7.6 Miles

CLASS	GRAD.	VOL.	SCENE	TIME	LEVEL
2-5	71	83	A	3	4-6

MAPS: USGS—Mount Storm Lake, Gorman and Mt. Storm
COUNTY—Grant

DESCRIPTION: This is the absolute limit of small river navigability. This is one of the steepest, most tortuous, most demanding runs in West Virginia. It is a little stream that starts right off with a bang and immediately gets worse by dropping over steep ledges. This isn't too bad, but the rapids become steeper, the drops become blind, and the maneuvering becomes intense. Most of the drops are complicated by boulders splitting the chute into more than one channel. If you choose or if your boat is forced into the wrong one, the results could be a demolished boat.

At one point the rapids are especially intense and the blind drops extremely severe one after the other. It is here that the river drops the horrendous 150′ within a mile. Countless opportunities exist for broaching or getting caught in a drop or chute.

DIFFICULTIES: All but the last mile or so. It is advisable to run the lower Stony first. If it is too much, don't think of getting on the upper. Also, it is suggested that you be in pretty good physical shape before attempting either section as they are both grueling runs requiring hard, constant paddling. It is impractical to detail each of the dangerous spots. There are too many and you are pushed into them before you know it. Few eddies exist and on such a small river, you shouldn't expect too much in the way of help from fellow paddlers. The biggest danger would be in broaching in one of the narrow chutes. Through much of the river, you are not very close to any road. Any run on this river is an expedition, not a cruise. In addition to a full repertoire of paddle-side strokes, the C-1 paddler will have to have a very dependable set of off-paddle side draws and braces as well. This is absolutely no place for a C-2.

SHUTTLE: Take out at U.S. 50 bridge. Take the road to Bismarck "50/3" leading from the bridge and drive to W.V. 93. Turn right and drive to the sluice at the VEPCO Dam. It is a long steep carry from the road down to the put in along the right side of the sluice. Put in on the pool below the turbulence.

B. U.S. 50 to North Branch of the Potomac—6 Miles

CLASS	GRAD.	VOL.	SCENE	TIME	LEVEL
3-5	76	83	A	2	4-6

DESCRIPTION: This, the Cheat, and the Savage are all well named, but this one especially so. Beginning placidly at the U.S. 50 bridge, this little brawler begins to head down hill fast. Not only is the gradient steep throughout and is there hardly any slack water, but the maneuvering around boulders, over ledges, and through complicated drops is extremely difficult and physically taxing. At low water the maneuvering is extreme and makes the most challenging run and the hardest paddling that you will find. Higher water makes the maneuvering easier, but the drops and turbulence are more significant. At low levels this section is "easier" than the upper, but becomes harder in high water.

The flow can be controlled by the power company dam, but runs are limited to high water run-off periods in winter and spring. The scenery from the river is pleasant woods, high cliffs, and picturesque falls, but too close by are strip mines, coal piles, mine dumps, and similar crud. The water is clear, but polluted with mine acids.

DIFFICULTIES: The whole cotton-picking run. The Class 4 designation relates more to constant, intricate maneuvering in low water and the 5 relates to the heaviness at higher levels. Singling out any one particular rapids as worse than the others is impractical with the exception of the last big drop at the sawmill just ¼ mile upstream from the mouth. This is a 6′ + waterfall which should be scouted to see if it is well enough padded.

Downed trees are a particular hazard on this stream.

SHUTTLE: Put in under bridge at U.S. 50. Take out can be reached by turning north on the "Kuhn Mine Road" just east of Mt. Storm. This hard road eventually splits. Keep to the left to avoid ending up in a strip mine. The last mile of road is bad for low clearance vehicles. Take out just above the falls and the bridge. It is recommended to combine this trip with a run on the best part of the North Branch and take out in Kitzmiller, Md., two hours and 9 miles downstream. See separate description.

GAUGE: Located on left side downstream from the bridge. The lower levels are going to be scrapers.

NORTH BRANCH OF THE POTOMAC

A. Steyer to Kitzmiller—13 Miles

CLASS	GRAD.	VOL.	SCENE	TIME	LEVEL
3-4	51	159	A-D	4	4.5-6′

MAPS: USGS—Gorman, Mt. Storm, and Kitzmiller
COUNTIES—Grant and Mineral (a Maryland road map would also be helpful)

DESCRIPTION: Whoopee! This stream is probably the longest and most continuous hard run around this part of the country. It descends rather steeply for its size thus accounting for the constant rapids, turbulence, and excellent action. The water isn't much to look at in that it is polluted with mine acids and is usually muddy from the surrounding strip mines, however the scenery from the river is usually beautiful until you reach the garbage laden banks, unpainted houses, and immense strip mines near Kitzmiller.

This is also the ledgiest river you will ever encounter and there must be at least 1,000 hydraulics. The first mile below Steyer is a very peaceful descent over Class 1-2 rapids then every once in a while a rather juicy drop through a narrow channel dampens your navel until without much other warning you are into it up to your eyeballs and you realize that the gradient is really picking up. Almost all of the rapids have at least one ledge, usually made more complicated by sinister turbulences. It is very narrow and rocky all the way to the mouth of the Stony where the volume of the river usually doubles.

Below the RR bridge ½ mile beyond the mouth of Stony is the first of a series of really big drops. After this the river broadens out into an almost continuous series of haystack filled rapids that do not require much maneuvering. You will appreciate this if you have just come down the Stony. This doesn't last long as the river renarrows and the rapids become more difficult. Maneuvering becomes more necessary and the descents become powerful. Padded boulders, powerful souse holes, and difficult crosscurrents add spice to the run. This continues mile after mile. When quiet water is encountered, it isn't longer than 50 yards.

DIFFICULTIES: Run the first island below Steyer on the right which contains a nice drop into a hole. The second island has a mean passage on the left consisting of the old sharp-left-hand-drop-into-a-vicious-curler-hole-combination-out-into-another-hydraulic trick! At least one other group refers to this as Corkscrew Ledge. Fitting. From here on to the mouth of the Stony, the river is steep and mean. In high water, you will really be pushing it.

There are four ledges below the RR bridge mentioned above. They are all within a distance of a half mile. The first two and the fourth are big drops into very heavy turbulence. The first and hardest is run from the left as is the steepest, the second one, which unlike the first is uncomplicated by maneuvering. You just drop down into the meringue. The third is obvious, but to run the fourth, you must get way over on the right. At 7.0′, a very dangerous level, some of these form *absolute keepers* and can not be run. There is a pool between each for rescue purposes, at least at lower levels. About three-fourths of the way to Kitzmiller are the remains of some old concrete bridge abutments. The one on the left has toppled over thus creating a dam in the main channel. The main force of the current smashes furiously against it, thus it is no place to get in trouble. It can be run on the left or snuck on the right (but this requires more water).

The whole run is not easy and is considerably long and strenuous. You will be working every minute. This is not a good river to test out intermediates—there are no midway takeouts, only a long walk along the RR tracks. Each paddler in the party should be competent and capable of taking care of himself. Much harder than the lower Yough.

SHUTTLE: The put in can be reached from U.S. 50 at Gormania by taking a dirt road down the Maryland side of the river for 2 miles to Steyer. A put in can also be made on the Stony River at the U.S. 50 bridge (see separate description). Take out at a ramp beneath the bridge at Kitzmiller, Md., on Md. 38 (reached from Md. 135 between Oakland and Bloomington, Md.) or from W.V. 42 via Elk Garden from U.S. 50. To save 2 miles of comparatively less action at the end, a take out can be arranged at the God-forsaken hole of Shallmar, Md., just upstream from Kitzmiller.

B. Kitzmiller to Bloomington, Md.—18 Miles

CLASS	GRAD.	VOL.	SCENE	TIME	LEVEL
3_4	8@42 10@32	418	A-D	5	4-6.8′

MAPS: Kitzmiller and Westernport
COUNTY—Mineral (also need a Maryland road map)

DESCRIPTION: This is a very long run, but has been described collectively because (1) it is a very fast run, (2) setting up an intermediate shuttle for the lower part is too time consuming, and (3) it will soon be obsolete anyway. If you want to just gobble up river miles through almost continuous big wave action, then this section in high water is for you. The first 8 miles down to Shaw transcribes two huge loops and the course offers much variety in that islands divide the course at several points. At 4.5′ on the Kitzmiller gauge (water just a couple of inches over the base of the bridge abutment), there is plenty of wave action with mostly Class 3 entertainment. With higher water the river would take on more of a Class 4 rating.

There are very few obstructions, the river being open and almost always down hill. There are only a few places where the entire river necks down creating a turbulent descent, otherwise each rapids is fairly wide. The turns are mostly gradual although a few channels around islands are fairly sharp. Most of the channels are on the left. Below Shaw the gradient is not as steep, but the volume is heavier. The rapids are usually turns in the twisting river or narrow chutes, all are somewhat heavy, but there are few obstacles to dodge. There are many surfing waves.

Other than for Shaw and a couple of miles from the take out, the scenery is rather striking, the river being lined with many cliffs. The water is polluted as above, but the total impression is pleasant. As with the upper river, you are running the Maryland-West Virginia border, our state being on the right.

DIFFICULTIES: There are several low (2-3′) ledges scattered along the first part creating hydraulics, back washes, and big curlers. In lower water, the correct passage must be located by good water reading. The best action and most of the ledges are about a mile upstream from Shaw. Some of these are so close that care must be taken to regain alignment after burrowing out of each hydraulic. Most of the other difficulties would only occur in high water (over 5-5.5′) when the rapids take on a meaner turbulence. At the narrow portions of the river, there are often large standing, keeper-sized waves that must be avoided. The nicest thing about this run is that there is an easy way around each nasty spot if desired. If in doubt, run each rapids on the inside of the bend for a less difficult shot. Well below Shaw, the appearance of a bridge across the river marks the hamlet of Barnum. Right below here one will find a series of long slide rapids over sloping ledges with huge stoppers at the bottom. These can be avoided if desired and caution is advised. The worst thing about the whole trip is the disgraceful air pollution emanating from the West Virginia Pulp and Paper Company at Luke, Md. The nauseating stench fills one's nostrils anywhere in the valley and in winter time, the snow is black.

SHUTTLE: Put in on the left side of the bridge in Kitzmiller. There is a convenient ramp down to the water. Take out on the left of an island just above the mouth of the Savage River in Bloomington, Md., on Md. 135. If you just want to run down to Shaw, drive out W.V. 42 to Elk Garden and turn left on W.V. 46. Do not attempt to use 46 down to the far take out. A trip from Shaw to Bloomington takes an hour and a half shuttle alone, and isn't worth it.

GAUGE AND SEASON: Usually up in the winter, but although it is big water, it goes down fast, usually in early April. Call (301) 440-7280, Weather Service, and ask for the Kitzmiller reading. A reading of 4.5′ is the absolute low for the river above Kitzmiller, and even then you will scrape a lot above Stony (because Stony contributes greatly to the

Kitzmiller reading). Five to $5.5'$ would be a real good run and $6'$ or above, awfully high. Below Kitzmiller, it can be run at lower levels, possibly down to $4.0'$ and high water would be considered in the 5+ region due to the formation of the keepers.

CODA: The U.S. Army Corps of Engineers, through an incredible bit of Class 5 maneuvering with former West Virginia state officials, and in an age prior to the environmental awareness of today, have developed and are proceeding to build a dam on the North Branch about 5 miles above the mouth of the Savage. The resulting reservoir will create a flat river back to the bottom of the first big island below Kitzmiller. The purpose of the dam is to create a flush box to augment low flows in the horribly polluted area downstream. Due to the acid content of the water, there will not be much recreational value to the new reservoir. The summer elevation of the reservoir would extend the rapids 1 mile below the island and the winter pool elevation, yet another mile, but this won't help the paddler as there would be no take out road to these points and the present road to Shaw will be gone. Indeed, Shaw will be gone. In times of extreme drawdown and if coupled with a gully washer, one could conceivably paddle through the Shaw ledges on down another couple of miles, but this is unlikely. Every paddler should therefore put this river in its present state on their high priority rivers to paddle soon. Projected completion date has been set for 1978. Canoeing may be enhanced a little below the dam, (the big slide rapids below Barnum will be unaffected by the reservoir) although the minimum augmentation of 305 cfs (equivalent to Kitzmiller 3.65) is pretty low and not enough for a good run. Besides the last couple of miles above the take out are pretty dreary and flat. There will be a new access road from W.V. 46 to the dam which will be located a couple of miles above Barnum.

C. Henry to Gormania—8 Miles

CLASS	GRAD.	VOL.	SCENE	TIME	LEVEL
1-2$_4$	40	159	D	2	5-7

MAPS: USGS—Kempton, Table Rock, Gorman
COUNTY—Grant

DESCRIPTION: This run starts in the shadow of Fairfax Stone, the historic survey mark dividing Maryland and The Old Dominion and indicating the headwaters of the Potomac. This section is an easy run with only one good white water section about one mile below Wilson. Look for a six-foot slide.

GAUGE: The Kitzmiller gauge is 13 miles downstream. It must be unusually high for this little headwater run.

SHUTTLE: W.V. 90 parallels the run.

SENECA CREEK

Forest Service Campgrounds to W.V. 4 and 28 Bridge—6 Miles

CLASS	GRAD.	VOL.	SCENE	TIME	LEVEL
4	70-90	S	B	3	2-3′

MAPS: USGS—Onego 15′
MNF
COUNTY—Pendleton

DESCRIPTION: Born high on West Virginia's tallest mountain, this lively little ripsnorter is pure delight if you can catch it up. Often after early spring thaws one can find suitable levels. It is essentially one 6-mile-long rapids with but one or two very short pools to break up the waves. The course is extremely narrow, especially in the upper parts, and very fast, however there is very little maneuvering required as there are few obstructions. You just skirt up and go. The course traverses pastoral farm lands around the northern edge of Spruce Mountain and heads east towards the imposing majesty of Seneca Rocks.

DIFFICULTIES: Very few at the levels indicated. Just above and just below the Onego bridge are some sloping ledges into some hydraulics that demand a reasonable amount of attention. About 300 yards downstream from a small white church there is a dangling cable that threatens to decapitate the busy paddler. Pass on either side. About a half mile downstream one encounters two pools that run out sharply to the left and S curve to the right. Each of these has a big hydraulic right in the main channel. Within view of Seneca Rocks and as one notices the banks littered with discarded cars, one encounters Junkyard Falls, an otherwise beautiful 8′ staircase descent into fairly turbulent water. Overhanging branches or downed trees offer the only other hazards at medium levels.

SHUTTLE: Put in at the USFS Seneca Campgrounds which incidentally is an ideal spot for a base camp when paddling in this area. Take out at the left side of the W.V. 4 and 28 bridge, the put in for the Petersburg Cruiser Race.

GAUGE: The level referred to above was from a gauge located under the left side of the bridge at the Seneca Campgrounds. It was washed out in 1974 and has yet to be replaced. The best predictor at present is a 4-8 foot level at Petersburg.

NORTH FORK OF SOUTH BRANCH—POTOMAC

A. Circleville to Mouth of Seneca Creek—16 Miles

CLASS	GRAD.	VOL.	SCENE	TIME	LEVEL
1-2_3	34	S	B	4	3-6′

DESCRIPTION: This is a zestful little stream that flows rather straight forwardly through an extremely scenic valley and hugs the base of North Fork Mountain. The rapids at lower water levels are mostly Class 2, but could get very interesting if water were high. Mostly continuous action although there are a few long flat pools.

DIFFICULTIES: Below Riverton, a fairly high ledge or small falls is encountered that has at least two good, obvious passages. Just above this, a fairly large sycamore has been uprooted and has fallen across the river thus blocking a very choice passage. In 1975 a kayaker was pinned under this tree and drowned. *Stay away from fallen trees, the current does not!* You may be strained out like wet tea leaves. About a mile above the take out one begins to find things picking up to Class 3. This is due to the many series of small ledges that cut across the river at 30 to 45° angles thus providing some interesting sport.

SHUTTLE: The whole run is never very far from the highway, so numerous choices can be made for trips of various lengths. Put in at the bridge at the edge of Circleville and you can take out at bridges at Judy Gap, Riverton, or on the Harper's Gap road just beside Hedrick's Motel. Take out at the parking lot where the swinging bridge crosses over to Seneca Rocks.

B. Mouth of Seneca to Dolly Camp Grounds—10 Miles

CLASS	GRAD.	VOL.	SCENE	TIME	LEVEL
2-3	22	S-M	B	2-3	2.4-5′

DESCRIPTION: This is the site of the Cruiser Class race at the annual White Water Weekend. This river is a most attractive one and a most solid, continuous Class 3 run at medium water heights. Almost every conceivable type of Class 2-3 rapids appears on this river; numerous fast rapids, large waves, the main current frequently takes the paddler under overhanging branches, long rock gardens, zesty chutes, sharp turns, and even a ledge. This is a tremendous run seemingly designed to test the mettle and the repertoire of strokes of the intermediate paddler. This unquestionably is some of West Virginia's finest canoeing and has probably been run by more canoeists than any other single river in the state.

Some of the state's most breathtaking scenery can be seen from the river—Seneca and Champe Rocks are in the immediate vicinity while the imposing majesties of Allegheny Front and North Fork Mountain loom in the distance on either side of the river providing a splendid backdrop for canoeing. Excellent trout and bass fishing can be had on this clear, unpolluted river, but its proximity to the road and numerous vacation cabins place the fragile beauty of the river in a precarious position.

DIFFICULTIES: Actually there are no really bad places, but a canoeist does tend to remember places he has gotten into trouble in the past. One of these occurs just downstream from Yokum's Motel. The stream splits and the only passable channel is to the right. Often, overhung branches or a fallen tree add spice to the tight passage. About halfway the river appears to be running through the woods. Apparently the course of the river has been changed due to natural causes in recent years and it hasn't yet quite made up its mind which way to go. Choosing the correct passage quickly without previous knowledge is not easy and changes from year to year. Watch for this shortly after passing an aluminum painted bus along the left shore.

About three-quarters of the way into the trip the river is flowing through trees on the left as it turns left around a point and through a stopper. Just past the stopper there appears to be a flat pool, but actually a very deceptive ledge splits the pool. This has flipped many an unwary paddler. The only passage in low or medium water is way over against the left bank under an overhanging tree.

SHUTTLE: Put in under the bridge over Seneca Creek on W.V. 4 and 28. This stream joins the North Fork in a few hundred yards. Take out at Dolly Camp Grounds near the Grant-Pendleton County Line. Take out opposite a curious triangle-shaped cave opening on the river from a towering rock formation.

C. Dolly Camp Grounds to Smoke Hole Caverns—5 Miles

CLASS	GRAD.	VOL.	SCENE	TIME	LEVEL
3-4	33	M	A	1	2.4-5

DESCRIPTION: This Hopeville Canyon section of the North Fork is a real thriller and can get pretty vicious in high water. This 5-mile section is the site of the Championship Downriver Class Race, held annually during the first weekend in April. It is a good river for intermediates to test their capability of moving on to advanced paddling. The rapids are all steep and require precise maneuvering around the boulders. It is definitely more difficult than anything appearing in the upper portions of the river and it has considerably more volume than above Mouth of Seneca.

DIFFICULTIES: There are at least 16 major rapids (Class 3 or better) in the canyon and a few more near the road before getting to the take out. It is difficult to describe any of the upper Potomac headwaters because they are still in the making, i.e., the rivers traverse such sheer canyons, the walls of which are subject to erosion and inevitably, landslides. The North Fork has been changed often because of this. In the late winter of 1971, a massive landslide from the left cliff created a new rapids. The slide is easily recognized as the new rapids drops out of sight (figuratively and literally). Scout on the right. By 1972 the newly deposited rocks had been shifted again. Look out for Piton Rock high in the rapids. Start on the right and get left. The bottom obstructing boulders of 1971 have now been rolled to benign positions.

Another change in the river is the disappearance of an island at the head of a rapids about a half mile below the Harman's Slalom Rapids at the canyon's exit. All that is left is a tree standing in the current on the left side of the river. Taking the tree on the left makes the rapids more difficult, but the lack of the island makes the whole thing less difficult than before. Eventually the tree will wash out creating an additional, but temporary hazard.

SHUTTLE: Easily made on W.V. 28. Put in at Dolly Camp Grounds and take out just under primitive bridge at Smoke Hole Caverns Campground.

D. Smoke Hole Caverns to Petersburg—9 Miles

CLASS	GRAD.	VOL.	SCENE	TIME	LEVEL
1-3	20	M	B	2+	4.5′

MAPS: For all Sections: USGS—Circleville, Onego, Petersburg 15′
COUNTIES—Pendleton and Grant

DESCRIPTION: This run into Petersburg is not paddled very often, but contains some nice water. Many of the rapids are visible from the road, but soon the river takes off to join its Mamma, the South Branch fresh out of Smoke Hole country. The river passes through fairly open, well-kept farmland and although it is leaving the mountains behind, there are still some spectacular scenes to come particularly at the place known as Royal Glen, the site of an old broken out dam.

Unfortunately, the Corps of Engineers consider the narrowness of this steep pass a naturally groovy spot for one of their concrete tombstones. Remember this if you have enjoyed your run on either the North Fork or on the lower Smoke Hole Run of the South Branch. One of their plans would have flooded the North Fork halfway through the Hopeville Canyon and the entire South Branch lower Smoke Hole Run almost back to the campgrounds.

DIFFICULTIES: Where the North Fork joins the South Branch, it divides into several channels some of which may be obstructed by logs or fallen trees. The old broken out Royal Glen dam may be run on the left with caution. Concrete reinforcing rods lurk just below the surface and may have trapped debris. The countercurrent below the chute is tricky. The long rapids immediately below here are not tricky, but may have some pretty good sized waves. Further down towards Petersburg the paddler will encounter an entertaining staircase of river wide ledges which deserve the usual caution regarding possible hydraulics associated with same.

SHUTTLE: Put in across from the Smoke Hole Caverns (worth a trip in themselves) on W.V. 4 and 28 and take out on the left bank before the bridge in Petersburg. This is next to the big parking lot and city park adjacent to the Petersburg Firehall.

GAUGE: For all sections, call (301) 899-3210 and listen for the Petersburg reading following the recorded weather forecast. This is the gauge referred to in all sections above. There is a visual canoeing gauge painted on the rock on the far side of the river at Harman's Pool located at the end of the canyon at the tourist cabins. You will need at least 1.5′ for section A on this canoeist's gauge. Three feet is a good maximum for all sections on this crude gauge. The differential between the government gauge at Petersburg and the canoeist's gauge is 2.3 feet. Some variation can be expected since the Petersburg gauge also includes the Smoke Hole discharge.

MOOREFIELD RIVER

South Fork of the South Branch of the Potomac

A. Fort Seybert to Milam Bridge—10 Miles

CLASS	GRAD.	VOL.	SCENE	TIME	LEVEL
2-4	25 4@40	204	A-B	3	1-3′

MAPS: USGS—Fort Seybert and Petersburg 15′
COUNTIES—Pendleton and Hardy

DESCRIPTION: The whole trip is characterized by fantastic beauty. All of the headwaters of the Potomac are characterized by massive rock formations that are awe-inspiring and the Moorefield ranks among the best. The water is magnificently clear and the banks absolutely unlittered. The wildlife to be seen is abundant—ducks, turkeys, beaver, kingfishers, woodchucks, and deer may be seen on a single trip. Yet, as of this writing, this magnificent gorge is considered to be a choice spot for one of an eastern electric company's pumped storage projects. The cost of kilowatt hours could never be high enough to pay for this unique setting.

DIFFICULTIES: After a couple of miles from the put in and just past a little church on the right, the river divides into three channels. Where they come together again is a pretty mean rapids which is choked by boulders. If you don't like this, you had better quit because it is only a prelude to what lies ahead in the canyon. There then follows an extremely beautiful cruise through a farm valley (Class 2). The farms, though isolated, are very well kept and progressive. At the end of this valley, a massive rock formation on the right stands as a sentinel guarding the entrance of the Moorefield Gorge. For the next 4 miles the rapids are steep and many are mean. The rapids are steeper than the gradient indicates because there are many flat pools between each set.

Most of the rapids are choked by huge boulders. This obscures the paddler's vision so that he must either paddle them by the seat of his pants or else do some judicious scouting. The latter is recommended, particularly in high water. Take your time through here, for safety's sake as well as for the enjoyment of the incredible beauty.

SHUTTLE: The take out is 2 miles south of Milam (upstream) on "7" almost at the county line. The put in is just a few more miles south at the bridge at Fort Seybert on Pendleton "3" (same road). One of the easiest shuttles.

GAUGE: There is a yellow painted gauge on the Milam bridge. There is also a gauge on the U.S. 220 bridge in Moorefield that roughly correlates.

B. The Moorefield Below the Milam Bridge—25 Miles

This is a delightful open boat trip through some of the most charming farmland in West Virginia. The small river winds placidly through the pastoral scenery with enough short, straight forward rapids to make things interesting. The rapids are more numerous at the upper end, but become sparser towards Moorefield.

There are numerous low water bridges that need to be carried in low water and could be dangerous in high. Immediately downstream from one of these concrete bridges, different from the rest in that it is characterized by arches instead of holes, there is a more difficult rapids than usual caused by large boulders in midstream. Other than for this, the whole stream has a Class 1-2 rating and it is very narrow throughout.

Milam can be reached by taking the South Branch River Road "7" south of Moorefield. The bridge is another couple of miles south of Milam. Take out either at the bridge in Moorefield or continue on 3 more miles to the Old Fields bridge on the South Branch (U.S. 220). Since the river is never very far from the highway, many shorter trips on this small stream are possible.

Readjusted yellow numbers on the Milam bridge are still too low. Don't run unless you have at least a foot. (Scouting report and based on experience with the upper river.)

SOUTH BRANCH OF THE POTOMAC

A. The South Branch Above U.S. 220 Bridge

The South Branch can be run from as far upstream as Franklin or even farther. Here it is a fast moving Class 1-2 trout stream with a 15-20′ gradient. It passes through a picturesque, broad valley through open farmland. The only hazards would be overhanging trees, low water bridges, and a small dam above Upper Tract. From Franklin would be a nice 16-mile run in high water to the U.S. 220 bridge. Franklin is an extremely attractive rural town with splendid overnight and eating facilities. It is the Spelunking Capital of West Virginia.

B. The Smoke Hole Run, U.S. 220 to Petersburg—25 Miles

CLASS	GRAD.	VOL.	SCENE	TIME	LEVEL
	5@35				
$1\text{-}3_{4,5}$	20@16	160	A	7	0-3′

MAPS: USGS—Petersburg and Onego 15′
COUNTIES—Pendleton and Grant

DESCRIPTION: This is a very long run, perhaps too much for one day, but it has been described collectively since it represents a significantly identifiable unit and most paddlers make a two-day overnighter of it. The first five miles is unquestionably the best white water on the South Branch and among the most beautiful of the whole Potomac, a river system that has plenty of beauty. In spades! Some will argue that the extremely rugged mountains forming the lower Smoke Hole Canyon are even more beautiful. Don't argue, just enjoy.

The river begins to pick up speed and action as it leaves the broad valley below Franklin, under the 220 bridge, and across a ford. It quickly turns a corner and enters a magnificent canyon which is a geologist's delight. The rapids through here are very closely spaced, fairly steep, and with enough complications to make your paddling interesting. Paddlers interested in action only will probably end their run after 5 miles at the Smoke Hole Campgrounds, but most will want to continue. Both should spend some time in this unique area as there are many attractive sights and trails in the area. Cave Mountain and Eagle Rock are two very noteworthy natural monuments.

As one leaves the Smoke Hole Campgrounds, he enters the most scenic, most historic, and most famous run in West Virginia. This is the land of whiskey stills, Indian and Civil War battles, and above all, mountaineer independence. For the most part the river is running through an isolated canyon of unparalleled grandeur. Mountaineer farms and homesteads add to the charm of the run and remind the paddler of the fortitude and austerity of the early settlers. They also remind the paddler of a tragic paradox. In order to protect the river for future generations from trash-laden riverbanks, fishing shanties, unplanned "developments" and the like, the Forest Service acquired this land to incorporate into the Spruce Knob-Seneca Rocks National Recreation Area. In so doing, these independent farmers had to be displaced. It was unfortunate that their way of life could not be preserved since their clean and well-kept farms harmonize beautifully with the surroundings.

The rapids are not as heavy as those above and seldom exceed a Class 2 rating unless the water is very high. About 4 miles from the Smoke Hole Campgrounds the paddler will encounter the newly built Big Bend Campgrounds (both are operated by the Forest Service). This makes a convenient overnight spot since cars may be left here. It will be the last contact point until Royal Glen is reached miles below. From here on there are few signs of civilization, only the occasional remains of the old homesteads. Several excellent primitive campsites exist next to the deep pools. As the miles progress, the canyon and the gradient decrease, making longer pools between the rapids. Soon the North Fork rushes in to join the parent stream and heads east towards Petersburg four miles away.

DIFFICULTIES: The major difficulty is encountered right off as one makes a right turn into the canyon. A massive rockslide is encountered where huge boulders block the river and the paddler's view. This is easily seen and one has plenty of time to take out. Pull off to the right and scout. Either portage by following the yellow triangles or if you are paddling a slalom boat, judiciously try it. At lower levels, the only way is on the far left over a steep drop into a boiling washing machine, against a huge boulder, and then a very sharp turn to the right. Tough for left-handed paddlers. At high levels, you are on your own. No immediate further difficulties will be encountered in the upper 5 miles except for heavy Class 3 rapids. At high levels, you will have your hands full. Watch out for a low water bridge at the picnic area. Portage necessary.

About 6 miles below the Big Bend Campground, a most unusual sight greets the paddler's eyes. An extremely massive landslide has occurred from high on the mountain on the left. This is Chimney Rock Slide and is visible for a considerable distance. The landslide has created a barrage on the river and a dangerous rapids. As you approach the rapids there is an island. Go to the right of it for portaging or scouting. The rapids is a short 10′ drop over a boiling cascade. Under each pillow is a very sharp boulder, so the route through should be attempted only by very skilled paddlers. It is not worth the risk to run this in an open boat.

As you approach the Royal Glen Dam and depending on the water level, you may want to land on the left and scout this, especially if you have an open boat. The dam is broken out on the left and can be run, but concrete reinforcing rods lurk just below the surface and of course are dangerous in themselves, but they may have entrapped logs and debris. The water going through the dam has tricky countercurrents which you may not be prepared for. The long rapids below here contains many high waves which could swamp an open boat loaded with camping equipment. Later on Smith Falls is encountered which is a series of low ledges and hydraulics.

SHUTTLE: If you are planning on making the entire run either straight through or with an overnight out on the riverbank, the shuttle is simple. Just put in at the U.S. 220 bridge below Upper Tract and take out at the next one in Petersburg, 15 miles away by car. Actually, a simpler put in can be had by driving down to the ford just beyond the bridge. A short 5-mile run can be made by leaving a car at the Smoke Hole Campground and a 9-mile run by leaving it at the Big Bend Campground. Arranging a take out at Royal Glen doesn't seem worth it in view of the horrendous shuttle involving driving clear over the mountain on W.V. 74, turning on W.V. 4 and 28 to the right, and right again at the Department of Highways maintenance yard. Great scenery up there, but you may as well paddle the remaining 3.5 miles into Petersburg.

GAUGE: No really good one visible. Corbett and Matacia define an ideal level as water wetting the top of the low water bridge at the Smoke Hole Picnic Area (4 miles from the put in). It can be run up to 8-10″ less. If you can't see the bridge, be careful. The Petersburg gauge reading gives an approximation by deducting 3 feet.

C. Petersburg to Old Fields—17 Miles

CLASS	GRAD.	VOL.	SCENE	TIME	LEVEL
1-2	8	672	B	4	0-2

MAPS: USGS—Petersburg, Greenland Gap, Moorefield 15′
COUNTIES—Grant and Hardy

DESCRIPTION: This is a flatter section of the upper Potomac traversing some of the finest agricultural land in West Virginia. The pools are long and the gentle (Class 1, occasionally 2) rapids few and far between. This is a good open boat run through excellent fishing water. Bass and trout may be taken the year round. In 1966, the water in the North Fork was so low that the Petersburg White Water Weekend race course had to be held here from Petersburg to the Fisher bridge just west of Moorefield.

The river branches many times below the U.S. 220 bridge between Petersburg and Moorefield. In one of the major branches, known locally as "Buzzard's Fork," high rock formations on the left are interesting in that they are populated with what appear to be wild goats. To see them run up and down the sheer cliffs is worth the trip itself. Just below here on the left are three large pools of backwater that can be explored by canoe by short portages. These are known as the "Sloughs" and are popular for bass fishing.

DIFFICULTIES: The only hazard to watch out for is a peculiarity of local laws and a very few strange landowners. Apparently titles to the land in this area extend under the river giving the landowner ownership of anything solid under the surface. This means if you flip, stop to dump, wade a riffle, or otherwise have to get out of your canoe, you are trespassing and at least one person will have you arrested by a conservation officer if he catches you. It is pointless to test this strange situation, so please cooperate by staying in your boat.

SHUTTLE: Put in at the city parking lot in Petersburg and take out at the Old Fields bridge just north of Moorefield on U.S. 220.

GAUGE: Same as for Part E.

D. THE TROUGH—Rt. 220 Bridge at Old Fields to Harmison's Landing—11 Miles

CLASS	GRAD.	VOL.	SCENE	TIME	LEVEL
C, 1-2	5	1226	A+	3	1.6-3.6′

MAPS: USGS—Moorefield and Keyser 15′
COUNTIES—Hardy and Hampshire

DESCRIPTION: This very beautiful and popular canoeing river on which many organizations sponsor large float trips, is an ideal river for novices or even non-canoeists to run. The first 4 miles of the trip are through very scenic farmland and actually contain most of the rapids. The approach of the RR bridge at the end of this stretch is tricky and marks the beginning of the Trough. As one makes a wide, right-hand turn in the river, he is on the left side and must quickly get over to the right 50 yards above the bridge in order to avoid an exposed ledge. In high water there will be good-sized standing waves below the bridge for nearly 100 yards. The paddler will then find himself entering the serenity of a deep canyon with 1500′ mountain walls rising steeply from each side of the river. The vistas are ever changing and provide spectacular scenery especially in the spring and fall when seasonal colors are at their peak. There is very little white water in the Trough itself, but the scenery more than makes up for this lack. This river also provides some of the best bass fishing in the state and one can find many primitive campsites along the sandy banks. There are a few more riffles as one leaves the Trough, but the river has widened considerably. A must trip for every West Virginia outdoorsman. Other than a reasonable amount of caution at the RR bridge, there are no DIFFICULTIES.

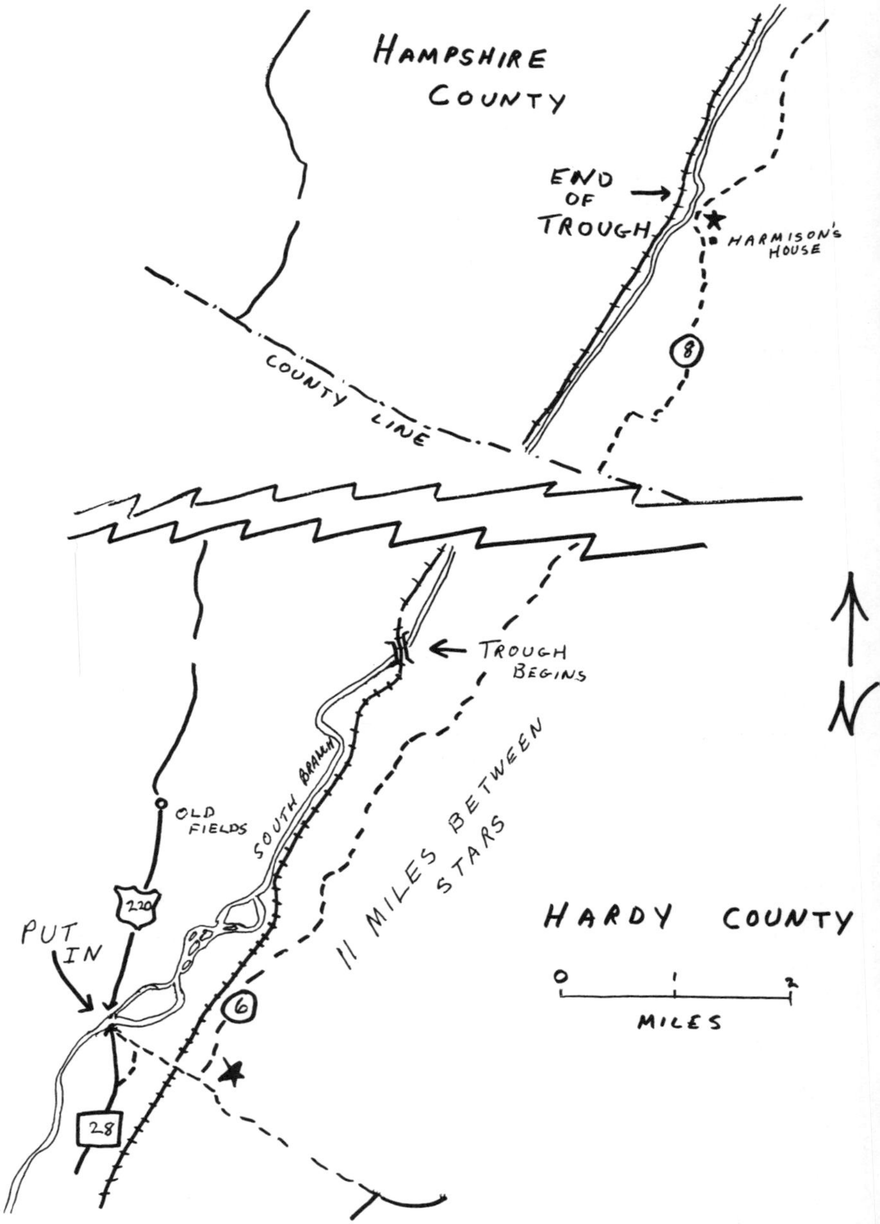
HAMPSHIRE COUNTY
END OF TROUGH
HARMISON'S HOUSE
8
COUNTY LINE
TROUGH BEGINS
OLD FIELDS
SOUTH BRANCH
11 MILES BETWEEN STARS
220
PUT IN
6
28
HARDY COUNTY
0
1
2
MILES
N

E. Harmison's Landing to U.S. Rt. 50 at Romney—13 Miles

CLASS	GRAD.	VOL.	SCENE	TIME	LEVEL
1	5	1226	A-B	4	2-4′

DESCRIPTION: After leaving the Trough, the river widens and slows considerably. Within the next 10 miles, the river passes through verdant farmlands and is characterized by extremely long placid pools punctuated by short riffles. It is an ideal float fishing stream and is considered by some to be the best for trophy-sized bass. Nearing Romney, arising from the right bank and extending for more than a mile are shale cliffs which jut upward 200′. However, much of this prospect is spoiled by the camps and cottages perched atop the precipice. The trip from Harmison's Landing is ideal for novices, johnboats, and weekend campers. A popular two-day open boat, camping trip starts by putting in at the U.S. 220 bridge, camping overnight at Harmison's, and then continuing to Romney the next day. There are no DIFFICULTIES in this lower part except an angry bull that will chase you if you get out at the wrong place.

SHUTTLE: The put in for Part D is easy to find—where U.S. 220 crosses the South Branch just south of Old Fields. Finding the take out at the end of the Trough (Harmison's Landing) isn't easy. Take the secondary road leading straight east from the put in bridge, cross the RR tracks, and turn left on the road at the farmhouse (it will be called "6" in Hardy County and "8" in Hampshire County). Continue on this road until the river comes back into view. Stop at either farmhouse on the right and request permission of Mr. Harmison to use the landing. There is a 50¢ per canoe charge for this and all canoeists are requested to honor this. The charge also covers camping for the night. Continuing on this same road will bring the shuttler to U.S. 50. One can take out at the old bridge pier on the right bank 100 yards upstream from the present span.

GAUGE: Call (301) 899-3210 and listen for the Springfield gauge reading following the recorded weather report.

F. The South Branch Below Romney

There is little interest to the white water paddler in the long slow 34-mile stretch of the South Branch to its junction with the North Branch at Green Spring. There is very little action, the banks are pretty muddy, and the scenery fairly developed farmland or fishing shanties. It is a good float fishing stream and well recommended for bass. It can get dangerous at high water stages and approaches big volume rivers.

LOST RIVER

Dry Gorge Section Between W.V. 55 Bridge Above and W.V. 259 Bridge Below Wardensville–6 Miles

CLASS	GRAD.	VOL.	SCENE	TIME	LEVEL
2-4	40	S	B	2	1.5+

MAPS: USGS–Wardensville 15′
COUNTY–Hardy

DESCRIPTION: This section of the Lost River, called the Dry Gorge section, is the most unique and best named river in the state in that it doesn't always exist! In low water, the river actually disappears into the ground just beyond the bridge above Wardensville thus leaving the section to be described indeed dry for most of the year. The river apparently traverses some unknown Stygian course only to emerge several miles away, seemingly *de novo,* to form the Cacapon River.

DIFFICULTIES: A run on this section can therefore only be made in high water when the underground river can't handle all of the flow and the river spills over into the flood channel cut around the mountain. Fantastic! For the first couple of miles there are frequent Class 2-3 rapids. Two islands mark a landslide choked channel necessitating a carry. Below the islands there is a series of steep ledges with their accompanying hydraulics. This is very steep and could be real mean in high water. Run these just to the right of center as there is a low water bridge right below them which must be portaged on the right. There are many chutes and drops through narrow passages that require maneuvering back and forth across the river to find the next passage. Another low water bridge must be carried near the end of the flood channel (on the right).

Soon the point is reached where the underwater river miraculously reappears from a series of small springs and the volume of the river fascinatingly doubles. Where the flood channel and the underground river merge, there is another series of steep ledges which produce heavier rapids than the first series. There are also several more good rapids before reaching the take out bridge. From here on, the river, now called the Cacapon, is much tamer. Catching the Dry Gorge wet is difficult, but well worth the wait.

SHUTTLE: Very simple–use the W.V. 55 bridges above Wardensville and take out at W.V. 259 bridge below Wardensville or at the low water bridge off W.V. 55 above Wardensville to eliminate some flat water.

GAUGE: Check the gauge under the Capon Bridge at U.S. 50. This reading may be gotten from Woolford's Grocery, 304-856-2750. There is a painted gauge at the upper bridge above Wardensville. A reading of 2.5′ on this gauge is enough. The Cootes Store gauge on the North Fork of Shenandoah is an indication of area discharge. Look for a 3-6′ range.

THE CACAPON

A. The Cacapon Above Capon Bridge (U.S. 50)—30 Miles

The long section of the Cacapon River from Wardensville to U.S. 50 offers little in the way of white water except for occasional riffles in medium water. It is however a good bass fishing stream and is popular, if not ideal for float fishing. A good secondary road follows the river from Capon Bridge to Yellow Spring and from there to Wardensville, W.V. 259 is handy. Hence, many shorter trips are possible. The pools in many instances are long and deep and at least one is the remains of an old millpond impoundment. Unfortunately this section of the river has been turned into essentially rural slums in many places due to the unlimited and closely spaced vacation cabins and trailers that line the banks, some in unbelievably poor taste. Sewage from these places as well as towns upstream have caused great increases in algal growth in recent years. A myth persists that the Cacapon is one of the few rivers in the state where you can still drink right from the river. The reverse would be closer to the truth.

B. Capon Bridge to W.V. 45 Bridge—12 Miles

CLASS	GRAD.	VOL.	SCENE	TIME	LEVEL
1-3	14	549	A	4	1-3′

MAPS: USGS—Capon Bridge
COUNTY—Hampshire

DESCRIPTION: This is a very popular eastern canoeing stream that contains exquisite scenery and challenging white water for the intermediate paddler. It is a good float fishing stream for open boats, but would require skills well beyond that of the novice to negotiate safely. It has drowned foolish, inexperienced paddlers. It is often up in the winter and the snow covered banks combined with the unusual rock formations make this a highly recommended run.

The trip begins with flat water and a few riffles through open farmland. After about 3 miles, the river heads to the left past high rocky cliffs and things get a little more interesting. There are 3 small to medium-sized ledges which require skill and possibly scouting for correct passage. Towards the end of the run, a spectacular rock formation may be seen high on the left, Caudy's Castle, which is worth an exploratory side trip. From here on to the bridge is a good deal of flat water.

DIFFICULTIES: The first low ledge is at the end of a right-hand turn against a cliff on the left and the best passage may be on the far right in lower water. Right below here is a nice sandy beach suitable for lunch stops. The second ledge is at the end of a spectacular rock formation called "Chapel Rock" and is always runnable on the far left. The third ledge is sort of big and intermediates may want to scout. In low water, the passage is on the right at the risk of banging your stern pretty hard. At 9″ or more, the best passage is just left of center, but requires more skill in maneuvering.

SHUTTLE: Put in under the U.S. 50 bridge on the left which is rather steep or drive down the left side of the river 3 miles to Cold Stream for a riverside put in that cuts off mostly flat water. Take out on the right under the W.V. 45 bridge which is a difficult climb. To reach this from Cold Stream, simply continue to Slanesville on W.V. 45 and turn right. Be sure to leave your car at the second bridge. (The first is over the North River.)

GAUGE: Both bridges have canoeing gauges, but one cannot improve on Corbett and Matacia's advice which cautions about scraping on the first riffle below the U.S. 50 bridge (can estimate by inspection). The Cacapon is simply boring if the water is too low. Taking a hike is recommended for such levels and more rewarding. Gauge readings may be obtained from Woolford's Grocery at Capon Bridge, 304-856-2750. The Cootes Store gauge on Shenandoah's north fork should be in the 3-5′ range.

C. The Cacapon Below W.V. 45—40 Miles

The river below the W.V. 45 bridge has very little gradient all of the way to the mouth on the Potomac at Great Cacapon. It transcribes huge loops through the mountains and ridges with very few rapids and many long, long flat pools. As such it is an ideal float fishing stream and even amateur anglers will tell you that it contains some of the best bass fishing water in the state. (Hint: Use eels, live or artificial for bait. Catfish minnows are also good.) Much of the scenery down to Largent is pretty good, but there are a lot of vacation cabins and summer homes along the way. They are apparently owned by a much wealthier class of people than those above U.S. 50 judging by the expensive appearance of many of them. New trailer parks and fishing camps are going in every day. Is this what is to become of all West Virginia rivers? Largent may be reached from near the W.V. 45 bridge by taking W.V. 29 north to W.V. 9 and then turning right. Continue straight on 9 to Great Cacapon. The only DIFFICULTY to warn you about is a high dam about 4 miles above Great Cacapon. Also, landowners are very particular about having paddlers camp on their lands due to many abuses in the past. Always check first. The river is incredibly rich in wildlife. It is not unusual to see beaver, wild turkeys, and deer in a short period of time. If you are making a float trip, it is suggested to get on the river at daybreak to take advantage of this. Eat your breakfast at mid-morning. Paddlers desiring to paddle below the dam to Great Cacapon are urged to be sure there is at least 1′ on the Capon Bridge gauge because the flow below the dam is much lower due to the impoundment.

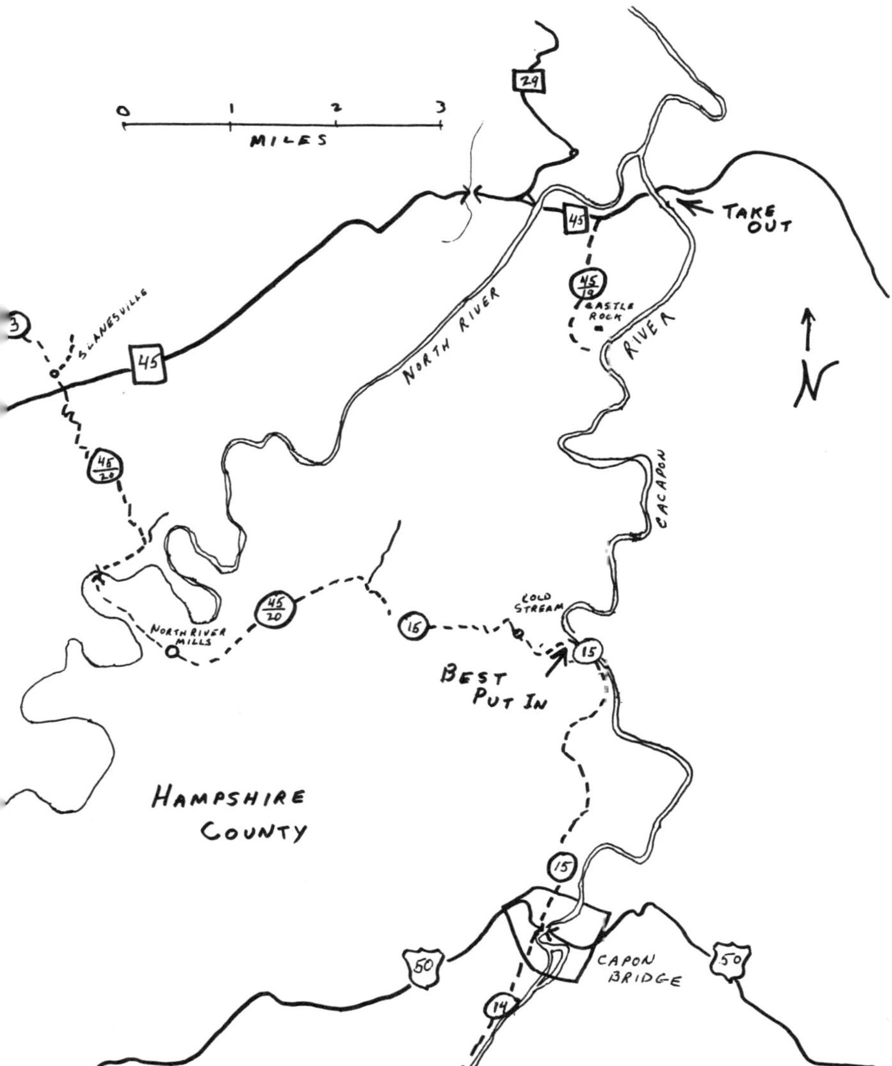
0 1 2 3
MILES
29
45
TAKE OUT
45/19
CASTLE ROCK
RIVER
N
NORTH RIVER
SLANESVILLE
3
45
45/20
CACAPON
COLD STREAM
45/20
16
15
NORTH RIVER MILLS
BEST PUT IN
HAMPSHIRE COUNTY
15
50
50
CAPON BRIDGE
14

SHENANDOAH

Millville, W.Va., to Sandy Hook, Md.—7 Miles

CLASS	GRAD.	VOL.	SCENE	TIME	LEVEL
$1\text{-}2_3$	¼@30 ½@20	2588	A-B	2	2-4′+

MAPS: USGS—Charles Town and Harpers Ferry
COUNTY—Jefferson

DESCRIPTION: This is a tremendously beautiful river no matter which way you look at it. The river passes between majestic cliffs, winds through interesting islands, provides homes and resting places for an incredible variety of water fowl, passes along the historic, nineteenth century charm of Harpers Ferry and the site of John Brown's fateful escapade, and finally joins the mighty Potomac through a magnificent gap in the Blue Ridge, the last West Virginia water to bathe mountains.

The fabled Shenandoah Staircase may be seen just under and upstream from the U.S. 340 bridge in Harpers Ferry. Like many rivers in the Eastern Panhandle, the rapids here are formed by the sharp upthrusting ends of the sedimentary layers of rock common to the East. This creates a long, interesting series of ledges that span the entire river diagonally from right to left. This provides the boater with a variety of entertainment under fairly safe conditions. The paddler can find a passage, eddy turn, ferry in either direction, find the next passage, and so on. The force of the river at normal levels (0-2′) and the shallow waters remind one of the rapids below the Hinton Bridge on the New River. Of course, if the river were high, it would be powerful and dangerous since it is so wide.

This is an excellent place for the whole family regardless of their interests. Some people just like to climb one of the many cliffs in the area, sit on a rock, and watch the river, the clouds, and the day go by. Although the effects of water pollution are irritatingly noticeable at low water and the river is located so far from the bulk of paddlers in West Virginia (3½ hrs. from Morgantown, 8 from Charleston!), it should be considered a must for every West Virginian.

According to Randy Carter, there are some 15 miles or so of the Shenandoah in West Virginia above the Millville put in and is mostly flat except for one fairly heavy rapids 1 mile above a power dam above Millville.

DIFFICULTIES: Not too many aside from getting there. The river begins as flat water and the first rapids begins against a high cliff as the river turns to the right. The good water is on the left. The river then pools up behind a river-wide barrage, Bull Falls, which is a 3-4′ ledge containing many passages. The ones on the left contain the heaviest water; the ones on the right may not have enough unless the river is high. The novice may do well to scout this first. There will be at least one hydraulic and a series of haystacks below each passage. Another nice 100-yard descent follows immediately which will be rather turbulent at levels over 1.0′.

The Staircase, already described, will then appear with the heaviest water just under and below the bridge. After joining the Potomac, the paddler should be mindful that the volume has now more than doubled and even the smallest waves are powerful. About a ½ mile below this junction, White Horse Rapids is encountered on the left which is a set of pretty good standing waves. Flips here are common and rescues difficult in high water.

SHUTTLE: Put in is reached by driving west of Harpers Ferry on U.S. 340 and turning left at the first crossroads to Millville (marked by a sign to the right "Harpers Ferry Caverns"). Put in at the large gauging station at river level. The take out can be reached from a back road out of the Maryland Roadside Park at the U.S. 340 bridge that spans the Potomac (not the 340 bridge in Harpers Ferry). Sandy Hook is located beneath the bridge. If you want to run the "Needles" of the Potomac (described separately), continue exactly 2 miles up the road from Sandy Hook to a convenient put in.

GAUGE: Use the Millville gauge reading. Usually figure on at least 2′ here. If over 4′, it is probably pretty high and Bull Falls will be dangerous. Randy Carter has a canoeing gauge on the left abutment under the Shenandoah bridge in Harpers Ferry. Over 2′ is considered high water on his gauge.

THE MAIN STEM OF THE POTOMAC

From two miles below Green Spring, W.Va. (Oldtown, Md.), where the North and South branches of the Potomac meet to form the great Potomac River, the beautiful, historic West Virginia-Maryland river border flows majestically for almost 115 miles towards Harpers Ferry. The river in most places is suitable for well-coached beginners in open boats. It is mostly flat water, but there are occasional Class 1-2 river-wide rapids. It should be remembered that this is a huge river and the force behind the little waves is considerable. It is an extremely dangerous river in high water.

The historic Chesapeake and Ohio Canal follows along the Maryland shore and at several points, historic or restored remains are worth visiting. In addition, a well-maintained hiking and cycling trail follows the old tow path on the left bank. Civil War battlefields and Revolutionary War sites add further historic interest to canoe runs in this area. Several developed campsites exist along the river which one can use as bases for canoeing operations. It is highly recommended to buy a copy of *Hiker's Guide to the C and O Canal* from the Mason-Dixon Council of the Boy Scouts, 1200 Crestwood Drive, Hagerstown, Md. 21740. This book is crammed with information about historic sites, camping areas, roads, and other points of interest in the area which the canoeist would find invaluable in planning his trip.

A highly recommended camping location is Fort Frederick State Park in Maryland, south of Hagerstown. It is the site of a historic Revolutionary War fort and a particularly impressive portion of the canal. Historic Antietam Battlefield is nearby. Finally the river is beautiful here, contains interesting, closely spaced rapids, and as with all of the river, is abundantly rich in wildlife, especially waterfowl.

The National Park Service is rebuilding and developing much of the Canal into a National Monument. One of the places scheduled for development in West Virginia is near Paw Paw on W.V. 29. It is a shame the state has never developed a state park along this magnificently beautiful and historic river.

DIFFICULTIES: Several of the old C. and O. dams still remain. Dam No. 6 just above the mouth of the Cacapon is broken out. About 10 miles below Fort Frederick, No. 5 creates a 5-mile long lake and must be portaged on the West Virginia side. There is a power plant dam right below Williamsport, Md. Dam No. 4 is a high one creating a 13-mile long lake (Big Slackwater) and is located near Falling Waters, W.Va. The last dam in West Virginia is No. 3 and backs up water for 5 miles above Harpers Ferry.

The 2 miles of the Potomac below Dam No. 3 down to Harpers Ferry, the mouth of the Shenandoah, and 1 mile farther to Sandy Hook, Md., below the U.S. 340 bridge, is definitely not for beginners. This beautiful stretch called the Needles is wide and powerful and is almost continuous Class 1-2. If the river is high, it could be dangerous.

A flipped or swamped boat could be very difficult to get out of or, if high water and cold temperature, *impossible* for the novice. A half mile below Harpers Ferry and an extremely beautiful gap in the river, White Horse Rapids appears on the left side of the river. Here one will find the biggest waves on this section and although they are regular, they are powerful. There are many rocky islands in this same area inviting other routes. The river on the right consists of small ledges between these islands.

GAUGE: The Hancock gauge gives a good estimation. Beginners should consider 2 to 4′ as ideal. The river becomes highish and dangerous between 5 to 7′ and above.

OTHER STREAMS IN THE POTOMAC BASIN

BACK CREEK: W.V. 9 bridge at Hedgesville to McCory's Ferry on the Potomac, a distance of 8 miles may be run with suitable levels. It is a very placid stream as it meanders through the Berkeley County countryside ranging in difficulty from Class B to 2. Two possible areas of difficulty are: a bend in the river approximately two miles from the put in where the river turns sharply to the right forming a Class 2 rapids and approximately a mile and a half from the take out as the river passes under a RR bridge and again turns sharply to the right forming another Class 2+ rapids. Back Creek joins the Potomac approximately 1 mile upstream from McCory's Ferry. McCory's Ferry may be recognized by a large sandstone outcrop on the right-hand side of the river.

NORTH RIVER: This is a very small tributary of the Cacapon which is occasionally paddled when the water is very high elsewhere. It loops and winds through great curves for some 21 miles between U.S. 50 and W.V. 45. The gradient is very little hence the white water isn't very challenging except at the sharp turns, under low branches, etc. There are many fences, dangling wires and branches to watch out for as well as a few low log dams. The most striking thing about this run is the access it provides to Ice Mountain, another of the Panhandle's incredible wonders. About 13 miles from the put in where the stream transcribes a sharp left-hand turn and is pinched in by steep rockslides to each side is a place to stop and climb this freak of nature. Even in late summer, ice may be found beneath rocks and in crevices high on this natural refrigerator. When the water is very high there is a horrendous run on the upper North around Rio with a boat eating ledge.

PATTERSON CREEK: This is an interesting stream passing through a very fertile, historic valley. It has been inhabited for centuries as evidenced by the wealth of Indian artifacts that may still be collected in the area. It is one of the gamiest areas of the state with deer, squirrels, and wild turkey being especially plentiful. The small stream is also rich in bass and, surprisingly, muskies. Again, it is runnable only when everything else is up, but the riffles do not add up to any particular difficulty. As usual, the fences, dangling wires, etc., must be considered. A potentially interesting open boat run could be made in high water between Burlington on U.S. 50 and Fort Ashby at the intersection of W.V. 46 and 20, a distance of about 18 miles. It is another 5 miles to its mouth on the North Branch.

NEW CREEK: Don't hold your breath on this one! This is about the absolute lower limit as far as size goes. When there is enough water on this tiny stream to float a boat, everything else has to be in flood stage. It is a straight forward Class 1-2 stream following major highways through largely pastoral settings. Other than the usual little stream difficulties, there is a low water bridge near Keyser. Put in near the intersection of W.V. 93 and U.S. 50 or anywhere else upstream or downstream as the highway is always close by. Take out on U.S. 220 somewhere in Keyser near the Potomac State campus.

LUNICE CREEK: This very shallow little trout stream can occasionally be run from near the vicinity of Maysville all the way into the South Branch at Petersburg near the tannery. The stream can be run when the water is very high elsewhere and affords fairly continuous Class 1-2 action.

THORN CREEK: This little headwater tributary to the South Branch has 7.5 miles of Class 2-3 water from near Moyers to the mouth. At a left turn 2.5 miles into the trip there are two interesting rapids. The second is blocked by a log. At the mouth is a terrible looking five-foot ledge. Paddle this when Petersburg gauge nears 5′. There are lots of limestone and caves along the run.

TEARCOAT CREEK: This is a short but extremely beautiful run cutting across the red shaley grain of Hampshire County. It tumbles over an endless series of ledge rapids separated by short pools at the bottom of a shadowy lichen-covered gorge. U.S. 50 is nearby but completely screened. It is a three-mile run to North River.

SLEEPY CREEK: This is an open boat trip alongside beautiful shale cliffs in the far Eastern Panhandle.

LITTLE CACAPON: This is a long Class 1 trip for high water periods from U.S. 50 to its mouth at Paw Paw.

CHAPTER II

THE BIG MOUNTAIN RIVER—THE MIGHTY CHEAT

The Cheat watershed is fantastic no matter which way you look at it. If you are a gung ho Corps of Engineers type, you drool in frustration at seeing water running freely every second over one of the largest uncontrolled watersheds in the east, but if you are a paddler, you see it as a place of almost infinite variety of water to test the mettle of your skill and your boat. If you are an outdoors buff, you are struck by the realization that the same water you see high on Bald Knob when traveling on the Cass Scenic RR, the same water you see pouring off Spruce Knob through the mountain hamlets of Job and Whitmer, the same water you see plunging over Blackwater Falls and the same water you see forming an enchanting Arnout Hyde photograph at Bruceton Mills, all eventually wind up in the same river, the mighty Cheat.

It begins in the real mountains of the state in the forms of four big forks, Shavers, Glady, Laurel, and Dry, each separated from its neighbors by massive high mountain ridges. Shavers Fork even begins by actually flowing *on top* of one of these ridges for many miles. In this country, the shuttles are as fascinating as the rivers. Although Shavers Fork is considered as the main source of the Cheat, and indeed is sometimes simply called "Cheat," Dry Fork is more important as a "tributary catcher"—the fascinating Gandy Creek, a stream that goes *through* a mountain, enters near Whitmer; Red Creek draining the unique Dolly Sods wilderness area has its mouth below Harman; the fabulous Otter Creek, which is a stream entirely within a wilderness area, enters above Hendricks; and finally at Hendricks itself, the wild and raucous Blackwater merges with Dry Fork with such volume that it is now called Black Fork and which in just a few miles joins Shavers Fork in Parsons to form the Cheat.

Two more significant paddling tributaries enter the Cheat, Horseshoe Run near historic Saint George, and the Big Sandy in the middle of the Cheat Canyon near Masontown. The Cheat comes to an ignoble end when it merges with northern West Virginia's sewer, the Monongahela, at Point Marion, Pa.

All of the Cheat tributaries and the Cheat itself below Rowlesburg are characterized by steep gradients, continuous action, pure, clean water (the lower Cheat, Big Sandy, and Blackwater excepted by mine acid), and spectacular scenery in largely unsettled areas. The Big Sandy is unique in that it begins in Pennsylvania, descends into West Virginia, and returns to its state of origin via the Cheat, the points of entry and exit on the Mason-Dixon Line being but 10 miles apart.

There are many primitive and developed camping areas along the rivers of the watershed. Along Shavers Fork in the Cheat Bridge area (F.S. 209), where "12" crosses Glady Fork, and at Jenningston on Dry Fork, one will find primitive camping areas. At the mouth of the Big Sandy, one will find an ideal campsite in a very wild setting. The Forest Service has excellent fee area campgrounds at Stuart Recreation Area right on Shavers Fork and a more primitive area at nearby Bear Heaven. There is another Forest Service fee area right on Horseshoe Run. The wilderness areas mentioned, Dolly Sods and Otter Creek, have attained wilderness protection by the Forest Service under terms of the Eastern Wilderness Act. There are two state parks in the entire area near the rivers, Blackwater Falls and Canaan Valley. All of the upper forks are good trout streams spoiled only by siltation of the strippers' shovels. Horseshoe Run is also a good trout stream as is the Big Sandy in the Bruceton Mills area. The Cheat itself offers good bass fishing all the way to a few miles below Rowlesburg where outrageous mine drainage sterilizes the river. There are even trout in the Cheat from Parsons to Saint George.

The dam builders are everywhere, but only a few fairly inconsequential products of their activities as yet exist. Very low, but dangerous dams exist on Shavers Fork at the Bowden Bridge and on Dry Fork just below Harman. A low power company dam near Albright on the Cheat and the Cheat Reservoir power company dam near the state line are the only others, but these latter two are in areas of little interest to the paddler. The Corps wants to put in a huge dam at Rowlesburg on the Cheat which would undoubtedly improve Cheat Canyon and Narrows paddling all year around for the expert paddler, but this book is for all types of paddlers and the dam would spoil the entire Cheat Valley between Rowlesburg and Parsons for the open boat canoe camper, float fishermen, and river trippers. This valley is rich in history, beauty, and most importantly, the major source of revenue for lovely Tucker County. At the present time, a power company is planning to dam up the upper Blackwater River, a very small stream and series of beaver ponds rarely paddled. The Corps and power companies have thoroughly studied the construction of impoundments on every single stream mentioned above. For those who would be interested in what such impoundments would look like, he is urged to visit either the Cheat or Tygart reservoirs, two very large silt catching basins of very low pH.

Recounting the history of the Cheat watershed would be the subject of a book in itself. The RR and early logging days buff will nod in recognition as he paddles by the sites of the old logging towns along the rivers: Spruce, Evenwood, Gladwin, Jenningston, Laneville, and many others. Some towns still exist today in the form of "bear camp" towns like Bemis, while some like the wild and woolly Brooklyn Heights, where a dollar would buy you anything, have returned to dust and known only as "a place across the river from Hendricks." The peaceful, outward calm of the mountain hamlets of Job and Whitmer belie their lawless past when murders, lynchings, and robbery were the rule. No town has such interesting history as does Saint George, destined to be buried by a Corps of Engineers reservoir. Dating from the Revolution, changing sides many times during the Civil War, having its county seat and records forcibly stolen and removed to Parsons by an outlaw army, this lovely little town, which has been repeatedly saved by the pluck of its people, seems doomed forever. George Washington knew of the lower Cheat and Big Sandy, exploring those parts near Morgantown for purposes of finding a waterway from the Potomac to the Ohio. George was told by ill-informed locals that the Cheat was navigable upstream for miles and wasn't too far from the equally navigable Potomac headwaters (the North Branch). It is a good thing George didn't try it! It is doubtful if our present leaders and policy makers get any better advice than this even today.

Logging is still a principal industry in the upper Cheat watershed although the logs are not floated to downstream mills anymore. Agriculture does not flourish in such rugged terrain and is limited mostly to high mountain hay farms except for fertile farms along the Cheat below Parsons and certain places in Preston County. The latter is noted for its production of much of America's buckwheat, a characteristic celebrated in Kingwood annually in September. Strip mining is becoming more popular and the results of this are far too evident to the paddler. Primarily, the Cheat watershed is encompassed by the Monongahela National Forest, a playground of vast natural and scenic attraction. The tourist potential of this area is great if planned for wisely.

Wildlife flourishes in the Cheat basin. Several black bear breeding areas are found. Deer and turkey are plentiful, but not as much as in the Eastern Panhandle. Some species are limited entirely to this area, e.g., the Cheat Mountain salamander. In other places a highly unusual association of several closely related species existing together occurs, as with the 22 species of warblers that live on Gaudineer Knob on upper Shavers Fork. The uppermost reaches of the Cheat forks contain native brook trout although their days are numbered if strip mining and clear cutting continue at the present rate. Beaver, muskrat, and occasionally fishers might be seen. The high country is also a botanist's delight whether his prize be the highly aromatic ramp or rare orchids. Balsam fir exists in several stands in the Cheat basin and American larch makes its southernmost stronghold near the head of the Cheat Canyon at Cranesville.

BIBLIOGRAPHY

Clarkson, R. B. 1964. *Tumult on the Mountains.* Parsons, W.Va.: McClain Printing Co.

Fansler, Homer. 1962. *History of Tucker County.* Parsons, W.Va.: McClain Printing Co.

Preble, J. 1965. *Land of Canaan.* Parsons, W. Va.: McClain Printing Co.

OTTER CREEK

Big Springs Gap to Mouth—2.6 Miles

CLASS	GRAD.	VOL.	SCENE	TIME	LEVEL
4	101	S	A	2	4.5-5.0

MAPS: USGS—Mozark Mountain
MNF
COUNTY—Tucker

DESCRIPTION: Otter Creek flows out of this roadless wilderness range of black bear, turkeys, and backpackers. It is little and steep and hard to get to. One has to be dedicated to paddling it to catch it at the right level. Otter Creek should be scouted from the old water level logging tramway trail along its entire length even if the paddler never catches it at the right level for a run. The headwaters can be reached from Alpena Gap off U.S. 33. There is a service road to a series of limestone filled tumbling drums which the state maintains as an experiment in trying to neutralize the naturally acid stream and improve its potential as a native trout stream. From there to Big Springs Gap it quadruples its volume as it meanders through a marsh area for four miles and then cascades at a steady 200 fpm for four more miles.

From the Big Springs Gap put in to the mouth there is no rest. It is hard work to find an eddy to catch one's breath. The creek is continuous, quick maneuvering in a small boulder patch, plus irregularly placed big boulders with hydraulics, pinning possibilities, and some downstream blind spots. Scouting Otter Creek is like trying to plan a course down a bobsled run. It's very exhilarating. It's very tiring.

DIFFICULTIES: About ½ mile into the trip there is a cross stream log on a ledge which will need to be carried. More logs could appear so be ready to eddy out. Eddying out on the right side is preferred since the trail is there. The left side is steep and laurel choked.

GAUGE: There is a gauge at the mouth of Otter Creek which can be surveyed by a short walk from W.V. 72. The Cheat gauge at Parsons will be in the 7-10′ range when Otter Creek is up. The Hendricks gauge on Dry Fork should be at about 5′.

SHUTTLE: Set up the take out at the Hendricks gauge for a fast 2.5 mile finish down the Dry Fork from Otter Creek's mouth. Shuttle back into Parsons and follow signs to Fernow Experimental Forest. Park at Big Springs Gap trail and carry 20 minutes down the trail to the put in.

SHAVERS FORK

A. Spruce to Cheat Bridge—17 Miles

The following account was made from a scouting trip taken along the entire course from the RR and actual paddling experience on the lower 5 miles of the course:

Your first problem would be setting up your shuttle and getting in to Spruce. Two private roads exist (Mower Lumber Co.), but experience has shown that they might be snowbound when you want in. When the roads are clear, the water might be too low. We would recommend commencing your shuttle at Cheat Bridge near U.S. 250. Turn right on Red Run Road just east of the river and continue upriver through the extinct town of Cheat Bridge. Don't cross the iron bridge, but stay on the upstream left all of the way (permission should be gained).*

Assuming you make it to the vicinity of Spruce, your put in would be 3900′ making it probably the highest run in the East. Here the river is very narrow, but fast. With adequate water it would be continuous 2 at least, a little 3 and with high water, there would be a lot of 3. Your first landmark would be 2 RR trestles a few hundred yards apart (Twin Bridges). In another ½ mile, Rocky Run or "Rocky Ridge Run" enters from the left. In another 2 miles, you will pass under a third trestle and then be joined by the Second Fork of Shavers from the right (known as Big Run among the locals). The bridge marks the end of the best action—the first 5 miles have 32 fpm gradient. The river then broadens out a bit, but still moves along pretty fast. The rapids are Class 1-2 with the 2's occurring at sharp bends. We did not see any particularly hazardous or difficult spots anywhere.

Other significant tributaries enter the stream from the left at roughly miles 8 (Beaver Creek), 9 (Buck Run), and 10 (Black Run). The road comes very close to the river at several points between these latter 2 runs, making access from Cheat Bridge easy. This part would make a splendid open boat fishing trip. The gradient averages 18-14 fpm and finally drops to only 10. The fourth bridge marks mile 12. From here down to Cheat Bridge, the river is very wide and shallow with very few riffles. These are Class 1's and occur at constrictions and bends in the river. The entire run would be a 17-mile trip through exquisite scenery. The regenerating spruce forest, the bogs, and mountain meadows remind one of Canada.

*People wishing to use the Mower Lumber Co. road for shuttle purposes should request permission from Mr. Ralph McDonald, Box 27, Durbin, phone 456-4422 (office) or 636-5106 (home).

B. U.S. 250 to McGee Run—10½ Miles

CLASS	GRAD.	VOL.	SCENE	TIME	LEVEL
	21				
1-2_3	2@32	S	A	3	—

MAPS: USGS—Durbin 15′
MNF
COUNTY—Randolph

DESCRIPTION: This is a very pleasant run on a beautiful river, one of the finest in the state, but also the one in the most jeopardy from industrialization. No stream in the state receives as many or as big individual fish from the state's trout stocking program. Indeed, the last 5½-mile section has been designated a Fish-for-Fun stream where angling is limited to barbless hooks and all trout must be returned. This is where you will find the fishermen in the state who are experts. The river is flanked by spruce, hemlock, and even balsam. The wildlife is fantastic, especially the birds. An interesting swallow nests under the bridge at the put in. The run is very easy down to Water Tank Run which enters from the right through large culverts. (If you want to keep track, the names of the runs that you will pass in order from the put in are Red Run, Stonecoal, Whitmeadow from the left, Glade and John's Camp from the right, Crouch from the left, then Water Tank, and finally Yokum and McGee from the left.)

DIFFICULTIES: At Water Tank, the river becomes steeper and the rapids more or less continuous although only Class 2. There are three pretty nice drops—one just below Glade Run, one right at Yokum, and one more before the take out. Just upstream from the mouth of Yokum, the paddler will pass under the bridge and coal conveyor of the controversial Linan Mines. There has been considerable question about whether an industrial development like this can co-exist with a beautiful, near-wilderness trout stream. If not, anglers and white water paddlers will be the first to know in the future.

GAUGE: None at present. If you can paddle around at the put in bridge without scraping, you will be O.K. You will need at least 1.5′ at U.S. 33 gauge (Part E).

SHUTTLE: Put in at the U.S. 250 bridge. To reach the take out, head back west along this highway and take the second road to the right, F.S. 92. From this Forest Service road there are many side roads that lead down to Shavers Fork along some of the runs named above. Not all of these roads are passable. Continue on 92 to the end and turn right down the hollow of McGee Run. There is a primitive campground there at the end of the Fish-for-Fun section.

C. McGee Run to Bemis—13 Miles

CLASS	GRAD.	VOL.	SCENE	TIME	LEVEL
$3\text{-}5_6$	58	544	A	6	1-2

MAPS: USGS—Durbin 15′, Beverly East, and Glady
MNF
COUNTY—Randolph

DESCRIPTION: After the longest shuttle in the state, the longest access paddle in the state, and carrying the most spectacular falls in the state, then one can pit his paddling skill and strength against 4 miles of the wildest water tumbling over 6 more falls, one of which is Class 6 and with no slack water between the drops.

The first part is wide and shallow at reasonable water levels, but it soon picks up speed slipping down over sloping rocks. A landmark at 5 miles is a RR marker visible from the river marked C-7, a mile later C-6, and at mile 7.5 R/S in green. Other than for watching for the RR signs, little else characterizes the first 3 hours of the trip except isolated wilderness.

Shortly after the last marker, there is an ominous looking blind rapids on a sharp right turn, but it is safe to run. The High Falls of Cheat will be met at mile 9, a river-wide abrupt drop of 15′, one of the most spectacular sights in West Virginia. There is a beautiful primitive campsite on the right used by backpackers. This is located at the mouth of Fall Run on the county map or Red Run on the topo.

DIFFICULTIES: One half mile below the High Falls is a Class 6 runnable falls. This complex consists of several ledges at the top and a thundering, slanting, right to left canted, 6′ drop. There is a large boulder immediately in the center run-out and jagged rocks in the ledge on the left. It is doubtful if one could keep to the right because of the diagonal shape of the ledge. It is a 6 because of the pinning possibility on the bottom boulder. The carry is easy on the right by lowering one's boat over the rock and climbing down.

Below this adrenaline pumping obstruction, the paddler has finally arrived at what this trip is all about. There is continuous Class 4 and 5 white water for 3.5 miles to Bemis. One is a bit busy to look for landmarks, but it is hard to miss the two RR bridges at 11 and 11.3 miles. The second bridge is at the sight of a runnable, sharp-dropping 6′ falls. It should be scouted at higher levels to be sure the paddler and his craft are not going to be invited to explore its base for an indefinite period. In the last 2 miles there are 3 more 4-5′ ledges which are all runnable.

In resume then, there is first the High Falls which are easy to recognize, then the Class 6 boulder smashing falls, and then the very dangerous falls at the second RR bridge, each separated by continuous, technically difficult water.

SHUTTLE: The shuttle for this trip is very long, but we recommend driving from the take out at Bemis back to Glady. Continue on through Glady turning right just beyond the town on F.S. 44. It is 25 miles through Wildell and May to Durbin. Turn right on U.S. 250 and on up the mountain to F.S. 92 (third right). Follow the signs to McGee Run, the end of the Fish-for-Fun section of Shavers Fork. These roads are not plowed during the snow season.

GAUGE: Use the U.S. 33 gauge described below. A 1-2′ reading will be necessary and the 2 will make those miles below High Falls very interesting. The Parsons gauge can be used as a rule of thumb by subtracting 2.5 and halving the remainder.

D. Bemis to Bowden Bridge—9 Miles
(to U.S. 33 Bridge—14 Miles)

CLASS	GRAD.	VOL.	SCENE	TIME	LEVEL
2-4	3@65 6@30	544	A-B	2	1-1.5′

MAPS: USGS—Glady and Bowden
COUNTY—Randolph

DESCRIPTION: What a way to start a canoe trip! The first 3 miles are straight downhill at a Class 4 pace, the next 3 are a delightful Class 3, while the last section levels out and divides into many small channels that provide a rather boring anti-climax. The river tumbles down vigorously off Cheat Mountain over beds of large boulders and provides very beautiful scenery (for the hiker; paddlers are so occupied, they don't see any scenery).

DIFFICULTIES: This section of the Cheat should be attempted by only advanced or expert paddlers. If you have to get out and scout any of it, you are probably not ready for it. A smashup leaves one stranded in the wilderness although one can walk out on the RR right-of-way. After completing about a mile and a half of Class 3-4 rapids, one enters a very long (almost ¾ mile) rapids that is more complex than mean. There are plenty of small eddies behind boulders so that one may "stairstep" his way down gradually. After this very long rapids, there is a quiet pool which is followed by a 50-yard lulu and contains three healthy souse holes that are best avoided. This is easier said than done as the heavy current tends to send the canoe in their direction. The river tames down considerably after this, but the paddler still needs to pay attention. There is one tricky place in the second section which seemingly is blocked by huge boulders and finding a passage may be difficult. Immediately under the Bowden bridge is a dam. Below this dam there is a 5-mile stretch of water along the highway until the U.S.

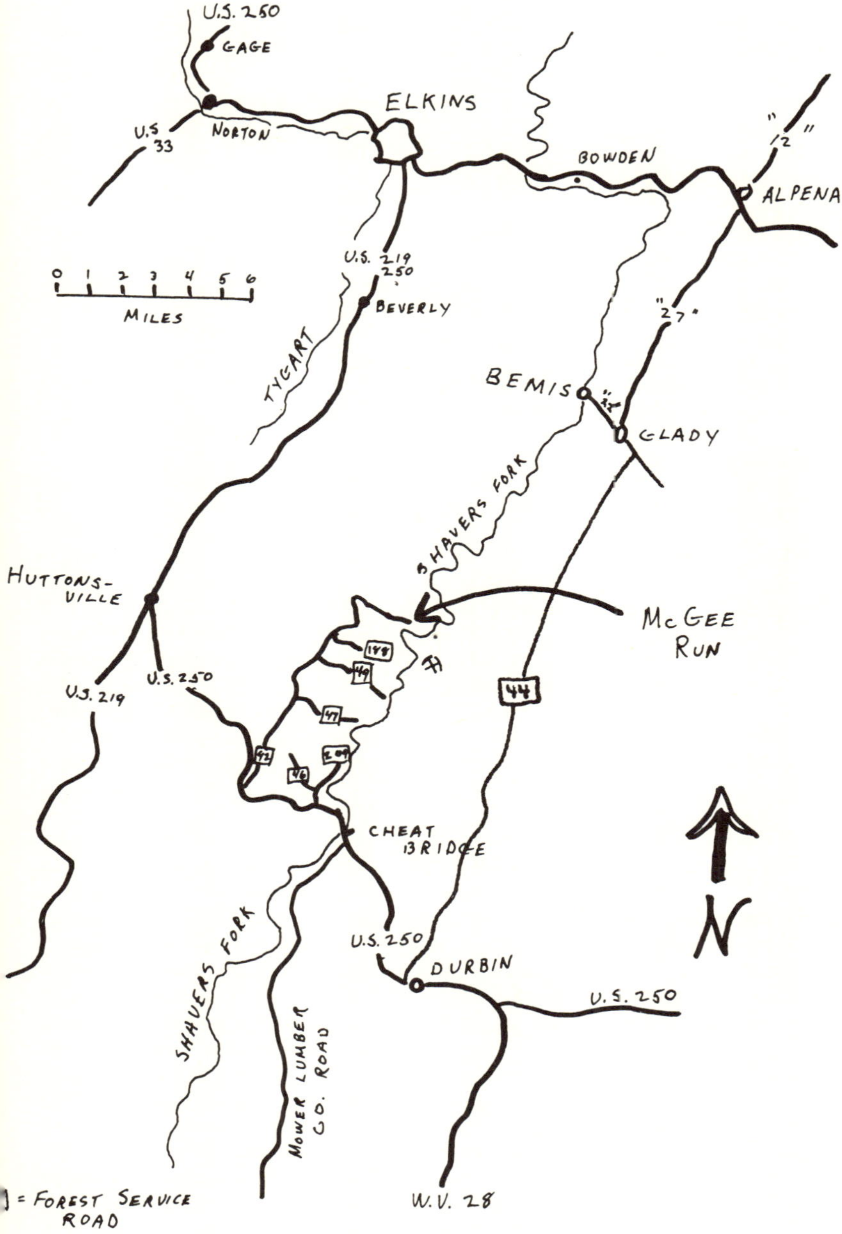
U.S. 250
GAGE
ELKINS
U.S 33
NORTON
BOWDEN
"12"
ALPENA
U.S. 219 250
BEVERLY
0 1 2 3 4 5 6
MILES
TYGART
"27"
BEMIS
GLADY
SHAVERS FORK
HUTTONS-VILLE
McGEE RUN
U.S. 219
U.S. 250
44
CHEAT BRIDGE
N
SHAVERS FORK
U.S. 250
DURBIN
U.S. 250
MOWER LUMBER CO. ROAD
W.V. 28
= FOREST SERVICE ROAD

33 bridge is reached. This section contains just a few riffles and is rather uninteresting due to the presence of many fishing cabins, trailer camps and the like. Along this section one should visit the Bowden National Fish Hatchery.

SHUTTLE: Take out just upstream of Bowden bridge. The bridge can be seen from U.S. 33. Bemis is reached by turning south from Alpena and taking "27" up to Glady. Turn right in Glady and take the two-mile road into Bemis. Put in under the bridge.

E. U.S. 33 Bridge to Parsons—22 Miles

CLASS	GRAD.	VOL.	SCENE	TIME	LEVEL
1-2	19	544	A-B	6-7	1-2.5′

MAPS: USGS—Elkins, Bowden, and Parsons
COUNTIES—Randolph and Tucker

DESCRIPTION: This part of the Cheat is a pleasant interlude between its raucous birthplace high on Bald Knob and the pastoral serenity of the Cheat Valley from Parsons to Rowlesburg where the mighty river begins its furious cascade through Cheat Canyon. The water volume in this section is fairly large, but soon doubles itself when it joins the Black Fork in Parsons. This river, one of the state's most scenic, will appeal to the novice as well as the expert. There are many ideal camping places and several vigorous rapids for playing around. The action and current are almost continuous with very little quiet water. The scenery through the deep hollows is spectacular. Many rocky bluffs and waterfalls line the river while the shores are studded with magnificent growths of hemlock. Some of the rapids reach Class 3 rating at the higher water levels, but the novice can always expect an easier passage should he desire.

DIFFICULTIES: None.

GAUGE: Located on the west bridge support on the upstream side of the U.S. 33 put in. Subtract 2.5 from the Parsons government gauge on the Cheat and halve the remainder for an approximation.

SHUTTLE: Can be set up in smaller segments. U.S. 33 to the steel bridge near Clifton Run is 6 miles by car, 8 by boat. From here on, the road on the right side of the river is rough. It comes close to the river at several points. If you want to do the whole thing, drive into Elkins and take U.S. 219 to Parsons.

GLADY FORK OF CHEAT

U.S. 33 Bridge to Mouth on Dry Fork (Gladwin)—16.5 Miles

CLASS	GRAD.	VOL.	SCENE	TIME	LEVEL
1-3	9@33 7.5@46	S	A	5-6	0.5-2

MAPS: USGS—Bowden, Harman, Mozark Mt.
MNF—Best
COUNTIES—Randolph and Tucker

DESCRIPTION: There are very few flat pools anywhere on this small, meandering stream. The rapids are continuous, but not difficult. The upper river is very shallow, but when the river is full, the turns on the smaller channel must be precise. Fallen tree hazards across the smaller channels are a real problem and caution is urged. The novice should be able to make good eddy turns.

Below the bridge to Sully (mile 9) the current keeps up a steady Class 2 pace, but soon the gradient begins to pick up. The last 3 or 4 miles are considerably more interesting in that waves, hydraulics, and passages become greater and more complex. The entire run is in a beautiful wilderness setting. Do not get too close to the low water bridge at the take out as the current is very powerful under it.

SHUTTLE: Put in at the U.S. 33 bridge. A take out for a 9-mile trip may be had by taking "12" north out of Alpena and parking at the bridge. Excellent camping may be done here or along the road to the left before the bridge. From the bridge to Gladwin is another 7.5 river miles. Continue on "12" taking a left at each of the next two forks. At the bottom of the very steep hill, turn left again and cross the low water bridge, the take out. It is possible to extend this trip by continuing on this road over the hill until it dead ends at Dry Fork. The paddler could carry the bridge, continue down to the mouth and paddle down Dry Fork 3 miles to the car.

GAUGE: There is a gauge on the Sully bridge. Also the water should be at least six inches over the drain pipe on the right abutment of the U.S. 33 bridge. You will need at least 5′ on the Parsons gauge.

LAUREL FORK

A. Laurel Fork Campground to U.S. 33—16 Miles

CLASS	GRAD.	VOL.	SCENE	TIME	LEVEL
1	21	S	A	5	1-2

MAPS: USGS—Sinks of Gandy, Glady, Whitmer, Harman
MNF
COUNTIES—Randolph and Tucker

DESCRIPTION: The upper Laurel Fork is an intimate easy stream that can float the canoe-camper almost back to the eighteenth century. Its availability is limited to periods of very high water in the winter and spring. Leaving the campground is the end of civilization for a day of chasing deer and beaver along a swift flowing river through marshy glades. The river is continuous fast water in a shallow narrow bed.

DIFFICULTIES: The paddler must be able to control his boat well enough to avoid being pushed into fallen and overhanging trees.

SHUTTLE: From the take out at the U.S. 33 bridge go west one mile and then south along the spine of Middle Mountain, "14", for 12 miles then left down to the campground on the road to Spruce Knob.

GAUGE: The gauge is located on the right upstream side of the U.S. 33 bridge. Do not expect it to be up unless the Parsons gauge on Cheat is over 7′.

B. U.S. 33 to Jenningston—13 Miles

CLASS	GRAD.	VOL.	SCENE	TIME	LEVEL
3-4	9@71	S	A	5	0.3-1.5′

MAPS: USGS—Harman
MNF
COUNTIES—Randolph and Tucker

DESCRIPTION: This is unquestionably the best run of the Cheat basin. It is a long trip through uninhabited and virtually inaccessible country in the high valley between the Middle and Rich Mountains. The remnants of an early logging railroad play tag with the meandering river for the first 3.6 miles crossing it four times on the artifacts of disappeared bridges. At this point, one hour into the trip, is the first of a series of 2-4′ ledges. These continue regularly for the next two miles to the granddaddy of them all, a 12′ unrunnable waterfalls which you should portage on the left along the tramway bed. After lunch at the foot of the falls be ready for seven miles of continuous Class 3 rapids to the mouth. There are a total of eight bridge crossings on the run. None of the bridges remain but the abutments are readily spotted as landmarks. Between the seventh and eighth bridges there is a 50-yard tunnel from one limb of a one-half mile loop to the other. The water visible at the mouth is typical of the entire river from the falls down. This is a very exhilarating run amidst the least spoiled scenery of West Virginia. After being flushed out into the Dry Fork, it is just ¼ mile to the Jenningston bridge.

DIFFICULTIES: Spotting the falls from upstream should be no problem. It takes about one and one-half hours of paddling time to reach the falls. There are six bridge crossings to the falls, the sixth one is about one mile above the falls. The falls is just around a right turn. Fluorescent strips have been tied in the tree branches on the left above the falls. The only other difficulty is the fatigue of 13 miles of wilderness travel topped off by nine miles of continuous maneuvering.

GAUGE: There is a gauge painted on the right side abutment of the U.S. 33 bridge. It will not be high enough unless the Parsons gauge is over 5′.

SHUTTLE: The put in is at the U.S. 33 bridge. The take out is at the mouth upstream along the left side from the Jenningston bridge. The best way between the two points is west along U.S. 33 four miles to Alpena, north on "12" by the Glady Fork and Sully. (See map p. 48.)

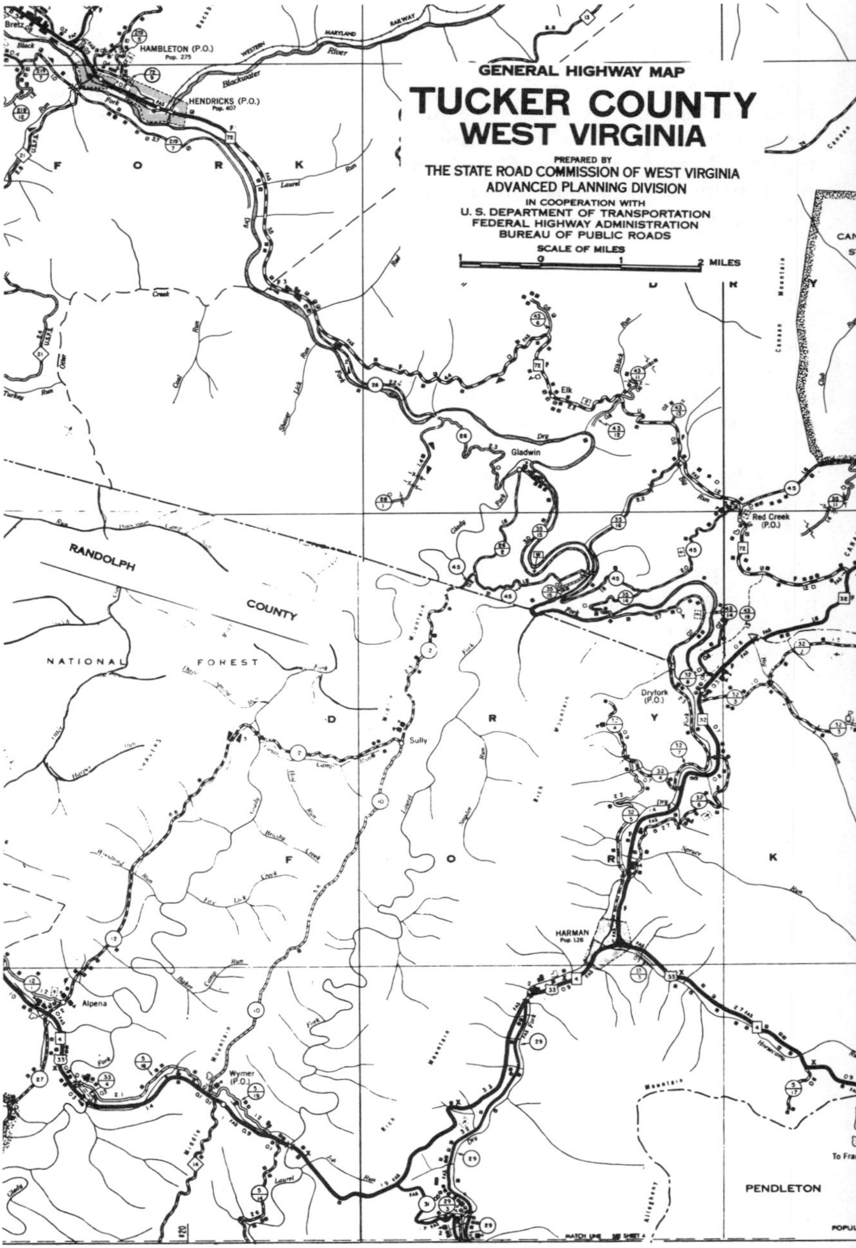
GENERAL HIGHWAY MAP
TUCKER COUNTY
WEST VIRGINIA
PREPARED BY
THE STATE ROAD COMMISSION OF WEST VIRGINIA
ADVANCED PLANNING DIVISION
IN COOPERATION WITH
U. S. DEPARTMENT OF TRANSPORTATION
FEDERAL HIGHWAY ADMINISTRATION
BUREAU OF PUBLIC ROADS
SCALE OF MILES
1 0 1 2 MILES
Bretz
HAMBLETON (P.O.)
Pop. 275
HENDRICKS (P.O.)
Pop. 407
WESTERN MARYLAND RAILWAY
Blackwater River
F O R K
Elk
Gladwin
Red Creek (P.O.)
RANDOLPH COUNTY
NATIONAL FOREST
Sully
Dryfork (P.O.)
D R Y F O R K
HARMAN
Pop. 128
Alpena
Wymer (P.O.)
PENDLETON
MATCH LINE SEE SHEET 4

GANDY CREEK

Sinks Outlet to Mouth—13 Miles

CLASS	GRAD.	VOL.	SCENE	TIME	LEVEL
2-3	37	S	A	2	4-5

MAPS: USGS—Spruce Knob, Whitmer
MNF
COUNTY—Randolph

DESCRIPTION: Gandy Creek disappears in a high meadow on the west side of Spruce Knob, swallowed by a cave. A mile and one half away over the ridge Gandy emerges as a white water stream. Only during flood periods is there enough volume for paddling. Then it's a sporty run. The most significant water is at a big diagonal stopper under a foot bridge half way down. There are three-foot waves and holes along the road above Whitmer.

DIFFICULTIES: Like all little steep streams there is the constant danger of being pushed into barbed wire and steel cable fences, strained under log foot bridges, and impaled on sturdy fallen tree branches. The paddler must be able to scramble for non-existent eddies like a pro quarterback buying time for covered receivers.

GAUGE: When Randy Carter's gauge at the U.S. 33 bridge on Dry Fork disappears Gandy is up. This requires about 11 feet on the Cheat gauge at Parsons (412-644-2890).

SHUTTLE: Easy. Pick your section along "29" from Dry Fork to the Sinks exit.

RED CREEK

North Branch Bridge to W.V. 32–6 Miles

CLASS	GRAD.	VOL.	SCENE	TIME	LEVEL
3-4	75	S	A	2	*

*No gauge at present. Consider water at the bottom of the downstream drain on right abutment of W.V. 32 bridge as adequate.

MAPS: USGS
MNF
COUNTIES–Tucker and Randolph

DESCRIPTION: This little river draining the Dolly Sods area is available only in very wet seasons. Put in at the bridge on the North Branch just above the confluence with the South Branch and be ready to maneuver because there will be no rest until the water seeping under your skirt dictates dumping. The river falls at a steady rate through the ghost lumbering town of Laneville, past the first footbridge and ford, and on to the second footbridge at the ancient Canaan Crossing. This second footbridge marks a section of low ledges and stoppers. The course continues with Mount Porte Crayon towering 2,500 feet on the left and Cabin Mountain on the right. Surprisingly soon the Rt. 32 bridge appears. The river continues for a mile to join the Dry Fork of Cheat. The most convenient take out is a quarter mile upstream from the mouth at an old bridge.

DIFFICULTIES: The upper part of the river may be described as busy, while that below the low water bridge at Laneville consists of bigger drops and waves. Approach the Laneville low water bridge with caution and carry on the right. The first big ledge comes up fast at the end of an "S" turn. The smaller channels are often clogged by downed trees.

SHUTTLE: The put in is reached by taking "45" east of W.V. 32 for 6 miles to the put in bridge. If the water in the upper part appears too low, try an alternate put in at the Laneville low water bridge (also reachable via F.S. 19). The take out bridge could either be on W.V. 32 or on downstream another half mile on a side road from the community of Dry Fork.

DRY FORK OF CHEAT

Dry Fork Above Gandy Creek

This stream is nestled snugly between Rich and Allegheny mountains, but has its source high up on Rich. The river is very small and exceedingly steep, but follows the Spruce Knob road very closely. In periods of high runoff following the spring melts, this stream could conceivably be run for quite a distance above the mouth of Gandy Creek with but a few carries. It would be a continuous Class 2 chute. The river is very high and the weather up there becomes exceedingly severe. The scenery is magnificently rugged.

A. Gandy Creek to Wayside Park, W.V. 32—12 Miles

CLASS	GRAD.	VOL.	SCENE	TIME	LEVEL
1-3	40	S	B	4	0-2′

MAPS: USGS—Whitmer and Harman
MNF
COUNTY—Randolph

DESCRIPTION: This is an exceedingly picturesque little stream winding through an immense high mountain valley that reminds one of travel ads from Switzerland. When viewed from U.S. 33 off Rich Mountain, the result is fantastic. The stream tumbles continuously at a Class 1-2 pace from the mouth of Gandy Creek through a series of highland meadow farms until the U.S. 33 bridge is reached. In this upper section, there are no difficulties unless a fallen tree or log temporarily dams the stream.

DIFFICULTIES: After passing under the U.S. 33 bridge, the stream begins to get more difficult. Several ledges are encountered and a wooden dam just below Harman can be run but scout to avoid the middle piling. From Harman to the take out, the stream returns to its continuous Class 2 character plus two Class 3 rapids in the last half mile.

GAUGE: There is a canoeing gauge under the U.S. 33 bridge. Also, inspection of the low ledges below this bridge should tell you whether there is enough water. When the Parsons gauge (see other sections) is greater than 5 , consider the run possible.

SHUTTLE: The put in may be reached from U.S. 33 by taking "29" south just upstream from the bridge. Continue through Job to the next fork. A put in can be made on either Gandy Creek or Dry Fork at bridges just upstream from the fork. The take out is located 2 miles north of Harman on W.V. 32 at the Wayside Park.

B. W.V. 32 to Jenningston—7 Miles

CLASS	GRAD.	VOL.	SCENE	TIME	LEVEL
2	36	S	A-B	2	.5′

MAPS: USGS—Harman and Mozark Mt.
MNF
COUNTIES—Tucker and Randolph

DESCRIPTION: This is a charming run lazily meandering through scenic farmland, rich in history from the boom days of logging. As one approaches Jenningston, more isolated parts of the forest are traversed, but even these are interrupted by the remains of old abandoned homesteads, schools and churches, reminders of more populous times. The river is steady Class 2 with the intervening pools being short thus providing almost continuous action. At higher water levels, the waves and turbulence could easily become Class 3 in the lower stretches. The mouth of Laurel Fork about a half mile above Jenningston bridge is a beautiful spot and the turbulence of the stream makes a fun "playing around" rapids.

Other than an occasional overhanging branch or low swinging bridge, there are no DIFFICULTIES. This would be an ideal stream for open boats if the water level were at 1′ or more. No maneuvering would be involved. Try and catch this one up when there is snow on the ground, it's beautiful.

SHUTTLE: Half way between the villages of Dry Fork and Harman, a bridge crosses the stream from W.V. 32. Launch the boats from the small Wayside Park on the opposite side. Take out at the homemade picnic grounds on the left bank below the bridge in Jenningston. Jenningston may be found by turning left at the first road past the village of Red Creek when traveling towards Parsons on W.V. 72. The river is 2 miles from this junction.

GAUGE: Right hand, stream side of bridge support in Jenningston. Also, since W.V. 32 is so close to the upper part of the stream, one can make a good visual inspection of the water level there. If you can canoe the first 50-100 yards from the put in, you will not have any trouble.

C. Jenningston to Hendricks—12 Miles

CLASS	GRAD.	VOL.	SCENE	TIME	LEVEL
3_4	25	723	A-B	4	0-2′

MAPS: USGS—Mozark Mt.
MNF
COUNTY—Tucker

DESCRIPTION: Although not as long as Shavers Fork, this tributary of the Cheat has a larger volume. This section of Dry Fork does not meander, but proceeds directly northwest to Parsons through a rather deep trough. The scenery, although beautiful, is more pastoral than the other Cheat tributaries for signs of civilization are always present such as quaint old homesteads, churches, rural schools, etc.

The rapids are fairly close together thus providing rather continuous excitement. Many drop over ledges and the waves are large and heavy. One of the most enjoyable rivers in the state.

DIFFICULTIES: About one mile below the put in the river divides. After the forks rejoin, a steep rapids veers off to the right and curves back to the left. The paddler is forced to the right. As he gets to the bottom, he must either scramble very quickly back to the far left or be prepared to blast through a big hydraulic at the bottom.

After passing under the second rickety swinging footbridge, things begin to pick up. About 400 yards below this bridge, there are a couple of steep river-wide hydraulics. These can be avoided in various degrees by sticking to the far right side of the river.

The two rapids below the mouth of Otter Creek (marked by the third swinging footbridge) could offer difficulty. The first is a right-hand turn that is obstructed by large rocks and care is needed to avoid broaching in the turn. The next rapids is probably the most difficult of the entire run. The approach is partly obscured by a bus-sized boulder on the left. One must make an S turn around this boulder, beginning at the right and then immediately going back to the left and then over a drop through some fairly heavy and complicated water. Consider all of the rapids below the second swinging footbridge as Class 4 in high water.

GAUGE: Downstream of the right side abutment of the Jenningston bridge. One could call the Monongahela Power Company office in various northern West Virginia cities and ask for the dispatcher. He can give you the Cheat River reading below Parsons. Do not attempt if below 4′. The Pittsburgh River District office can give the Parsons reading. There is also a government gauge at Hendricks which should be above 2.5′.

SHUTTLE: This is exciting! Hendricks is located on W.V. 72 which is a very narrow, tortuous road over high mountains and deep hollows. The scenery up there is superb among the high mountain meadows, but if you want to look, stop your car. You can take out just below the mouth of the Blackwater or upstream one-half mile from Hendricks gauge off W.V. 72. A shortened trip with a simplified shuttle is to put in at Rich Ford on "26". See map p. 48. Jenningston can be reached via "35/16" near the village of Red Creek. If you come to this village from Parsons, you have passed the turn off.

BLACKWATER

A. Canaan Valley Section—11 Miles

CLASS	GRAD.	VOL.	SCENE	TIME	LEVEL
A-3	9	193	A	4	3-4.5

MAPS: USGS—Blackwater Falls, Davis
MNF
COUNTY—Tucker

DESCRIPTION: Appalachian Power wants this river. They wish to "enhance" the beauty of the Land of Canaan by flooding it. Until they do this is a unique highland marsh drained by the Blackwater and its dendritic tributaries. The river is flat, but swift with clear brown ("black") water. Signs of beaver business highlight the trip. The character of the river changes when it passes through the gap in Brown Mountain. The last couple of miles are enjoyable ledges. The trip ends in the pool of a ten-foot dam at Davis.

GAUGE: There is a gauge at Davis. You can get a reading from Frank Jernejcic, Department of Natural Resources, Fairmont (304-366-5880), but give him at least a day's notice. These are the numbers given above. A general index is that the Parsons gauge on Cheat should be over five feet.

SHUTTLE: To reach the put in take "35" south off W.V. 32 three miles to the bridge over North Branch. Turn toward the east. A gate blocks the road in one-half mile. Carry one-quarter mile to the river. Take out at Davis.

B. North Fork Junction to Hendricks—7 Miles

CLASS	GRAD.	VOL.	SCENE	TIME	LEVEL
5	5@112	193	A	4	2.5-3.5

MAPS: USGS—Mozark Mt.
MNF
COUNTY—Tucker

DESCRIPTION: This is West Virginia's longest continuous rapids. It flows through a narrow, steep defile draining the Canaan Valley. The Valley is a flat upland swamp on the west side of the Allegheny Front. Multiple branches of the upper Blackwater funnel the 150-square-mile drainage basin into two main forks which respectively pass the former logging capitals of Davis and Thomas. Near these nineteenth century towns, they suddenly leap off the mountain as two 50′ falls and begin their unrelenting rush to the Dry Fork 8 miles and 1,000 feet below.

The two main divisions of the river, the Blackwater and its North Fork, confluence about a mile below their initiation drops and slow their descent to a more "realistic" paddling gradient. Both falls, the one preserved by a State Park and the other on the North Branch should be viewed by the paddler, but the gradients are too steep to paddle.

From the put in at the junction and with only minimal veering from left or right, it is one continuous blind bend—downwards. From the paddler's eye level he can never see more than 50 yards to where the river disappears over the edge of the world. It has a fantastic 112 fpm gradient for 5 miles to Lime Rock, an abandoned community 2 miles upstream from Hendricks. This is a gradient which is 50% greater than that of almost any other paddlable river. Fortunately this descent is not broken into alternate stretches of rapids and pools, but is evenly distributed. It is a gigantic sluiceway between mountains rising 2,000 feet on either side with almost no riverside bench.

Paddling the Blackwater is a constant challenge of reading and negotiating chutes over staircase ledges randomly strewn with 5-10′ boulders. The paddler is constantly maneuvering in the ever pushing current. Moving side eddies are the only rest or rescue spots along the course. The waters of the river are a non-silted brown covered with suds—a form of pollution which has been present since the time of Thomas Lewis, a 1746 explorer who appropriately called this stream "the River Styx." The color is attributed to organic acids from the upland swamps leaching iron oxides from the red shale lining much of the riverbed.

In the first 1½ miles, there is a unique rapids that serves as a landmark. The water races 75 yards over a flat, sloping red shale floor. With this minimization of friction, the current reaches horrendous speeds before abruptly dropping into a giant washing machine at the bottom. Shortly below this is Tub Run, a tributary on the right.

The last 2 miles into Hendricks drop at an interesting 48 fpm and could be run separately beginning at Lime Rock. The trail to Lime Rock is accessible via permission from the Hinchcliff Lumber Company at Hendricks on week days only and at the risk of traversing a very marginal looking log and plank bridge.

DIFFICULTIES: To single out any part of this trip as difficult is ludicrous. Everything about it from getting to the put in to the take out is difficult beyond the scope of all but the expert paddler. While the river is mostly Class 3 or 4, the overall series without pools and considering the inevitable fatigue of constant maneuvering makes this a Class 5 run. Another complication to consider is that the river runs in a southwesterly direction against the afternoon sun. Using the AWWA point system of classification, the Blackwater almost adds up to a Class 6 run.

The Washing Machine Slide referred to above which is an optional carry is preceded by 2 or more carries dictated by undercut or passage obstructing boulders. In the next mile a mandatory carry will be on the left side of a 9′ high, 30 yards wide diagonal ledge choked with rubble. This is marked by being several hundred yards downstream from the only 2 islands along the river. The next landmark is Big Run, entering from the right and somewhere below this is another memorably mean rapids in the vicinity of a spectacular left side tributary waterfall.

GAUGE: The above gauge readings refer to the Davis gauge. See Section A. A paddlers' gauge at Hendricks is misleading because of the river width. If it is more than 0.3′ above or below zero go somewhere else. The Parsons gauge rule of thumb for the run is 4-5.5′.

SHUTTLE: The shuttle is easy, but the put in is a bear. From the take out under the W.V. 72 bridge in Hendricks, take U.S. 219 to Thomas and then right to Coketon and on to Douglas via "27". Park where the road leaves the river, shoulder your boat and walk one mile, that's right—one mile, along the RR track then slide it down 250′ over a wooded 60° incline to the river. By walking about 300 yards below the confluence before descending to the river, the first two carries can be avoided. Incidentally the RR parallels the river some 300′ above the water and serves as an avenue back to civilization in case of accidents. The river has been run from as high as Pendleton Run, but the approach to the put in was even more strenuous and almost every rapids had to be carried. It wasn't worth the half day of labor.

BLACK FORK OF CHEAT

Mouth of Blackwater River to Parsons Tannery—4 Miles

CLASS	GRAD.	VOL.	SCENE	TIME	LEVEL
2-3	25	1109	B	1	4-6′

DESCRIPTION: The Black Fork's name, like its water, is the contraction of the Blackwater and the Dry Fork rivers. It is not to be confused with its untamed shrew of a mother—the Blackwater—but rather a chip off the old block—the Dry Fork. The Black Fork is an end-of-the-day type of trip ideally topping off a lower Shavers Fork or Dry Fork trip. The river courses between wooded mountain ranges only partially spoiled by traces of civilization. It is an extension in scenery and type of water of its major parent, Dry Fork. Little maneuvering is necessary, but the volume and gradient combine to provide a rocking-horse ride over three foot, uniform standing waves.

GAUGE: The above readings are for the Parsons gauge on the Cheat. The Hendricks gauge can be read on the spot and should be over 2.5′.

SHUTTLE: Put in on the Blackwater River under the bridge at Hendricks and go down 400 yards of Class 3 rapids to the junction with Dry Fork. One can take out at the Parsons tannery (this is private land, permission should be secured) or extend the trip 2 miles by paddling down to the junction with Shavers Fork and on to the Holly Meadows bridge for a much more scenic take out. This can be reached from W.V. 72 below Parsons by turning right on "1".

BUFFALO CREEK

Etam to Macomber—3 Miles

CLASS	GRAD.	VOL.	SCENE	TIME	LEVEL
3	86	S	A	1	1.6-

DESCRIPTION: The put in is in the shadow of the Etam satellite signal receiving station. The entire run is white water with many ledges and frequently up against an overhanging cliff of limestone. It is never over 25 feet wide.

GAUGE: There is a gauge on the left 50 yards above the put in.

SHUTTLE: Put in a mile below Etam at a bridge. Shuttle on W.V. 72. Take out at U.S. 50 bridge.

SALTLICK CREEK

Amblersburg to Rowlesburg—4 Miles

CLASS	GRAD.	VOL.	SCENE	TIME	LEVEL
3	52	S	B	1	–

DESCRIPTION: This is what to do in Rowlesburg on a weekend when the Cheat is too high and it has been raining steadily for a day. The run is parallel to the main line of the B&O as it descends Briery Mountain from Terra Alta.

At adequate water levels the water is continuous Class 3 with some stoppers and haystacks. There is a five-foot dam at the B&O switching yards that can be run but is usually carried.

DIFFICULTIES: Higher on this little tributary logs and trees are a significant hazard. In this section they are still a potential threat. Look out for the dam.

GAUGE: There is not any. When Calamity Rock on the Cheat Narrows can not be located and the Parsons gauge is six feet and there is not time to get to the upstream tribs of the Cheat, go to it.

MUDDY CREEK

W.V. 26 Bridge to Mouth—2.5 Miles

CLASS	GRAD.	VOL.	SCENE	TIME	LEVEL
4	92	S	B	1	0-1′

DESCRIPTION: It is dodge 'em all the way—rocks and logging debris. The creek is entirely along W.V. 26. Stop and visit the antique iron furnace midway along this roller coaster for a view of the Big Muddy Rift. Below the rift the run is a series of boulders.

DIFFICULTIES: Below the put in is Little Muddy Rift, a narrow, twisting drop of ten feet in 20 feet with undercut rocks. A mile later the river drops over a wide, slanting shelf about twenty feet high and 100 yards long, Big Muddy Rift. This is a very steep young stream with few eddies and sharp rocks. Because of upstream logging there is a danger of being forced into a jam of debris.

GAUGE: The above readings are for the Little Sandy. This is the next watershed north along W.V. 26 and would reflect the same necessarily wet conditions.

SHUTTLE: Put in at the W.V. 26 bridge. Take out at side road bridge in sight of the Cheat.

HORSESHOE RUN

Shaffer to Bridge Above Saint George—9 Miles

CLASS	GRAD.	VOL.	SCENE	TIME	LEVEL
1-3	41	S	B	3	6′

MAPS: USGS—Saint George and Lead Mine
COUNTY—Tucker

DESCRIPTION: This is a simple, clear little stream draining the northernmost portion of the Monongahela National Forest and flowing past Forest Service and YMCA camps bearing the same name. The run is named for the huge loop in the Cheat just upstream from the mouth of this run. The lower end of this run is scheduled to be turned into mud flats when and if the Rowlesburg Dam goes in. At full pool level, the lower 3 miles of this beautiful stream will be ruined.

After 2.6 miles of small sloping, uncomplicated moving water, the paddler negotiates a series of low ledges near Lead Mine. One mile downstream, the river passes under the bridge going up Hile Run. Between here and the YMCA Camp is the most interesting section with the run channeling and dropping over easy Class 3 ledges. From Camp Horseshoe to the bridge near the mouth are easy gravel bars with one half the gradient of the upper stream and passing through farmland.

DIFFICULTIES: There are essentially no difficulties except that of catching this tiny trout stream when it is high enough to run. While it is an easy run suitable for the novice, it is not a bore to the intermediate or advanced paddler because of the continuous drop and scenic surroundings. CAUTION: If you happen to catch it up in the summer, each of the camps may not have had time to take down temporary dams made out of pipes and planks. These would be dangerous and both would have a fast water approach.

SHUTTLE: Put in can be reached from W.V. 72 by driving through Saint George and out "1" to Camp Horseshoe on to Lead Mine and then "7" to Shaffer where several small streams join to form Horseshoe Run. The first bridge you cross on your way from Saint George is the take out.

GAUGE: None. The level refers to the Parsons gauge and is only a general guide. The bridge on the side road up Hile Run should not be showing more than 7 stones on the right side abutment to have adequate volume.

CHEAT

A. Parsons to Rowlesburg—36 Miles

CLASS	GRAD.	VOL.	SCENE	TIME	LEVEL
B-1	7	1653	B	10	3-4½′

MAPS: USGS—Parsons, St. George and Rowlesburg
COUNTIES—Tucker and Preston

DESCRIPTION: This is a lazy but extremely beautiful river meandering alternately through well-kept farmland and spectacular bluffs. There are occasional Class 1 rapids that offer no problems unless the water is very high with resulting high waves. One of the better rapids is just before the Holly Meadows bridge (3 miles from Parsons). The next bridge, 8 miles downstream, leads to the historic village of Saint George. About 2 miles below Saint George the river leaves the highway and enters a beautiful gorge. Some nice rapids occur here, also.

Below Hannahsville, the area known as Seven Islands is encountered and is particularly scenic. The highway does not come near this section, but there is a dirt road along the left side of the river. There are many deep pools suitable for swimming and fishing. Bass may be taken all along the river while trout may be caught in the riffles of the upper stretches. Many primitive camping sites exist and the river is ideal for extended open boat touring.

It is recommended that all paddlers tour this scenic river and join in the fight against the Corps of Engineers who consider this an ideal location for a huge silt catching reservoir.

SHUTTLE: Due to the nearness of roads, a shuttle can be set up most anywhere for shorter runs, particularly along W.V. 72.

GAUGE: Call Monongahela Power Co. (292-9404 in Morgantown) and ask for the dispatcher. He can give you the Cheat River reading at Parsons. It would be too low if less than 3′ which corresponds to about .9′ on the Albright canoeing gauge.

B. Rowlesburg to Albright Power Dam—14 Miles

CLASS	GRAD.	VOL.	SCENE	TIME	LEVEL
2-4 low 3-5 high	5@20	2207	C	3-4	0″-4′

MAPS: USGS—Rowlesburg and Kingwood 7½′
COUNTY—Preston

DESCRIPTION: Leaving Rowlesburg quietly and broadly, the river soon becomes narrower and starts to pick up speed. Approximately 3 miles below Rowlesburg, after having passed several Class 1-2 riffles, the first big waves are encountered opposite a worked out limestone mine (Cave Rapids). For the next 5 miles the rapids become increasingly more difficult and is the choicest part of this section. There are good rescue spots after each rapids, but in high water (3-4′), they are even difficult to get out of. After passing several Class 3 rapids, the paddler enters a long series of similar rapids, the "Narrows." The entire river is necked down by the presence of an automobile-sized boulder (Calamity Rock) in midstream which makes passage at any level difficult. Although this boulder is largely out of the water at 1′ on the Albright gauge, it is completely submerged when the reading is a little over 2′. This should give the paddler a healthy respect for what just a few inches increase in water level means on the Cheat. Usually it is recommended to run the boulder on the passage to the right. Keep in mind that there are two problems—entering the passage correctly which is not always easy due to the combination of waves immediately above it and managing the powerful drop right at the end of the short chute. This passage will swamp an open canoe at any level and will fold up a raft in high water.

There are three major rapids below this boulder that also pass through narrow confines. This creates a tremendous turbulence and results in powerful crosscurrents and eddies. In high water, one simply blasts through the standing 5′ waves and tries to maintain stability while at lower levels one must be more precise in maneuvering around the exposed boulders. The paddler inexperienced with big water might be fooled by thinking that he can "sneak" down the sides of these narrow rapids in the relatively calmer water, but what usually happens is that the paddler is sucked over into the big stuff by the high velocity of the main channel (sort of like Bernoulli's principle).

The first of these major rapids (Wind Rapids) is the most difficult in high water and consists of a wide hydraulic before one gets to the chute. The hydraulic is best taken on the far left. There is also a severe hydraulic about halfway down the chute on the left—always an interesting scene. The second (Rocking Horse) is the longest narrow passage—100 yards of turbulence. The last rapids is less severe, but still interesting. The remaining rapids to the RR bridge consist of boulder dodging and catching the best chutes. By now strip mine pollution has seriously damaged and scarred the river. The scenery at Preston is depressing and the river again widens out leaving few places for rapids to form. Two miles below the State Rt. 7 bridge there is a short Class 2 rapids, but not much else except the scenery improves a good deal. W.V. 72 parallels the river on the left to this bridge while a local road continues on the right below it giving plenty of opportunity for scouting and/or setting up shorter trips.

SHUTTLE: Rowlesburg City Park is a good put in while the right side of the river 200-300 yards above the Albright Power Station provides a take out. Paddlers interested in the choicest part may put in opposite the limestone caves and take out at the mouth of Lick Run for a 5-mile trip.

C. Albright W.V. 26 Bridge to Jenkinsburg Bridge—11 Miles

CLASS	GRAD.	VOL.	SCENE	TIME	LEVEL
3-5	25	2207	A	4	–½-4′

MAPS: USGS—Kingwood and Valley Point
COUNTY—Preston

DESCRIPTION: Once regarded as one of the most difficult rivers in the East, the Cheat Canyon has been moved down a few notches as better paddling skills have evolved and new rivers like the Gauley have been "discovered." However, this does not mean that the river has gotten any easier and it should not be taken lightly, especially by those unskilled at intricate maneuvering and in handling heavy water. At low water it is a notorious boat buster and at high levels it has been a killer, literally. Yet it is an extremely beautiful river tumbling through essentially a wilderness canyon. Massive boulders litter the riverbed thus blocking the view through each rapids and contributing to the complexity of the run.

Some chutes of the canyon are very narrow, but the river gauge is located in a wide shallow spot. Hence, a 2″ difference on the gauge makes a whale of a difference downstream, translated to feet in many instances. Anyone undertaking this run should realize that this is a very long run far from any roads. A smashup puts the paddler miles from any help in country that is extremely difficult to traverse by foot. To walk out of the canyon straight up takes 2 hours and you still may be miles from the nearest farmhouse when you get there. There is a good trail on the right side of the river, but it is much higher than the river.

A detailed description of all of the difficult rapids in the Cheat Canyon is impractical due to their number and complexity (there are at least 38 of Class 3 or greater difficulty). There are no long flat pools although each set of rapids is separated from the next by a small quiet spot. In high water (2′ or more) the rapids tend to run into each other, thus creating the Class 5 conditions.

DIFFICULTIES: The most difficult part of this run is its length and inaccessibility. The river carries a Class 3-4 rating at levels up to about 1.5′, but at levels higher than this, many of the rapids take on a Class 5 character. The force and size of the waves and holes increase dramatically so that by 2 to 2.5′, it is another river. It is not recommended to run this river at levels greater than 3.0 unless one is extremely experienced.

The first rapids is a long wide rock garden that soon narrows down and drops over a series of eroded ledges. There are some major hydraulics here in a complex countercurrent. If this is too much, take out immediately on the left as it will be the last chance and they don't get any easier.

Beyond Decision Rapids the next rapids of note is Beech Run Rapids. At high water it has some center and right side holes. The 9th rapids into the canyon will get your attention. Old Nasty is a 50-yard furious drop over a boulder garden. You can't see the bottom from the top. Enter at the left center and gradually work to the right.

Two rapids below this the paddler will encounter Even Nastier which is a very long rapids. About 2/3 down the main stream drops over a ledge on the left, through a hydraulic, then smack into a hugmongous boulder and peels off into a whirling hole on the left side. This wicked hydraulic-curler combination is the most flipping rapids on this river. It's a long swim from here to the next pool. It is safest to run this rapids on the tight left or to right of the Even Nastier Boulder.

The next long portion of the canyon is known as the Doldrums. Lunch Spot Pool with its limestone fossils, Prudential Rock, a few playing waves, and lovely scenery. The flat sections ends when a louder than usual roar echoes off a spectacular left side sandstone cliff in the distance. Que Ball and Anticipation Rapids herald the approach of the toughest section of the Cheat. Teardrop is a long rapids run on the right-left-right-left. The veering back and forth across the 200-yard rapids is dictated by some notorious holes and snaggling rocks, hence the pun name denoting both ripped boats and weeping paddlers. The above mentioned cliff is dissected by a 60-foot falls and marks High Falls Rapids. The rapids is a wide sandstone dam spilling water turbulently into a natural amphitheater. A good passage is over the highest center green wave and then off to the left with the mainstream.

The next rapids gets harder the lower the water becomes. In this Maze Rapids the paddler often gets sucked into a dead end. The second rapids below High Falls, known as the Trap, is very long, steep, and complicated. Do not miss the beautiful right side waterfall high along this rapids. Enter in the center then run right by the waterfall or if left be wary of trap number one—a pinning rock below a two-foot ledge followed by Box Canyon, trap number two. If not pinned or not shunted into the blind passage get left for the most formidable portion of this rapids. In stream center is the Devils Trap, a large smooth demon rock nurturing a swirling hole in its wake, trap number three. If you missed it, as advised, by being to the left then it is damn well time to get right to avoid flipping on the front side of Pillow Rock, trap number four. The next rapids was named in honor of Pete Morgan of Albright, gauge reader for many years, but is more widely known as Coliseum because of the column like erosion in the limestone strata bordering the rapids. Some have suggested that the name is because it is here that the Christians are thrown to the hydraulics. Coliseum can be run on the right or down the center. The rest of the canyon is decrescendo from fun to fatigue.

SHUTTLE: Put in at the Albright bridge or, to avoid some flat uninteresting water, at the riverside campground about a mile downstream on W.V. 26. The take out at Jenkinsburg is not easy to find. Take W.V. 26 south to Kingwood and right on W.V. 7 to Masontown. Turn right at the drugstore on Main and Depot streets and take this road to the fork. Turn left and continue on to Bull Run and a second fork. Take this to the right down the extremely steep, narrow road to Jenkinsburg. A shorter but rougher shuttle is via Valley Point and Mount Nebo on the right side of the river. (See Big Sandy shuttle and map on p. 65.) From the river, paddle on down below the bridge to the mouth of the Big Sandy. An easy trail leads up to the parking area.

D. Jenkinsburg Bridge to W.V. 73—8 Miles

CLASS	GRAD.	VOL.	SCENE	TIME	LEVEL
3, B, A	4@16	2632	A	3	0-4′

MAPS: USGS—Masontown and Lake Lynn
COUNTIES—Preston and Monongalia

DESCRIPTION—This interesting run is seldom paddled because there is only 4 miles of rapids followed by a long flat paddle and the shuttle takes so long. It is a good indication what some of the easier rapids in the upper canyon are like. The first rapids is encountered about 50 yards below the mouth of the Big Sandy with the best passage being towards the right in low water. If this is too low, forget it. One will encounter 4 good rapids (Class 3) and several riffles in the first 4 miles. The last rapids is divided by a gravel bar (Grassy Island) and that's it. High above this island on the right is the impressive Cooper's Rock State Park. The only danger one gets into from here is the risk of being run over by powerboat cowboys and, on at least one occasion, a damned seaplane! The long flat paddle to the take out is beautiful, but very wearisome kneeling in a white water boat. Soon Mont Chateau State Park is reached, but there is no easy take out there. You will be charged to take out at the marina next door, so you may as well paddle on down to W.V. 73 bridge.

SHUTTLE: Horrendous! Jenkinsburg is described above. To reach the take out, go back out to Masontown, turn right on W.V. 7 and head for Dellslow or Pioneer Rocks. Turn right on Tyrone Road and go to W.V. 73. Turn right and drive to the east side of the bridge.

GAUGE: The three lower parts of the Cheat can be run year around, even often during the summer, but one must be careful that the river is not too high. It is a huge watershed and the river is very powerful in high water. The canoeing gauge is located on the Albright Bridge and the reading may be obtained by calling Morgan's Gas Station at 329-1748. The Parsons gauge reading may be gotten by calling the Monongahela Power Company and asking for the dispatcher. A conversion between the two gauges may be obtained from: Parsons gauge—2.3 = ¾ Albright gauge. The extremes of −6″ and +4′ were both ridiculous. It is a good run at 1′ to 2.5′.

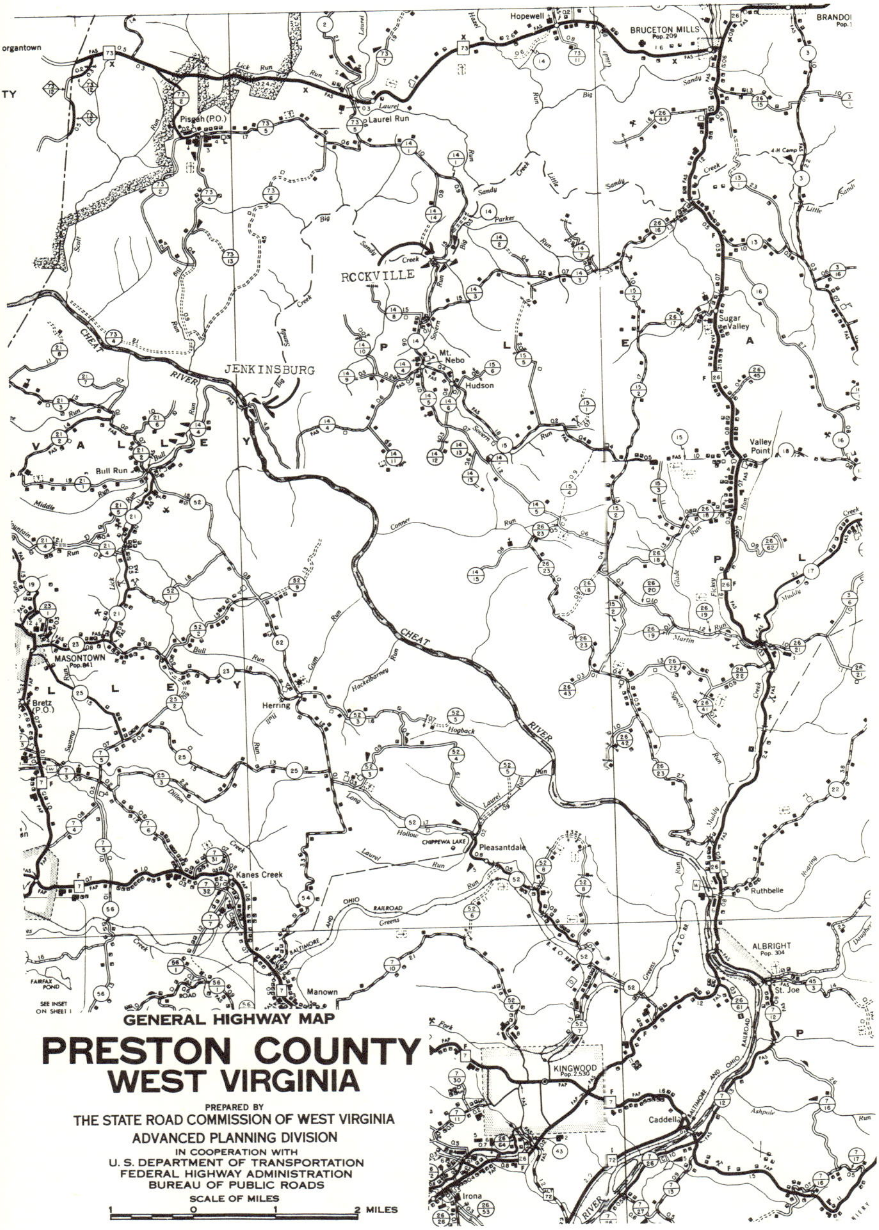
GENERAL HIGHWAY MAP
PRESTON COUNTY
WEST VIRGINIA
PREPARED BY
THE STATE ROAD COMMISSION OF WEST VIRGINIA
ADVANCED PLANNING DIVISION
IN COOPERATION WITH
U. S. DEPARTMENT OF TRANSPORTATION
FEDERAL HIGHWAY ADMINISTRATION
BUREAU OF PUBLIC ROADS
SCALE OF MILES
1 0 1 2 MILES
Hopewell
BRUCETON MILLS
Pop. 209
Pisgah (P.O.)
Laurel Run
ROCKVILLE
JENKINSBURG
Mt. Nebo
Hudson
Sugar Valley
Valley Point
Bull Run
MASONTOWN
Pop. 841
Bretz (P.O.)
Herring
CHIPPEWA LAKE
Pleasantdale
Kanes Creek
Manown
Ruthbelle
ALBRIGHT
Pop. 304
St. Joe
KINGWOOD
Pop. 2,530
Caddell
Irona
CHEAT RIVER
BALTIMORE AND OHIO RAILROAD
FAIRFAX POND
SEE INSET ON SHEET 1
4-H Camp

BIG SANDY (PRESTON COUNTY)

A. Pa.-W.Va. State Line to Bruceton Mills—5 Miles

DESCRIPTION: No danger spots. A very small intimate stream with a 3 fpm gradient flowing through rhododendron thickets and small farms. Bed is sandy to muddy, but good fishing for trout and bass. Best rapids at Clifton Mills. All flat water from here to dam. Put in at steel bridge on road north of Brandonville, W.Va. The put in is actually on a tributary of the Big Sandy, Little Sandy Creek. (This should not be confused with another Little Sandy Creek below.) The take out is above the dam at Bruceton Mills on the right. Be careful in high water.

B. Bruceton Mills to Rockville—6 Miles

CLASS	GRAD.	VOL.	SCENE	TIME	LEVEL
1-4	4@9 2@45	415	A	2	5.8-7′

MAPS: USGS—Valley Point and Bruceton Mills
COUNTY—Preston

DESCRIPTION: This is 6 miles of progressive slalom training starting at Class 1 and sequentially working up to Class 4 as this little stream tips down beside Chestnut Ridge to the Cheat Gorge. Suitable for intermediate paddlers in open boats at lower water levels, but decking recommended. Automobile camping at nearby Cooper's Rock State Park.

DIFFICULTIES: Hazel Run Rapids is the first one of any problem and appears as an impassable barricade of boulders. Try the second one from the right. Below the mouth of the Little Sandy (on the left), one will encounter a long slide rapids where the water zips quickly over very shallow rock tables and then terminates in several wide hydraulics. Below the mouth about 500 yards is a 6-8′ falls. It can be recognized easily by the large shelf of rock jutting out from the left forming a dam. The first shelf can be carefully run by cutting hard left below this ledge then back across to near center for the main ledge. At higher levels run straight over left or far right.

A very long rapids or one rapids right after the other occurs just below the falls and this is where the big action is. This will get to Class 5 if the level is over 2.0′. Several steep drops over ledges around blind bends require quick decisions and paddle responses and continues this way until the take out. It is usually a good Class 4 except in very low water. Paddlers in trouble may want to take out at the rustic cabin on the right just below the mouth of Laurel Run and Corner Rapids. The approach to the bridge is tricky. The right is blocked by a fallen tree, the left is choked, you will have to go through the island in the middle (look for a hemlock growing in the middle of the river). It is a very deceptive drop involving two very quick turns.

SHUTTLE: Put in below the dam on the right at Bruceton Mills. Take out is just under the Rockville bridge on the left. When parking, be careful not to block access to the cottages. Rockville can be reached from W.V. 73 crossing over Laurel Run. Take the left fork twice. The Big Sandy can also be run starting on Laurel Run at W.V. 73.

C. Little Sandy to Rockville—5 Miles

CLASS	GRAD.	VOL.	SCENE	TIME	LEVEL
	41				
3-4	1@70	S	A	2	6.5-7.5′

DESCRIPTION: A tougher white water trip than the Bruceton to Rockville section requiring a more skilled paddler and more water. It is wilderness all the way. After a 20-minute paddle on flat water the first of several ledges is reached. The river then becomes a very continuous Class 3 rapids dropping 70 feet in one mile to the Big Sandy. The last two miles of this trip is on the tough part of a swollen Big Sandy. Note that the level required to get down the Little Sandy puts the Big Sandy above the recommended level for Section B. If you are feeling confident the run from W.V. 26 to Jenkinsburg, Sections C & D, will be one of the most memorable white water trips of a lifetime.

DIFFICULTIES: A sloping ledge on the Little Sandy is complicated by a boulder standing at the bottom catching the main current. Take care to avoid a pinning at lower levels. Avoid to the left at higher levels. Also all of the Big Sandy at this level is an interesting place.

SHUTTLE: Put in at W.V. 26 bridge two miles south of Bruceton Mills. The shuttle to Rockville is rough but direct (see map p. 65).

GAUGE: The reading above refers to the Rockville gauge. There is a paddlers gauge at the put in. It rarely reaches zero. Go ahead if it is -0.2′.

D. Rockville to Cheat River—5.5 Miles

CLASS	GRAD.	VOL.	SCENE	TIME	LEVEL
	2@30				
4-5	4@80	415	A	3	5.8-6.5

MAPS: USGS—Bruceton Mills and Valley Point
COUNTY—Preston

DESCRIPTION: The lower Big Sandy is an exciting, beautiful, piquant mistress who shows occasional flares of bad temper to even the most experienced canoeists. This is the most remote, most scenic, and most challenging white water in northern West Virginia. The banks are choked with laurel making the necessary scouting and portaging very difficult. If a walk-out is necessary, there is an old RR bed on the right to within a mile of the Cheat River. Then you would have to figure out how to get over to the left where the only road reaches the river at Jenkinsburg.

DIFFICULTIES: Plenty! Parts of the course are hazardous and require scouting and carrying. At 1.5 miles is a rather difficult sequence terminating in 18′ falls. It begins with a fairly steep three part drop on the left into a pool just above the falls. Scout and use safety measures. Carry the falls on the right. The falls has been run to the left side of the main current. The next series of rapids is busy for ¼ mile then followed by a broad ledge split by a large rock in midstream. The passage on the right ends in a big curler which throws good boaters under an undercut rock. Run more safely just to the left of center. The next biggie is Zoom Flume, a steep 8-10′ drop which is easier than it looks and even more exciting. Scouting again recommended to see the twisting flume. Think left through this one. Get back out of your boat if you are still in it and scout the next rapids, Little Splat. It is safest to finish on the right. The second falls, Big Splat, is next and is a complex falls dropping a total of 25′. Carry on the right. Three and a half miles and 272′ (down) later, the paddler, who may be hiking by now, will reach the Cheat River near Jenkinsburg. In this section there are two islands. Scout the first one. It is easier on the left; more exciting on the right. Run the second one on the right.

GAUGES: The reading above refers to a government gauge on the bridge at Rockville. There is a paddler's gauge under the Bruceton Mills bridge. The correlation between the two is complex but good. Rockville = ¾ (Bruceton + 1) + 5. The recommended levels at Bruceton are 0-2′.

SHUTTLE: For Section C, one can put in at Rockville (described above). The take out is on the left at the mouth of Big Sandy on the Cheat. Take the steep trail up through the laurel thicket to the parking area. Jenkinsburg may be reached by continuing on the road from Rockville (from the left side of the river), turn right at the top of the hill, then take a left at the next crossing and proceed to Mt. Nebo School. At Mt. Nebo bear hard right to Jenkinsburg. This is terrible driving and almost as rough as the paddling.

CHAPTER III

FASTEST WATER TO THE NORTH
THE TYGART SUB-BASIN

Of the rivers that flow out of the mountainous heartland north towards the Ohio, the Tygart ranks among the mightiest in the state being a big mountain river with a vast watershed. The Tygart begins high in the mountains of Randolph County, not too far from the headwaters of the Elk, and flows through a valley rich in history and natural beauty. Up there the river is known locally as "Tygart's Valley." Near Philippi, it picks up two very significant tributaries, the Middle Fork and the Buckhannon. It meets its sister river, the West Fork, in Fairmont to form the Monongahela.

The West Fork is fairly flat and winds gently through largely settled areas whereas the Middle Fork, most of the Buckhannon, and part of the Tygart pass through extremely wild country. A minor, but interesting tributary of the Tygart, Three Fork Creek, has its mouth in Grafton below the Tygart Reservoir and the nearby trout stream, Whiteday Creek, has its mouth on the Monongahela not many miles away.

Much of the watershed receives acid pollution, and siltation. The fact that there are no municipalities that have secondary sewage treatment facilities, coupled with the industrial wastes of the lower valley, causes serious pollution on the lower watershed. The upper part of all the Tygart branches and tributaries are good trout streams and, near Huttonsville, offer superb bass fishing as well. The Buckhannon has suffered many devastating fish kills recently from abandoned mines. Strip mining on the Buckhannon and lower Tygart is routine.

State parks exist at Audra on the Middle Fork and at the spectacular Valley Falls on the lower Tygart. The Corps of Engineers has a dam above Grafton creating a reservoir and there is a state park there as well. This reservoir has a phantasmagoric drawdown and is managed solely for navigation releases on the Monongahela, not at the barge companies' expense, but at yours. A new reservoir, Stonewall Jackson, is planned for the West Fork near Weston. This dam will create recognized benefits for the state in the way of flood control between Weston and Clarksburg, well-planned recreational facilities in conjunction with state agencies, and is locally desired, thus making it somewhat unique in the state.

Points of interest on the Tygart include the area around Valley Head and Mingo Flats, long known as a site of Indian travel and encampment, Civil War trenches and the site of Robert E. Lee's headquarters at one time near Huttonsville, the site of the first land battle of the Civil War and the unusual double lane covered bridge, both at Philippi. Ghost towns are common along the Buckhannon where mills once stood harnessing its power. Beverly, located on the Tygart above Elkins, was once the largest town around and Randolph County's seat. Bitter animosities still remain over Elkins having assumed this role in modern times. Hammond, below Valley Falls, is also an interesting place, once the site of the largest brickyards in the east. At one time it was a very large community with trainloads of bricks leaving every day. A disastrous fire followed by some hanky-panky in the till folded the industry in the early forties. The remains of the kilns exist today and are very interesting. The distinctive bricks made by the firm may be found everywhere in the vicinity.

The Tygart's Valley in Randolph County has some nice farms in the rich bottoms and there are some mines in the nearby mountains, but the main industry is timber and wood products with Elkins being the center. Elkins is the annual host to the Mountain State Forest Festival held each year in early October and is also the headquarters of the Monongahela National Forest. It would be an ideal place for a white water paddler to live due to its proximity to so many superb rivers, but the sport is unknown there.

Barbour and Upshur counties do not have such supportive industries. The county seats of Philippi and Buckhannon are principally small college towns. Although these counties are not usually thought of as mountain counties, both are extremely rugged and underlain with vast coal deposits. Together with a poor alternative economic base, this factor has made them prime targets for the strippers' bulldozers. Taylor and Marion counties are small, but underlain with rich natural gas fields. This and glassmaking are the supportive industries. Grafton was once an important RR center, then declined, but is now returning economically. Fairmont is both a small college town and a busy industrial city. There are many active paddlers in the Fairmont-Clarksburg area.

BIBLIOGRAPHY

Burch, J. July 6, 1968. Brick Furnace Rests in Peace. *The West Virginia Hillbilly.* Richwood, W.Va.: Comstock-McClung.

Hornbeck, B. 1967. *Upshur Brothers of the Blue and Gray.* Parsons, W.Va.: McClain Printing Co.

Maxwell, H. 1898 (Reprint 1961). *History of Randolph County.* Parsons, W.Va.: McClain Printing Co.

MIDDLE FORK

A. Laurel Fork to Audra State Park—5 Miles

CLASS	GRAD.	VOL.	SCENE	TIME	LEVEL
1-3	26	330	A-B	1-2	3.5-6.0′

MAPS: USGS—Sago 15′, Audra
COUNTY—Barbour

DESCRIPTION: This interesting and lively little trout stream starts off quite tranquilly over Class 1 riffles past delightful little islands and then gradually changes character. The rapids become more numerous, more continuous, more complicated, and steeper. As one passes the halfway mark, the paddler's view is obscured by numerous boulders and rock gardens making a thrilling Class 3 slalom course for the intermediate paddler. As the edge of the state park is reached, the intensity, but not the continuity of the rapids lets up.

Once a beautiful wilderness river, the left-hand bank is currently undergoing "development" by realtors who have cut an ugly, land-scarring road into the woods so that cabins, trailers, etc., may be located along the stream. One aspect that bears watching is a large oil or gas well installation uncomfortably close to the river.

DIFFICULTIES: None except opportunities exist for broaching on the numerous boulders. One rapids about halfway may appear to be choked with such boulders and locating the correct passage in low water may be difficult. There are many 2-3′ ledges in this run and one fairly vigorous 6-8′ stairstep drop, but most are uncomplicated. This run could be mean in very high water (over 6.0′). In general, the best passages including around islands are to the left. Do not run the last rapids under the bridge unless you plan to run Section B since the area around this part of the river is fenced in. This rapids is much more difficult than anything in the upper section.

SHUTTLE: The take out is immediately above the bridge. A parking lot is located immediately on the right. To reach the put in, take the road upstream that leaves the park on the left side of the river. This hardtop road soon makes a sharp right towards Buckhannon, but a dirt road continues straight (to Mt. Nebo) and should be taken. Soon this dirt road forks again. Take the left fork down the steep hillside to a clearing and another fork. Bear to the left and just past a vacation cabin, there is a spot to park and easily launch the boats (known by the locals as "Finnegan's Ford"). This road continues upstream a considerable distance, but the paddler will find the water rather flat, although beautiful. A fast Class 1 run in high water may be made by putting in at a Boy Scout Camp 5 miles above.

B. Audra State Park to Tygart Junction—6 Miles

CLASS	GRAD.	VOL.	SCENE	TIME	LEVEL
4	2½@79	330	A	3	3.5-5′

DESCRIPTION: Look at the thinly paddled rapids under the bridge at Audra State Park, look at the lush sylvan surroundings, subtract the road, bridge, and bathhouse, and then you will know what to expect for the first 2.6 miles of this run. It's a beautiful, busy, boat buster. The rapids under the bridge can be run on the right side straight for the retaining wall of the swimming area and then slipping to the left down into the pool when the water is low. When it is high, it is more entertaining to fandango down through the center. Beyond the pool requires careful picking of channels for the next 60 minutes to the first of three major rapids above the mouth of the Middle Fork.

The river empties into the Tygart Gorge about at its midpoint. The only way out is to paddle the remaining 4 miles to the mouth of the Buckhannon. This results in an interesting two trips for the price of one. First there is the steep, rocky, technical paddling of the lower Middle Fork and then the much heavier, pushy Tygart with its tripled volume.

DIFFICULTIES: About an hour into the trip a hemlock bedecked isle looms midstream. Paddle most easily on the left but it is interesting on the right. At higher levels there is a stopper that tends to shunt the unwary into a left side whirlpool that will require several cycles before breakout. The big 3 rapids in the last half mile of the Middle Fork are next and will require scouting. The first is long and goes around a corner to the right after about 100 yards. The worst drop is before the turn. Enter in the middle and then paddle to the right. The next big rapids, recognized by a 50-foot boulder on the bottom left, looks bad on the right, but go there anyway because the broken ledge at the left bottom is terrible. Go to the right over high, clean ledges. The third and last rapids before the mouth can be run on the left where the water smashes into a high bank wall. Below that the water runs through an impassable sluice and the boat must be scraped over the right side wet slope and then fall off a 2′ ledge before running through the last drop and waves.

GAUGE: The government gauge just upstream from the bridge has been partly washed away, but one can extrapolate to get a reading. The Belington gauge on the Tygart should be 4′+.

SHUTTLE: Audra State Park may be reached by "11" from either U.S. 119 or 250. See map p. 79. For the take out, see the Tygart, Section C. The ingeniously designed campgrounds at the state park offer the finest riverside camping of any place in West Virginia.

BUCKHANNON

A. Alexander to Tenmile—9 Miles

CLASS	GRAD.	VOL.	SCENE	TIME	LEVEL
1-3	27	584	A-B	3	7-10′

MAPS: USGS—Sago 15′
COUNTY—Upshur

DESCRIPTION: This is a deceptive river in that the extremely sluggish, placid river known to most people below Buckhannon and its small size in the headwaters area near Alexander belie what is in store for the paddler between Alton (pronounced Elton by the locals) and Sago. The river begins as a very small scenic stream where the Right and Left Forks join at Alexander. There is hardly anything more than straight forward riffles for 5 miles until one gets well below Alton. Here the gradient picks up to 40 fpm, the rapids become complicated, and closely spaced. Each rapids is fairly steep and in low water, a good deal of tight maneuvering will be necessary. There are very few, large sight-obstructing boulders, but vision is still limited by the gradient and the many bends in the river. All but the advanced paddler should arrange a take out at Tenmile as the river's character changes drastically from there on. Since the best action is below Alton, most will not want to bother with the Alexander to Alton stretch.

DIFFICULTIES: There are none to speak of other than the usual difficulties encountered in rock garden types of rapids. Most of the rapids below Alton are 50-100-yard descents through such patches.

B. Tenmile to Sago—4 Miles

CLASS	GRAD.	VOL.	SCENE	TIME	LEVEL
3-5	53	584	A	2	7-10′

MAPS: Same as above

DESCRIPTION: This is an isolated stretch of expert level water on an unlikely river running through nineteenth century Appalachia. It is one of the crude nuggets the good paddler seeks. The first 3 miles are very difficult and much scouting will be required. The last mile into Sago is fairly flat with comparatively minor rapids.

DIFFICULTIES: Shortly below Tenmile the river pools behind a boulder-choked natural dam. The water flows primarily to the right side and seemingly sluices in a boulder-studded 15′ channel at a right angle across to the left side, however, most of this sluice leaks out under 8′ boulders from the downstream side creating a very dangerous trap. This trapped a paddler under and between the big boulders in 1970. Fortunately he was spit out of the current, but recent observations have shown various obstructing pieces of debris in this opening which could snag an underwater body. Avoid this Class 6 channel entirely and hop your boat down the secondary stream on the left side of this obstruction.

The river slides along over interesting rapids for a mile below this nightmare to the second bad rapids. This one is a long boulder-strewn slide complicated by an S-shaped entrance, which frequently results in involuntarily eddy turns. If this happens, the paddler should back down the rest of the rapids rather than chance broaching on the rapids-dividing, wet boulder halfway down.

The third meany eats boats on every trip and can be respected from the right side portage. The river drops 3′ through narrow passages at the top and then races over irregular rocks on a left slant to batter against an ugly shelf. This can sometimes be run as far left as possible sneaking out a spot between two entrance boulders.

Beyond this the river slides and drops over innumerable ledges between and around sight-obstructing boulders. This is a Class 4 run without major problems until the rotted bridge piers of the ghost town of Ours Mills is reached and the end of the action.

GAUGE: There is a government gauge at Buckhannon. A reading can be obtained at (412) 644-2890. About 10 stones showing on the right abutment of the Alton bridge will ensure adequate water.

SHUTTLE: This is a dandy place to get lost. See map p. 75. Sago, Alton, and Alexander are all reachable by hard roads from W.V. 4 and 20. Difficult, unmarked roads connect Sago with Tenmile, Tenmile with Alton, and Alton with Alexander and all are very time consuming. We would suggest a put in at Alton and arranging a take out for intermediates at Tenmile and a final take out 1 mile above Sago for a 9-mile trip by river. Finding Sago and Alton is no problem. Tenmile can be reached from Sago via Tallmansville by stopping often for directions. Take plenty of gas, maps, and a flashlight.

C. The Buckhannon Below Sago

Below Sago, the river winds placidly for 36 miles to Carrollton dropping only 2-3 fpm in the process. This part would make an excellent canoe-camping-fishing trip. The last little ¾ mile section below Carrollton really tries to look big and impressive before joining the mighty Tygart and has been described separately under Part D of that river.

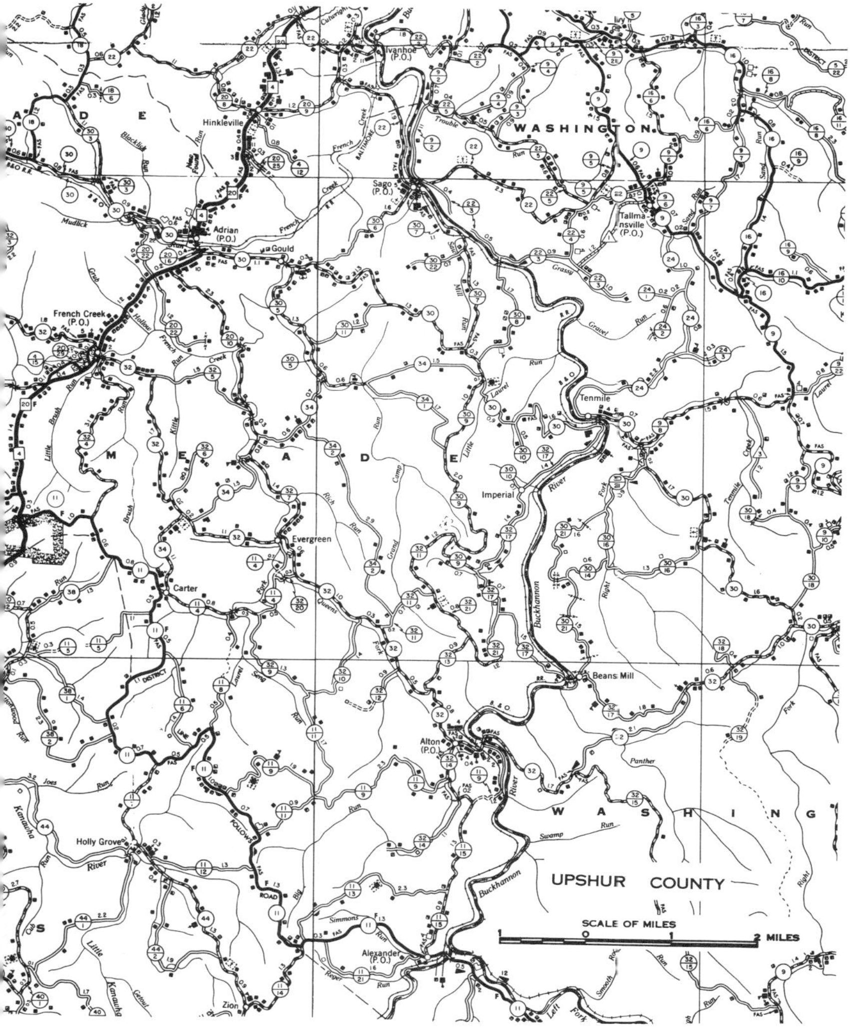
UPSHUR COUNTY
SCALE OF MILES
1 0 1 2 MILES
WASHINGTON
W A S H I N G
M E A D E
Ivanhoe (P.O.)
Hinkleville
Sago (P.O.)
Tallmansville (P.O.)
Adrian (P.O.)
Gould
French Creek (P.O.)
Tenmile
Imperial
Evergreen
Carter
Beans Mill
Alton (P.O.)
Holly Grove
Alexander (P.O.)
Zion

TYGART

A. The Tygart above Elkins

From Mill Creek to the bridge at the western edge of Elkins is a distance of 32 miles. The river drops only 100 feet in this distance and is *thought* not to exceed a Class 1 rating. It is a small river most of the way, but gets larger near Elkins. The Tygart Valley is a broad picturesque valley studded with prosperous farms and walled off in the distance by the mountains. The river meanders lazily through this scenic country, but would only be canoeable during the spring or wet periods. We have run only a small section of this river between Burnt Bridge and Beverly and have observed much more of it from the road. We assume that this run was typical of the entire stretch. We were impressed by the changing scenery and the tremendous amount of wildlife seen on the river. This part of the Tygart could be broken up into several such short runs.

B. Norton to Beaver Creek, The Tygart Loop—5 Miles

CLASS	GRAD.	VOL.	SCENE	TIME	LEVEL
3-5	25	790	C-D	2	4-5

MAPS: USGS—Junior
COUNTY—Randolph

DESCRIPTION: The river from Elkins to Norton is rather slow and dreary containing only one 3′ ledge and a few riffles. At Harding the river leaves the highway and, like a naughty child, while it is hidden from sight it acts up, only to resume its party manners when it comes back to the road near Gage. In general this is true with much of the Tygart. Where it is easily seen, it looks like a Sunday float trip, where it cannot, it Class 5's you. Below Harding the river drops through long, challenging Class 3 rapids. It picks up as it tumbles over a rocky eroded ledge veering to the right and ends squirting between 20′ boulders in three 10′ channels which may be choked by obstructing logs. This Class 4 complex pauses in a small pool where the river turns sharply to the left dropping 10′ over a 50-yard sloping rock bed disappearing around the next bend to the right behind the Twin Giants. Beyond this nightmare are two rapids with stoppers.

DIFFICULTIES: The Twin Giants is frightening. After the Class 4 rapids and pool described, the 50-yard-long flow dropping out of the pool is punctuated by 3 diagonal stoppers all slanting from left to right and driving the paddler toward two 35′ boulders which are perched on small pedestals. Most of the water gets around to the left of these huge rocks, but some runs out under them via a 30′ long tunnel, 4′ high, 10′ wide and 50-100% full of swirling water. It is no place to go, but the diagonal stoppers are shoving, shoving, shoving! This horror chamber is a likely place for a floating tree to lodge and become a very effective body snatcher. Scouting is a must and the carry on the right is tough.

GAUGE: In Belington ½ mile downstream from bridge on left bank. Gauge can be read through door. Daily readings are made by Richard Winas 823-2183 and called into Pittsburgh Weather Service (412) 644-2881.

SHUTTLE: Put in under the U.S. 33 bridge at Norton reached from U.S. 250 just north of its junction with 33. Turn west and swing down around the hill to the left. The take out is 3 miles north of U.S. 250 south of Gage where the highway bridges Beaver Creek. The river from here into Belington is dull and unattractive.

C. Belington to the Mouth of the Buckhannon—11 Miles

CLASS	GRAD.	VOL.	SCENE	TIME	LEVEL
3-5	37	790	A	3-4	2.5-5.5′

MAPS: USGS—Belington and Audra
COUNTY—Barbour

DESCRIPTION: This is the most rugged portion of the Tygart. The rapids are continuous, complex, and bodacious. The river tumbles through a spectacular gorge civilized only by the RR tracks on the right bank and it is worth the slight disfigurement as a walkway for emergency. The water is clean, but acid-polluted and flows through second growth deciduous and coniferous forests.

The trip starts out with a literal bang in that three huge ledges must first be negotiated. Then it is one narrow, steep rapids after another for several miles. In most of these rapids, vision is limited by the huge boulders blocking the view. The river then broadens somewhat and the rapids gentle down to a Class 2 or 3 level before joining the Middle Fork.

The current is now noticeably more forceful and although the gradient hasn't picked up (yet), the rapids are heavier. In about 2 miles the paddler comes to the most interesting part of the river which necks down and drops 80′ in about 1¼ miles, which is terrific for such a big volume river. After this, many interesting rapids with absolutely sinister countercurrents, boils, and assorted goodies occur with amazing frequency. Finally the river broadens out considerably just before reaching the mouth of the Buckhannon.

DIFFICULTIES: About 3.7 miles below Belington or just below the alternate put in, the river begins tumbling over 6-8′ ledges between boxcar-sized boulders separated by 3-4′ sluiceways. The first of these is the Keyhole and consists of two very tiny passages that disappear between the huge boulders. Take the one on your left which is just a hair wider than your boat, making sure your paddle doesn't get stuck, especially if you are driving a kayak, and zoom down what looks like a gun barrel. The next two ledges are blind and ought to be scouted to see where the correct passage is. Most will want to carry the fourth one, Hard Tongue Falls, which roars over the ledge and caroms off a boulder wall to the right into an incredible cauldron of boiling foam. A left hander is out of luck, but kayakists and right handers try to lean way over on a right brace, but they are usually bracing on aerated suds and are apt not to make it. Below this look for the Gates, a row of boulders across the river forming three slots. Run the middle drop please. The left is undercut.

In the steep section 2 miles below the mouth of the Middle Fork, the river pools against a river-wide barrage of boulders and then disappears to the left dropping 25′ through an S-shaped Class 5 chute 75 yards long. At the bottom of the chute stand 2 smaller boulders. One generally turns hard left beyond the second one although it is hairily possible to go between them. The very next rapids is a carry for most paddlers (on the left). This is Shoulder Snapper Falls, an 8′ sheer drop into a pile of boulders. On some occasions when attempted, the boat has gotten stuck in an almost vertical position behind boulders at the bottom. One unlucky paddler who couldn't wiggle loose, dislocated his shoulder while attempting to leave his boat in the fast current. A half mile below Shoulder Snapper look for the Hook Drop. This is a sharp left turn in heavy water. Just below are some waves which have been branded Instant Ender.

This is not a river for rafts, although it has been done, the passages are too narrow and there are too many undercut rocks for trapping flipped rafts and raftees.

GAUGE: Pittsburgh River District office (412) 644-2890. Ask for Belington reading. Located on left bank in Belington and can be read directly.

SHUTTLE: See map p. 79. Put in at bridge in Belington or, to avoid 3 miles of uninteresting flat water, shuttle via Philippi turning right off U.S. 250 at Mt. Pleasant Road then left for 0.7 mile and right 1 mile down over something that is imitating a road to the riverbank (Papa Weese's Paradise—a fishing camp). Take out is reached from U.S. 119 taking "36" to Carrollton. Take the dirt road on the left side of the Buckhannon as far as you can or dare. This is privately owned. Please ask permission and observe closing the gates and parking out of the way so as not to obstruct traffic. From the river, one must paddle upstream when he reaches the mouth of the Buckhannon and land on the sandy bank 100 yards upstream on your upstream right. It is a tough take out through a lot of brush.

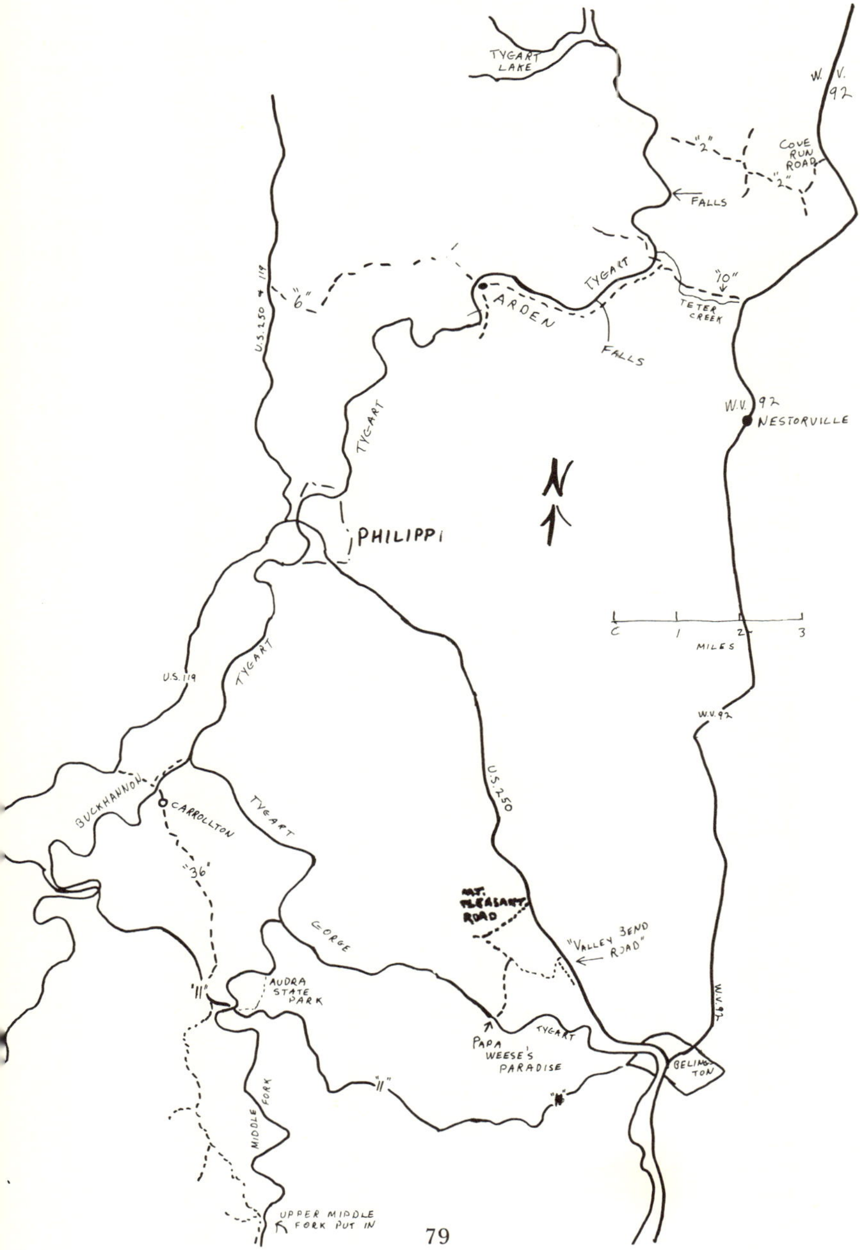
TYGART LAKE
W.V. 92
COVE RUN ROAD
"2"
"2"
FALLS
"6"
U.S. 250 & 119
ARDEN
TYGART
"10"
TETER CREEK
FALLS
W.V. 92
NESTORVILLE
TYGART
N
PHILIPPI
0
1
2
3
MILES
U.S. 119
TYGART
W.V. 92
BUCKHANNON
CARROLLTON
TYGART
U.S. 250
"36"
MT. PLEASANT ROAD
GORGE
"Valley Bend Road"
"11"
AUDRA STATE PARK
W.V. 92
PAPA WEESE'S PARADISE
TYGART
BELINGTON
MIDDLE FORK
"11"
UPPER MIDDLE FORK PUT IN

D. Mouth of Buckhannon to Philippi—5.3 Miles

CLASS	GRAD.	VOL.	SCENE	TIME	LEVEL
1-2	7	1782	B-C	1½	3-5′

MAPS: USGS—Audra and Philippi
COUNTY—Barbour

DESCRIPTION: This is a pleasant short trip close to Philippi consisting of several rapids curving gently around large boulders. At low to medium water levels (3.5-4.5′), the rapids are of Class 1-2 difficulty, but could become much more difficult in high water since all of the rapids are formed at narrow spots in the river. The scenery begins in a nice woodsy setting, but soon breaks down when an extremely long strip mine is encountered on the left bank. This then gives way to pastoral hillsides and then the small college town of Philippi. The first half of the trip contains most of the action while the latter is mostly flat. Contrary to what the Philippi topo map shows, there are no "falls" on this section and it is an excellent undecked boat run. There is one river wide ledge (2′ in low water) just above the historic, double lane, covered bridge and in sight of the Alderson-Broaddus College which is high on the hill in the background. Run at center. Below the bridge is a 5.5-mile flat water paddle through mostly depressing scenery until the first rapids of the Arden Run are encountered.

SHUTTLE: It is suggested that one put in at Carrollton on the Buckhannon River which is only ¾ mile above the mouth for a total run of 6 miles (Buckhannon River is a smaller stream of Class 1-3 rating at this point with fairly continuous action over easy drops and around corners). The put in is at a covered bridge in Carrollton reached by turning onto "36" from U.S. 119 south of Philippi. This is a uniquely historic run in that rare covered bridges may be found both at the put in and the take out. Take out behind a filling station just upstream and to the left of the Philippi bridge.

GAUGE: See next section.

E. Above Arden to Big Cove Run—8 Miles

CLASS	GRAD.	VOL.	SCENE	TIME	LEVEL
3-5	27	1782	C	3	2½-4½′

MAPS: USGS—Philippi and Nestorville
MNF is good for shuttle roads
COUNTY—Barbour

DESCRIPTION: The Tygart is a big flat river for 5.5 miles below Philippi while it gathers courage for the 170′+ jump to the reservoir behind the Grafton dam. All but the last 3 miles of the run below Arden may be scouted from a secondary road from Philippi to the ancient concrete bridge at Teter Creek. Some of the best water is in the remaining run to the reservoir. The scenery at Arden is depressing while the Moats Falls has been continuously desecrated by nearby college students. The river above Arden consists of several Class 2-3 rapids, but Arden bridge marks the turning point. The river drops over big rock ledges and reefs and is strewn with huge boulders. As one approaches the reservoir during the drawdown season, ugly mud slopes detract from the otherwise remoteness of the area.

DIFFICULTIES: About one mile below Arden there is a ledge channeled on the left. The current continues down the left side 50′ dropping over a boulder and ending in two stoppers. The larger, upstream wave must be skirted to the right if one is to maintain alignment and speed for running a ledge and the second stopper. The second rapids downstream from Laurel Creek (enters from the right under a steel bridge) the river narrows and piles over a rapid succession of three ledges with unavoidable 5′ standing waves. Three hundred yards below this rapids, the river funnels over a ledge to the left and undercuts a shelf of rock with a 1′ clearance. This can be negotiated, but it is dangerous.

Five hundred yards farther downstream the river spills over a 15-20′ river wide falls. This can be scrambled on the right at low water after sneaking under the natural bridge. It is better to carry along the road on the right. One mile below this the river is narrowed and split by a partially submerged, house-sized boulder in a powerful drop. It is fairly flat until the Teter Creek bridge.

About 2 miles below Teter Creek bridge is a game called Blindman's Bluff. The river pools up behind a natural rock dam, turns to the left and immediately to the right, all of the time being necked down considerably. There are big diagonal stoppers pushing to the right in this turn and as (if) one regains alignment around the last corner, he is faced with a huge tongue of water called Well's Falls dropping 10′ over a slide into a formidable stopper. If one slides off the left side tongue to the right, he would slam into a four-foot wall of water. This is the most powerful, runnable rapids in the entire Monongahela Basin, a river system full of challenges. It should be scouted each time. The very next rapids is also mean—essentially a sheer drop into a very nasty hole. Both of these rapids are runnable, but they are also easily carried on the right. All of the other rapids below Teter Creek are nice Class 3 drops that offer no special problem (in low water). The entire Arden section is something you wouldn't even want to get near during periods of high water. This can get awfully messy in the spring.

GAUGE: One can call the Pittsburgh Weather Service (412) 644-2881, and ask for the Tygart River reading at Philippi. These are the readings referred to above.

SHUTTLE: Use the dirt road on the right side of the river. Drive about 2 miles upstream to the first rapids for an easy put in. Beginners should take out at the Arden bridge. Intermediates can take out at Laurel Creek. Experts proceed with caution and carry the falls. One can take out at Teter Creek for an easy shuttle with a road alongside throughout. To reach the Cove Run take out, turn right at Teter Creek and go out to the main highway, W.V. 92 and turn left. Take Cove Run Road "2" to the left, then a right, another right, and then a left at the succeeding forks. The last part takes you down a very steep unimproved road to near the river. Be sure you recognize this point from the river. You will not find rapids on the lower part until around the first of October. Peak drawdown is generally reached about the last of February. At such time there would be another 1.8 miles of rapids dropping 30 fpm to the flatwater. You would then have another 2 miles of flatwater to a take out on the left side at Wildcat Hollow Boat Club.

F. Valley Falls to Hammond—1.5 Miles

CLASS	GRAD.	VOL.	SCENE	TIME	LEVEL
2-6	60	2259	A	1	0-1′

MAPS: USGS—Fairmont East
COUNTY—Marion

DESCRIPTION: This section of the Tygart should be considered an expedition requiring experienced paddlers, a close scrutiny of the dam discharge from Grafton, and a certain cavalier attitude. The major DIFFICULTY in addition to the large gradient is the fact that this section of the river has been narrowed down 80% as it enters the steep gorge. This is considerable for such a large volume of water. In this section there are at least 8 major drops. The first ledge, Valley Falls, is about 10 miles downstream from Grafton. It is the site of an old mill, artifacts of which still remain. This is a river wide ledge about 7′ high which has water coming over at least 3 sites (low water level). The chute on the right is sloping and can be run with more water although it does pile angrily into and off the shore rocks at its base. The next ledge of about 14′ is sharp and appears to be unrunnable. At low water it can be run to the left of the right half. At higher water the boat disappears deep into a pool and pops up into the falls where it stays and stays and stays. The third ledge is a Class 4 rapids with two runnable channels both requiring right angle turns to the left after running tight along the right bank and just before dropping into the main current which piles over an impassable rocky course. The fourth ledge is clearly Class 6 at even moderate water levels. The river narrows to a single channel and drops 8′ over a boulder with a thin flow at the center and a boiling flume at each side.

The fifth rapids is a series of three drops in rapid succession in a 20′ channel. The bottom two have huge souse holes up against the undercut right shore. The last three are straight forward rapids. The last can be reached from the take out and is an excellent white water training site.

Due to the discharge of the Grafton Dam, can be "run" any time, but if several gates are open, this whole narrow valley is a nightmare of explosion waves,* *moving* 12-15′ waves, and terrible souse holes. An interesting site from the RR tracks, but no place for anyone's boat.

GAUGE: The Grafton Dam has a gauge, but readings are meaningless to the authors. The above gauge reading is for Colfax. See below. Decision to run this can only be made after on-the-spot observations have been made.

SHUTTLE: Valley Falls State Park is easily found by following the signs from either Fairmont or Grafton along the county roads "13" and "5" respectively. The Hammond take out is reached by a yellow brick road (honest) from this same county road. Also, Colfax in the next section.

G. Hammond to Colfax—5 Miles

CLASS	GRAD.	VOL.	SCENE	TIME	LEVEL
	1@20				
1, 2-B	4	2547	A, C	1.5	0-3′

MAPS: USGS—Fairmont East and West
COUNTY—Marion

DESCRIPTION: There are no danger spots on this run unless there are several gates open at the Grafton Dam. Normally a pleasant Class 1-2 run for 1 mile below the brickyard. Take the first island to the left and the rest on the right for the best rapids. The remaining four miles are fairly flat through attractive scenery. Take out at Colfax on the left just past the bridge or one could continue on to Fairmont for another 4.5 miles of flatwater.

GAUGE: Homemade gauge located on bridge support at Colfax. Has been run at 8′, but this latter run was ridiculous! Three feet would be a reasonable upper limit.

*Explosion Wave—A very violent and unpredictable wave.

THREE FORK CREEK

Near W.V. 92 to Thornton—12 Miles

CLASS	GRAD.	VOL.	SCENE	TIME	LEVEL
1-4	2@30 1.5@60	S	B-C	3	0-6″

MAPS: USGS—Thornton, Gladesville, and Newburg
COUNTIES—Preston and Taylor

DESCRIPTION: This is a very small stream that can only be run when there has been a lot of rain. The water is very acidic, the rocks orange, and the scenery poor in many places, but it has some very interesting rapids. The upper 2 miles below W.V. 92 are steep and can only be run when the water is very high. Runs may also start at a bridge on the Gladesville-Independence road "33". The scenery here is very attractive as the laurel and hemlock crowd in on the stream, but the water is fairly flat with only occasional riffles. As the water begins picking up speed and complexity to Class 2, the next bridge is met which ends this 3-mile segment and is the signal for the beginning of the Class 3-4 action-packed 1.5 miles. In this latter section, there are 3 falls.

After passing the third falls, the water tapers off to a Class 2 for another 2 miles and marks the end of the action. You might consider taking out at the second bridge beyond the last falls. The water below here to Thornton is fairly fast, but contains very few riffles. It is not recommended to paddle beyond Thornton as the water is even flatter, the scenery uninteresting, and very few opportunities for take outs exist.

DIFFICULTIES: Just before, under, and beyond the second bridge from the put in, is Victoria Falls, a steep slide rapids into very turbulent water and then over a 2-4′ ledge into a powerful hydraulic. The rapids after this are all closely spaced, steep, and complex. The second and third falls are near the end of this 1.5-mile course. The first of these, Yosemite, is a steep staircase descent taken on the right and the next rapids, the third falls (Niagara), is a river wide shelf with several passages. Scouting is recommended for the first and third falls. The falls have been given these grand names not only for the power they connote, but also to bring a touch of beauty to this otherwise forlorn land.

SHUTTLE: Put in at the first bridge below W.V. 92 on the Three Fork Creek Road "35", or at the bridge next to the tavern on "33", 2.5 miles south of Gladesville. Continue on this road to Independence and bear right following the road to Doortown. Take outs can be made at the bridge there, the next one downstream at Irontown, or under the U.S. 50 bridge at Thornton. For just the action part, put in at the Victoria Falls bridge reached by taking the road next to the cemetery from Gladesville. Take out under the power line right-of-way below the last falls if no one is around. The people owning the property just upstream from here get pretty uptight about this though. It would be better to paddle another half mile down to the Doortown bridge.

GAUGE: There is a canoeing gauge at the bridge south of Gladesville, but no experience has been gained with the river at really high levels. The zero is very liberal, however, and was set to indicate scraping on the first ledge at Victoria Falls. It can be run a lot lower than this with a lift over that ledge.

CHAPTER IV

MISCELLANEOUS STREAMS IN THE OHIO DRAINAGE

North-central West Virginia doesn't contain much white water. Although it is very hilly, the valleys do not have the gradients or the volumes necessary to create anything more than minor riffles in most places. The land is sparsely populated, rural in character, and given mostly to agriculture and strip mining. There are few areas of natural or scenic interest and none located along the streams. Other than for the river cities along the Ohio, the major cities are Harrisville, West Union, Glenville, and a lot of other places most paddlers have never heard of. A few rivers, the Little Kanawha, Decker's Creek, and Whiteday Creek are described individually, while a few more are described in general terms.

DUNKARD CREEK—This is a very long, winding stream that parallels the Mason-Dixon Line through northern Monongalia County. Its mouth is on the Monongahela in Pennsylvania. Parts of it have been run by canoe. Float fishing in rowboats is popular. In high water, there is little more than Class 1 riffles. The stream is very rich in waterfowl and bass and muskie fishing is good. It could be run as far west as Blacksville all the way to Mt. Morris, Pa. Although the road distance between bridges may be short, the river distance may be as much as twice as far due to its meandering qualities.

HUGHES—This is a popular float-fishing stream whose mouth is on the Little Kanawha River above Parkersburg. It also furnishes good muskie fishing. The forks of the river appear to have some gradient in the vicinity of North Bend State Park and *possibly* might be runnable in high water although this has not been determined.

MIDDLE ISLAND CREEK—This is northern West Virginia's most popular float fishing stream yielding lunker-sized muskies. It winds for miles through Doddridge, Tyler, and Pleasants counties and has its mouth at St. Marys. This is a big creek—612 cfs average.

WHEELING AND LITTLE WHEELING CREEKS—These streams that barge their way through beautiful downtown Wheeling aren't much to look at, but are capable of coming up quickly, causing property damage, and loss of life. They definitely have white water (actually brown) and the former occasionally gets rafted by college students. Low water bridges and interstate construction have added formidable hazards to any attempted run. As far as we know, they haven't been paddled responsibly yet.

The most famous resident of this area was pioneer hero Lewis Wetzel who among other things used to *run* between Morgantown and Wheeling (all the way) and would think nothing of swimming over to Ohio in the winter. Sort of West Virginia's Davey Crockett.

BIBLIOGRAPHY

Allman, C. B. 1961. *Lewis Wetzel.* New York: Devin-Adair.

DECKER'S CREEK

A. Preston-Monongalia County Line to W.V. 7 Bridge—5 Miles

CLASS	GRAD.	VOL.	SCENE	TIME	LEVEL
$2\text{-}3_6$	40 1@200!	99	A-C	1	1′+

MAPS: USGS—Masontown and Morgantown South
COUNTY—Monongalia

DESCRIPTION: This is the only white water stream that Monongalia County owns all by itself and it's a humdinger. The put in is just below an unrunnable cascade of successive water falls. It moves right along at a fast small stream, Class 3 pace through dense laurel thickets, ledges, fallen logs, and low hanging branches. It is a very rocky stream and follows W.V. 7 very closely. The scenery gets crudded up as it passes through two large limestone mining areas and one must actually paddle through culverts at these places.

DIFFICULTIES: Watch out for downed trees, trapped debris, and a possible clogged culvert. At high water three bridges at Greer are too low to go under. Other than for these ordinary dangers, all you need worry about is the 200 fpm drop to the W.V. 7 bridge at Pioneer Rocks, a so far unrunnable "Class 7" rapids. It is one horrendous drop after another for a whole mile. You could be hurt real bad if you goofed. Not recommended to paddle, but you ought to take a look at it. We don't know what all is actually in there except a whole lot of hell!

SHUTTLE: Park at the county line sign on W.V. 7 for a fairly gentle slope to the put in. Take out somewhere above the highway sign "HILL." This marks the start of the Pioneer Rocks Hell.

B. Dellslow at W.V. 7 Bridge to Monongahela River—6 Miles

CLASS	GRAD.	VOL.	SCENE	TIME	LEVEL
1-3	28 2@50	99	D	2	0-2

MAPS: USGS—Morgantown North and South
COUNTY—Monongalia

DESCRIPTION: Once one of the most beautiful streams in northern West Virginia, this little stream is now polluted with strip mine acids, crushed limestone, industrial pollutants, and raw sewage. The scenery is terrible—one literally canoes through the bowels of Morgantown, but it has plenty of action for late winter canoeing after severe thaws.

DIFFICULTIES: Within 25 yards of the put in there is a 4′ S-turn ledge which is Class 3 at medium water. The first 2 miles drop 104′ with most of that occurring in the first mile. Several hazards line the way: at mile 1 the broken down bridge at Richard may be choked with debris. After turning the corner below the bridge at Rock Forge one enters a long sterile channel built by the Department of Highways to replace the river they bulldozed aside. As one approaches the large factory on the right there is a dangerous fall consisting of very sharp boulders left behind by the construction. Scout for the best passage since you can't afford to hit these rocks. One may need to carry the low water bridge at Marilla Park if the water is high. At mile 5 the river drops sharply over a series of ledges and heads under a high overpass. The water gets up to Class 3 and turns sharply to the right through high standing waves. The left hand "bank" is a concrete wall; just below this there is another ledge which must be run on the far left in a tight passage between the bank and a fallen tree; the final ledge is a few hundred yards below this and should be scouted to find the best passage. The biggest danger on this run would be an upset because you would be swimming in almost raw sewage in the last 3 miles.

GAUGE: None. The top of the right footing of the Dellslow bridge can be considered zero.

SHUTTLE: Put in just above the W.V. 7 bridge at Dellslow. Take out can be reached by paddling down the Monongahela under the Westover Bridge, being careful to dodge the spit from the playful urchins above, and take out at the foot of Walnut Street one block beyond the bridge.

LITTLE KANAWHA

Wildcat to Falls Mill—13 Miles

CLASS	GRAD.	VOL.	SCENE	TIME	LEVEL
C-1_4	10	274	A-B	4	–

MAPS: USGS—Orlando, Newville, and Hacker Valley
COUNTIES—Lewis and Braxton

DESCRIPTION: This is a good trip for novices in winter or early spring when the water is up. The entire proceedings will take place in remote and scenic surroundings. Don't expect much in the way of rapids, especially in high water. The gradient is such that only Class 1 riffles predominate. There is a lot of flat water, but it is moving along at a good flow at such levels. The pool below the falls has been a popular fishin' and swimmin' hole for generations.

DIFFICULTIES: There is only one and it is a real lulu, that of the falls giving the hamlet at the take out its name. Novices can easily take out above the falls while the more experienced may want to run it. There is nothing to it actually, just over the top, down over the steep drop, and into an almost keeper-sized hydraulic. Perfectly straight forward. If there is enough flow to run the falls and you flip, the fast current below will take your boat for quite a ride. There are practically no rapids from here to the mouth at Parkersburg.

GAUGE: None. If water is 6″ below the footing of the Wildcat bridge, there will be plenty of water. An easier place for observation is the Falls Mill bridge. A reading of 6½ stones down on the right upstream abutment proved adequate.

SHUTTLE: Use W.V. 4 from Falls Mill east to Ireland and turn right on "50" to Wildcat.

WHITEDAY CREEK

Camp Calico to Monongahela River—9 Miles

CLASS	GRAD.	VOL.	SCENE	TIME	LEVEL
1-3	3@55 6@23	S	B	3	1-3′

MAPS: USGS—Rivesville
COUNTY—Monongalia

DESCRIPTION: This anxious little screamer is the Monongalia-Marion County line. The first 2 miles are continuous Class 3 with no pools and very few eddies. This has been compared to a small Savage River and a road runs alongside for an abbreviated run. The second or middle part down to W.V. 73 consists of more open Class 2 water while the final 3 miles consists of mainly big waves and drops up to Class 3. The stream is only 20-40′ wide. The tiny steep section above the Girl Scout Camp has been run during a very high water period. It is hazardous with tree problems.

DIFFICULTIES: In the first quarter of a mile there is a left-hand bend against an auto-sized boulder. Stay to the right of center to avoid another partially submerged rock in the bend. You can eddy out immediately to pick up paddlers, etc. Several islands and fallen trees invigorate the next two miles. A quarter mile below the W.V. 73 bridge is a 4′ dam that can be run at reasonable levels but better scout for logs and strength of keeper.

GAUGE: There are gauges on W.V. 73 bridge and on the first bridge downstream along "36". Both have the same zero and are similar in the paddling range. The downstream gauge can be read by Thomas Thomas, 304-363-3661. It will likely be up after a heavy winter rain. A 0.5 reading is adequate for playing on the three miles below W.V. 73.

SHUTTLE: Take "79" east from W.V. 73 at the golf course and turn right at a sign identifying Camp Calico. Put in at pool above bridge below the camp. To reach the take out take "36" from W.V. 73 at Smithtown and proceed to the third bridge over these troubled waters, a half mile short of the Opekiska Locks. There remains a 6-mile run above Camp Calico which hasn't been checked out yet and that could keep a paddler very busy in high water.

CHAPTER V

THE BEAUTIFUL VALLEY RIVER– THE GREENBRIER

In a state with so much beauty, it is difficult to pick out the most beautiful this and that, but many look to the long and broad Greenbrier Valley for such titles. Beginning high in the mountains in the "Birthplace of Rivers" whose opposite slopes give rise to the Cheat and Potomac rivers, the lovely Greenbrier winds its way for some 150 miles through some of the most beautiful and productive land in West Virginia. It would take less than an hour's drive to cross the headwaters of four major rivers–the Tygart on U.S. 250 near Huttonsville, Shavers Fork on up on the top of the mountain, the forks of the Greenbrier on down the other side at Durbin, and the North Fork of the Potomac's South Branch on out W.V. 28 to Circleville.

The West Fork of the Greenbrier is an extremely popular, tiny trout stream beginning very near the source of Glady Fork which flows the opposite way. The Greenbrier and Shavers Fork parallel each other, but one flows southwest in the valley and the latter flows northeast on the top of the mountain. The East Fork is also a very small trout stream draining the western slopes of Spruce Knob. The forks join in Durbin and head for scenic Cass and busy Marlinton.

Below Marlinton the valley broadens and as the river moves from Pocahontas to Greenbrier County, it drains some of the richest, most productive farms in the state. This portion of the Monongahela National Forest is particularly well kept, the roads are all good, and there is an abundance of scenic attractions. The river has one final fling at wildness below Talcott before merging with the teeming waters of the New at Bellepoint below the Bluestone Dam.

As yet there are no real dams on the Greenbrier watershed. In fact the river below Marlinton and its major tributary, Anthony Creek, have both received protection against such fol-de-rol by both strong local support and state legislative action. The Corps of Engineers, however, is greedily eyeing dams to be put in on Knapp's Creek, on the Greenbrier above Marlinton near Clover Lick, and on the East Fork. This latter dam would inundate the site of the National Youth Science Camp and miles of native brook trout habitat among other things.

The upper Greenbrier has been immortalized by the late Warren Blackhurst in his historical novels depicting life there in the early logging days. Knapp's Creek, Deer Creek, and the Greenbrier were used to float out the winter cut during times of spring high water following the big thaws. If you are ever on the Greenbrier at 3′ or more bouncing along the swollen river in the safety of your canoe, think of how it must have been for the old rivermen who would ride for miles in such dangerous water balanced on a big white pine log with his heavy caulked boots and cumbersome peavey gripping the wet bark. The state has wisely captured the romance and history of this era by developing the Cass Scenic Railroad as a prime tourist attraction, but much more of this needs to be done in our state. The Greenbrier hustles right by the depot.

It also flows through many other quiet and beautiful towns such as Ronceverte (French for greenbrier) and Alderson. All of these towns developed as important stops along the C. and O. RR, then the only means of transportation in this country aside from the rivers. Remains of old sawmill towns like Seebert and Watoga still exist. As the RR construction approached the big loop of river below Talcott, the RR people decided to save time and money by drilling a tunnel through the mountain to Hilldale rather than following the river. This was the Big Bend Tunnel in which big John Henry of folk music fame met his well-known demise trying to compete against the steam drill. This same region has produced other folklore and songs familiar to the folk music and RR fan. John Hardy, a C. and O. employee, who "killed him a man on the West Virginia line," sprang out of the folk idiom here and one of the most celebrated train wrecks in history and song, that of the No. 143 the F.F.V., took place just east of Bellepoint near the tunnel.

In addition to agriculture and cattle production, the entire region is also well known for timber production, especially in the Durbin-Bartow area. Other industry is very light in spite of the presence of the RR. Due to the wealth of scenic attractions and the fishing in the Greenbrier, tourism and recreation should be considered primary industries. In addition to the native brook trout mentioned above, the forks are heavily stocked with hatchery trout. The river is also well known for bass, catfish, and walleyes below Marlinton although fish kills in this area occur with distressing frequency.

The paddle or drive from Durbin to Hinton is not only very scenic and rich in the very interesting side trips one can take, it is also a trip rich in history. In addition to the Cass Scenic RR, the river also flows by Seneca and Calvin Price state forests and Watoga State Park. Although the latter has a crummy campground, it is not near the river. The Forest Service has two excellent campgrounds on Anthony Creek (Blue Bend and Blue Meadow) and there is a private campground at the mouth of this same stream. The Forest Service also maintains an interesting campground on an island in the middle of the East Fork above Bartow. Other than that, primitive campsites would only be found on private land and permission would have to be gained. The Corps permits camping in trailers below Bluestone Dam.

Canoeing has been popular on the Greenbrier for decades and Marlinton, Lewisburg, or Hinton would make excellent bases of paddling operations. An outstanding vacation could be made touring the entire length of the river and taking in all of the attractions in the area. Most of the trip with the few exceptions noted in the descriptions would lend itself quite well to open boat canoe camping. Perfect for Scouting groups.

BIBLIOGRAPHY

Blackhurst, W. E. 1954. *Riders of the Flood.* (Second Printing, 1968. Parsons, W.Va.: McClain Printing Co.)

———. 1963. *Sawdust In Your Eyes.* Parsons, W.Va.: McClain Printing Co.

———. 1965. *Of Men and a Mighty Mountain.* Parsons, W.Va.: McClain Printing Co.

Dixon, T. W., Jr. 1967. *The Rise and Fall of Alderson, West Virginia.* Parsons, W.Va.: McClain Printing Co.

Price, W. T. 1963 (reprint). *Historical Sketches of Pocahontas County.* Parsons, W.Va.: McClain Printing Co.

GREENBRIER

A. The Greenbrier Forks

The West Fork is runnable from at least the mouth of Little River along F.S. 44 to Durbin. It is a fast paced Class 1-2 stream with a few low, angled ledges. The best rapids may be seen from the U.S. 250 bridge. The take out is ½ mile below U.S. 250 at a bridge on the WEST side of Durbin. This is a beautiful stream passing through the forest.

The East Fork is runnable from Camp Pocahontas, located at the junction of W.V. 28 and F.S. 14, to Durbin. This is a busier stream than the West Fork and it passes through pastoral settings along the highway. Low hanging branches and barbed wire are greater hazards on this smaller fork. One can take out at the U.S. 250 bridge at Bartow near the motel or 2 miles downstream at an iron bridge on the EAST side of Durbin. This latter section is heavily polluted and not as nice as the other part. There is a paddler's gauge on the Camp Pocahontas bridge and you will need at least 2′ on the Marlinton gauge or 4′+ on the Buckeye government gauge.

B. Durbin to Cass—17 Miles, Gradient 18 fpm

MAPS: USGS—Durbin and Cass 15′
COUNTY—Pocahontas

DESCRIPTION: This is a beautiful small trout stream that pours easily but steadily through rock gardens and eroded ledges. Stay in the middle at about one half mile from the junction of the East and West Forks in order to avoid the concrete pier on the right side of a bridge. For three miles below this, the water is fairly calm, but soon the river becomes narrower as the mountains squeeze in. The water in this area is Class 2 with some boulder dodging required. The river flows fast through wilderness country. The bed remains narrow and 3′ haystacks are common at the ends of the rapids, but there are no boulders or souse holes to complicate the passages. No major DIFFICULTIES.

SHUTTLE: Put in on the West Fork at the U.S. 250 bridge near the edge of Durbin. There are two ways to drive to Cass. Secondary State Rt. 3 enters U.S. 250 about a mile above the West Fork bridge and proceeds directly to Cass. A longer route over somewhat better roads is U.S. 250 to W.V. 28 through Green Bank and turning right on secondary "7" to Cass.

C. Cass to Marlinton—27 Miles, Gradient 11 fpm

MAPS: USGS—Cass, Mingo and Marlinton 15′
COUNTY—Pocahontas

DESCRIPTION: The river below Cass has more volume, but moves slower through uncomplicated rapids with no obstructions. The scenery remains beautiful although some signs of civilization appear. Many wilderness campsites along the way make the whole trip from Durbin to Marlinton an ideal overnight camping trip in open canoes. In the spring, numerous small mountain streams supply fresh water, and trout or bass fishing may be done almost anywhere.

SHUTTLE: Put in at Cass and take out at the W.V. 39 bridge in Marlinton.

GAUGES: Look at the level of water under the bridge at Durbin. A depth of water there of about 3′ will give a good run. Trips beginning at Cass could similarly be determined by examining water conditions under the bridge. There is a canoeing gauge on the Marlinton bridge which should read at least 2′ for these upper runs.

The Greenbrier Below Marlinton

The Greenbrier below Marlinton begins to take on the characteristics of a big river. It has a large volume having been added to appreciably by streams such as Knapp's Creek and Deer Creek, and in many places may be quite wide and powerful. The rapids are usually formed at narrow places in the river or in curves. There are many long flat stretches between such rapids and the gradient seldom exceeds 8 fpm. It can be floated most of the year, but is unrunnable in dry summers. In each section, we have indicated points of caution and difficulty.

The river can be run down to ½′ on the Marlinton gauge located on Rt. 39 bridge in Marlinton, lower right bank bridge pier. Readings may be obtained from Brill's Esso Station 799-8229. Referring to gauge, you would have an ideal run about 1½-2′ although runs up to 3′ and higher have been made. At 2′ or greater, the current is swift and large haystacks or long fields of haystacks appear. At 3′ the flat water is moving fast and very powerfully, most of the boulders have been covered up, and the waves, particularly on the outside of the curves may reach 5-6′. Obviously, at this level, it is no place for inexperienced paddlers or undecked boats. A government gauge exists at Buckeye and can be obtained by calling 453-2482. You will need about 4′ on this gauge in the Marlinton area.

D. Marlinton to Denmar—16½ Miles

MAPS: USGS—Marlinton 15′
COUNTY—You are still in Pocahontas!

DESCRIPTION: There are not many exposed rocks and this is an easy run at all levels. Mostly Class 1 riffles when rapids. From Seebert on, the left bank is either state park or state forest. Seebert is at the second bridge from Marlinton. Set up shuttle from U.S. 219 and take "27" into Seebert (the road to Watoga State Park) or "20" into Denmar.

DIFFICULTIES: There is a low water bridge just under a new high one which must be portaged. For this section as well as any of the lower Greenbrier, novices should make decisions well before approaching any rapids as the water may be very swift. If in doubt, always stick to the inside bend of any curving rapids on this river (although this is not always a good rule to follow elsewhere).

E. Denmar to Renick—17½ Miles

MAPS: USGS—Marlinton, Lobelia and White Sulphur Springs 15′
COUNTIES—Pocahontas and Greenbrier

DESCRIPTION: The river continues winding its way into Greenbrier County picking up volume from numerous side streams which can be appreciable during summer cloudbursts. Don't try to take out at Spice Run Station located about 4½ miles from Denmar. Apparently boaters aren't welcome by the locals. About a mile below Spice Run after the river bends to the left, there are some big waves which can get over 5′ at high levels that develop on the right hand outside bank.

SHUTTLE: Use U.S. 219 to find Denmar (use "20") and Renick (use "11").

F. Renick to Anthony Station—10 Miles

MAPS: USGS—White Sulphur Springs 15′
COUNTY—Greenbrier

DESCRIPTION: The Greenbrier has a much larger volume from Marlinton to Hinton, being very broad and powerful in places. Rapids are usually formed at narrow places in the river. There are long flat pools between such rapids. It can be floated most of the year, but it is ideal to catch it in high water when the current is swift and large haystacks appear for greater stretches.

There are no danger spots on Section F, but there is one rapids three miles above Anthony that open boat paddlers should scout. Before the rapids begin, the river curves slightly to the right, toward the RR track. There is a concrete post beside the tracks with a "W" on it. The rapids parallel the tracks for 100 yards and pile up against car-sized boulders before it curves to the left.

The mouth of Anthony's Creek may be seen on the left near the take out. This is a fine stream and has been described separately.

SHUTTLE: Put in on right side of river in Renick below U.S. 219 bridge. Take out on right bank below bridge at Anthony Station. This is also a good camping spot. Take "21" from Frankford to reach Anthony.

G. Anthony Station to Ronceverte—18 Miles

MAPS: USGS—White Sulphur Springs and Ronceverte 15′
COUNTY—Greenbrier

DESCRIPTION: The river is still moving rather slowly through occasional rapids. There is a rock dam at Ronceverte that is pushed up every summer during the dry season. High water washes it out so there may be a passage. Scout if appropriate.

SHUTTLE: Put in on right bank below "21" bridge at Anthony and take out on right bank at Ronceverte City Park just before going under the bridge.

H. Ronceverte to Alderson—15 Miles

MAPS: USGS—Ronceverte, Clintonville, and Alderson 15′
COUNTY—Greenbrier

DESCRIPTION: The river begins to take on characteristics of our classification of a big river. The current is more powerful and the rapids below Fort Spring become more numerous and interesting. They consist of nice runnable ledges up to 2′ and boulder patches with waves up to 3′. Catching this section in high water would be an exciting run, but open canoes would need decks. You should begin thinking about Class 3 water from now on.

SHUTTLE: Put in at Ronceverte City Park and take out on the right bank near the bridge in Alderson. This is rather steep. You are now on W.V. 63.

For those that don't give a rap, the Federal Women's Reformatory is located just downstream on the left.

I. Alderson to Talcott—14 Miles

MAPS: USGS—Alderson 15′
COUNTIES—Greenbrier and Summers

DESCRIPTION: The river is fairly flat most of the way in this section and offers few rapids. An excellent float fishing part of the river for bass or just a beautiful place to indulge in general indolence.

SHUTTLE: Made from W.V. 3. Put in where you can at Alderson and if you find a good one, tell us. Take out at Talcott at the "17" bridge.

J. Talcott to Bellepoint—16 Miles

MAPS: USGS—Talcott and Hinton
COUNTY—Summers

DESCRIPTION: The novice and inexperienced white water paddler should end his trip at Talcott because from here on the Greenbrier can get pretty nasty in medium to high water. The river is fairly flat for 2½ miles below Talcott as it begins to transcribe a big loop, the famed Big Bend.

DIFFICULTIES: Bacon Falls, below Talcott, can be easily recognized upstream by the sheer rock cliff on the right bank. The correct approach is on the left side from which the falls can be scouted. This is unrunnable most of the summer due to the many exposed rocks in low water. When runnable, the easiest passage is on the left, while the right may be considered dangerous. Here the water piles furiously over the steep drop right into the cliffs and then over large boulders. About a mile below Bacon Falls is a tilted ledge known as Linsey Slide. Above this is a series of small ledges. The easiest passages are on the left. From Linsey Slide to the take out, the river moves faster and there are several long rapids which are easily run. Consider Bacon Falls as Class 4.

SHUTTLE: Put in at the "17" bridge in Talcott and take out on the left near the mouth on the New below Bluestone Dam.

ANTHONY CREEK

Neola to the Greenbrier River—15 Miles

CLASS	GRAD.	VOL.	SCENE	TIME	LEVEL
$1\text{-}3_4$	10@12 5@24	S	A	4	1′-?

MAPS: USGS—Callaghan and White Sulphur Springs 15′
MNF
COUNTY—Greenbrier

DESCRIPTION: This is a small stream tumbling through beautiful and largely unsettled country. It is an important tributary of the Greenbrier, and one of the few in the state protected by legislation. The river from Neola to Blue Bend Recreation Area is a very small trout stream descending gently over gravel bars and in general, follows "15" and "16." The rapids do not exceed Class 2 difficulty, but there are many sharp turns and fallen limb hazards to watch for.

From Blue Bend to its mouth on the Greenbrier, Anthony Creek passes through *de facto* wilderness and drops more steeply as it cuts beside Gunpowder Ridge. The rapids for the first 3 or 4 miles are easily negotiated Class 2 drops over minor ledges.

DIFFICULTIES: After a rather long flat stretch, the river is separated by an island with the most difficult passage being to the left. The next rapids consists of a curious ledge that runs almost parallel to the banks of the stream. One must avoid broaching over this drop. Soon the river enters a pool and it appears to come to a dead end, but it actually turns sharp right, as near as any river can make a 90° bend, through a barricade of boulders and the first of a series of intricate Class 3 rapids. These are boulder strewn stretches with many chutes and ledges and could easily get to Class 4 in high water. After a mile of this, the narrow gorge opens up and levels out into the wide Greenbrier Valley.

SHUTTLE: Put in at a bridge in Neola or, for a shorter 5-mile trip, at a bridge immediately above Blue Bend Park. A dirt road just downstream from this latter bridge leads directly under it. Take out about ¼ mile above the mouth on the right. This can be reached from a dirt road along the east bank of the Greenbrier, marked "Camp Anthony."

SEASON AND LEVEL: There is no gauge at present. Examine the water at each put in. More water (at least 1.5′ under the bridge) is needed for the section beginning at Neola. If you scrape when leaving the swimming area of Blue Bend itself, do not attempt to proceed. Enough water to carry you over this little ledge without doing so would be regarded as zero. In general, this is an early spring runoff stream, but it has been caught at high levels at later times even in summer following prolonged rains. If you were to find it "up" in summer, it would be too low by the time you got there. During one such summer run when a lucky canoeist just happened to be in the area when the stream was up to a runnable level, it dropped 6″ in the hour it took to run from Blue Bend to the take out.

MISCELLANEOUS GREENBRIER TRIBUTARIES: The Greenbrier must have hundreds of small tributaries draining into it, many of which could probably be runnable if the water were extremely high and you could arrange a put in. Sitlington's and Deer creeks near Cass should theoretically be runnable since both were once used to float logs down to the Greenbrier. Knapp Creek is of good size some times and has been run. A put in can be arranged on W.V. 39 at the bridge or even farther up if the water is high enough. A primarily Class 2, 9-mile run may be had down to the Fifth Avenue bridge in Marlinton. There are many sharp turns and a lot of fast action, especially in the upper part. The scenery is excellent. Short fast rides may be had at several places, just how many we will probably never know. For instance, the last mile of Stony Creek at Campbelltown near Marlinton and Swago Creek at Buckeye south of Marlinton have each been run in very high water. Spring Creek which has its mouth 3 miles below Renick has a very bad reputation of coming up very quickly during hurricane type weather, causing flash floods, and loss of life. The Corps seizes on events like this to justify dams on the Greenbrier (the loss of life occurred high on Spring Creek) instead of embarking on plans of sound watershed management.

SECOND CREEK: There is a 16-mile run from Hollywood to Fort Spring which is available when the gauge at U.S. 219 bridge is above 2′. The run is isolated and beautiful with some interesting Class 3 water.

CHAPTER VI

WILDEST WATER FROM THE CENTRAL HEARTLAND

This section of West Virginia is both at the very heart of the state and of the Monongahela National Forest, specifically the very rich Gauley Ranger District. This region contains not only the greatest variety of water, but also the most difficult and uninhibited water in the state. Most of the action may be found in Webster and Nicholas counties, two very rugged and isolated areas of immense vastness. Nicholas alone probably has more white water than any other county in the state.

The rivers in this section comprise two distinct watersheds, the Elk and the Gauley. The Elk Basin is one of the few in the state that has been studied extensively by the State Department of Natural Resources (but ignored completely was the subject of this book). It has few major tributaries, but many small creeks. The Back Fork of Elk, which has its mouth in Webster Springs, has been designated by the state as a Fish-for-Fun stream which is absurd since at the present time siltation from strip mining and logging has precluded this noble activity (the watershed is not in the MNF). Other important tributaries of the Elk are Birch and Little Birch rivers and both Forks of Holly. The headwaters of the Elk are very close to those of the Tygart, another great river, but one which flows in the opposite direction. The Elk's mouth is in Charleston on the Kanawha, the site of a famous winter camp made by an early white water swimmer, Simon Kenton.

The fantastic Gauley has an amazing number of tributaries. The Gauley begins high in the recesses of Webster County as a small rootin' tootin' scrapper and then settles down for a long placid cruise near the border of the national forest. It then picks up the Three Sisters of the Monongahela National Forest, rivers of incomparable action and in most places unparalleled beauty, the Williams, Cranberry, and Cherry. By the time it has done this, it is fairly good size and begins to become active again as it carves its way through Nicholas County. Below Summersville, it begins its vicious, unrelenting journey to meet the New at Gauley Bridge to form the Kanawha, but not before being further swollen by the equally vicious, but smaller Meadow River. Both of these streams are the unquestioned leaders of white water difficulty and small boat navigability found in West Virginia.

Webster and Nicholas counties are incredibly rich in natural resources, but little significant industry is located there. Historically, areas such as this have been exploited by absentee industries with but little return to these areas and therein lies West Virginia's most pressing problem. The land is too rugged for agriculture and the recovery of its two main resources, coal and timber, is environmentally destructive. The riches leave the area and capital never develops to build nice things or attract industry for its people. Unemployment is chronic and leads to poverty, apathy and poor education which in turn perpetuates the trouble. If only some way could be found to make the incredible beauty of these counties pay off to the inhabitants without being so socially degrading or environmentally destructive. Webster Springs was once an important tourist center featuring fine hotels and quality recreation and Richwood was once a booming lumber center, but the glory of both are gone and recovery has been difficult.

All of the Monongahela National Forest provides superb recreation near the rivers. There are many primitive camping sites along the upper Williams River and two Forest Service campgrounds are on the Cranberry. An additional one is nearby at Summit Lake between the North Fork of Cherry and the Cranberry. The Williams and Cranberry drain a roadless area known as the Cranberry Back Country which state groups are trying to get protected under the National Wilderness Act. There are no public camping grounds on any of the Elk white water except the Corps of Engineers facilities on the Sutton backwaters.

Speaking of the Corps, they haven't ignored the area. There is a large reservoir at Sutton on the Elk, one of the oldest in the state, and a relatively new one in Summersville on the Gauley. Both are popular for broadwater recreation. The latter begins drawdown in the fall permitting runs on the lower Gauley. The rest of the rivers run free, but what frightens everyone are the plans of the Corps with state backing to construct a chauvinistic dam 4′ higher than the Russians' latest effort. This 875′ dam would go in at Swiss and flood the entire Gauley back to the Summersville Dam as well as 7.5 miles of the lower Meadow. Are we so insecure that we must destroy every evidence of Nature's might?

The Cranberry drains a magnificent area of natural wonder, the Cranberry Glades. This natural refrigerator has created a life zone featuring plants and animals more in keeping with Northern Canada. Naturalists flock there to see wild orchids and other rare plants in profusion. Collecting native Cranberries is an adventurous outing. The entire area is an amateur botanist's delight with many garden clubs sponsoring wild flower tours in the area.

The area was naturally the scene of early logging activity, but more of the hardwood variety than the spruce-hemlock-white pine types. Many old towns have disappeared as have a myriad of early railroads—West Virginia Midland, Stroud's Creek and Muddlety, Erbacon and Summersville, etc. One of the most recent to disappear was the Buffalo Creek and Gauley near Clay that was the largest coal-fired operation east of the Mississippi. It hauled coal, timber, and oddly enough, milk, as recently as the mid-sixties. Sawmills come and go, but one of the most impressive was the completely steam operated one in nearby Swandale that was dismantled along with the demise of the BC&G. The lower Elk was the scene of a great deal of Indian activity, such peoples having used the area for centuries as a hunting grounds as the river's name suggests. A significant Civil War battle was fought high over the Gauley at Carnifex Ferry, now the site of a historical state park. The battle along with several other similar ones was responsible for West Virginia breaking away from the Old Dominion and becoming a separate state. Most of us now believe that Virginia should change its name.

Richwood and Webster Springs are both ideally located near excellent white water although there are few areas one can stay at the latter. Summersville has good access to the lower Gauley and the middle Meadow in season. Native white water paddlers do not exist in this area at the present time.

BIBLIOGRAPHY

Clarkson, R. B. 1964. *Tumult on the Mountains.* Parsons, W.Va.: McClain Printing Co.

Comprehensive Survey of Elk River Sub-Basin, Vol. I. 1969. West Virginia Department of Natural Resources.

Sutton, J. D. 1919 (reprint). *History of Braxton County and Central West Virginia.* Parsons, W.Va.: McClain Printing Co.

WILLIAMS

A. The Williams Above Tea Creek

The Williams begins as a tiny trout stream with many branches high in the mountains of Pocahontas County. From where the bridge crosses the Williams "17" and on around the mountain, the river leaves the road. When it reappears, the Williams is simply a flat river. It then begins picking up to a Class 2-3 near Sugar Creek and continues for ½ mile to the Tea Creek bridge where most runs begin. It is 3½ miles between these bridges. F.S. 86 follows the Williams from the flat water all the way to Three Forks and there are many primitive camping sites along the way.

B. Tea Creek to Three Forks of Williams Bridge—11 Miles

CLASS	GRAD.	VOL.	SCENE	TIME	LEVEL
3-5	53	317	A	2	-0.5-0.5

MAPS: USGS—Mingo 15′; Webster Springs SE
MNF
COUNTIES—Pocahontas and Webster

DESCRIPTION: This is a little river with very big ideas. When it is in season it is comparable to the Savage only with rocks to avoid. The rapids are continuous with individual segments surging to Class 5 and never dropping below Class 3. Any pools are tilted downhill. This run is along a favorite trout fishing area in the Monongahela National Forest. It is picturesque and remote, but populated by fishermen.

DIFFICULTIES: There is a particularly bad rapids, Bannock Shoals, at the county line where the river converges as it is tumbling down a rocky hill to squeeze into a 15-foot passage between two boulders.

Three miles above the Three Forks bridge is Three Part Rapids: 1) A sloping river-wide ledge off to the right, 2) A double hydraulic that must be blasted, and 3) A sheer four-foot falls studded with bottom side boulders and bordered with a holding wave. The third part can be avoided by crossing the river from the right side while running the stoppers and bumping down a rock pile at the far left. Depending on what has happened in the first eight miles the in-trouble paddler won't even consider this baby and the good-run paddler will be so high he will be walking on water down this rapids.

GAUGE: There is a faded canoeist's gauge at Three Forks bridge which is set at least ½ foot too high. Think twice if it is up to one foot. The USGS gauge is just downstream on the left from the Dyer Bridge. It reads three feet higher than the Three Forks gauge. The Craigsville gauge can be used as an estimate and should be 11.5 to 12.5′, call Huntington Hydrology number (529-2318, ext. 604).

SHUTTLE: Both ends of run are reached from W.V. 20 two miles east of Cowen via "46" or from U.S. 219 north of Marlinton via "17". Both secondaries meet as F.S. 86 along the Williams. Put in and take out easily at the bridges listed, but trip can be shortened to any length along the road.

C. Three Forks to Gauley River—10 Miles

CLASS	GRAD.	VOL.	SCENE	TIME	LEVEL
1-3	20	317	A-C	3	0-2

MAPS: USGS—Webster Springs SW, Webster Springs, and Cowen
MNF
COUNTY—Webster

DESCRIPTION: This section of the Williams is considerably tamer, but no less interesting. All of the rapids are straight forward, open rapids with good wave action as the river turns corners, cuts through islands, or is occasionally split by a large boulder. With the right level, it would make an excellent open boat run. The river here is wider and shallower than that above Three Forks. The volume increases greatly, however, due to the many tributaries it picks up in the first two miles. The best action is in the first half of the run, but the river gradually becomes wider and flatter as the Gauley is approached. The scenery from the road is rather depressing, but the paddler sees little of this from the river.

DIFFICULTIES: About two miles below the put in the river branches many times around small islands. Many of these passages may be choked with debris or fallen trees. There is a low water bridge about eight miles from the put in which must be portaged.

SHUTTLE: See section B. Take outs can be arranged at many places along "46".

GAUGE: See section B.

CRANBERRY

A. The Cranberry Above Cranberry Recreation Area

The Cranberry River drains a fabulous wilderness area known as the Cranberry Backcountry. Technically, travel within the backcountry is closed to the public, but in practice is open to well drillers, coal prospectors, loggers, trail bikes, snowmobiles, and a lot of other people who don't belong in there. The South Fork of the Cranberry drains the famous Glades and would be accessible by car, however the water would have to be very high and you would have a great deal of difficulty lifting around deadfalls, etc., on such a tiny stream. F.S. 102, a good gravel road, is closed to public traffic so if you wanted to use it, you would have to secure special permission from the Forest Service or else be a fairly agile kayakist and motorbike in with your boat on your shoulder. It is 4½ miles to the Forks of Cranberry, a good theoretical put in. From here to the lower gate at the Cranberry Recreation Area and Campgrounds is about 9 miles. A dirt road, F.S. 76, follows the river closely. The river in this part has a gradient of 100+ fpm and hence should be as interesting, if not more so, than the next section. There is one section known to the fishermen as "the Roughs" which sounds interesting and *apparently* contains some big drops although this remains undetermined at present from the wildwater boater's viewpoint. The MNF map is helpful, but the USGS topos are too old to be of any benefit. Anyone wishing to travel by primitive means in the Cranberry Backcountry should obtain a West Virginia Highlands Conservancy guide for the area (see bibliography).

B. Cranberry Recreation Area to Big Rock Camping Area—6 Miles

CLASS	GRAD.	VOL.	SCENE	TIME	LEVEL
3-5	80	215	A	2	3.5-5.0′

MAPS: USGS—Webster Springs SW
MNF
COUNTY—Webster

DESCRIPTION: Very little, very steep, very busy. That pretty well describes this prelude to the Cranberry. Although a Forest Service road follows the river, it is a very remote stretch of thrilling action and impressive scenery. It is a good stream for maneuvering and there are many ledges and boulders complicating the descent. The action is fairly continuous after passing the first mile of fairly flat water. Below the county line, the gradient eases up, but it is still a steep slalom descent. At low levels the maneuvering is intense, but high water covers up a lot of the boulders and makes for a more straight forward albeit very turbulent descent.

DIFFICULTIES: There is a low, practically washed out bridge about a mile below the campgrounds which may need to be carried. There is another carry where there is an eroded ledge below which there is a boulder right in the middle of the channel only one boat length away from the ledge. Cannot be run in low water. In high water you may hear a loud crunch from the bowels of your boat. Next below and one mile above the county line is another rapids or waterfall that will need scouting. There is a huge boulder blocking the view on the left, right at a point where a steep drop begins. As you draw abreast of the boulder you run into a stopper which forces you to the right into either a smaller boulder straight ahead or into an eddy even farther to the right. You should try to keep to the left through the stopper and avoid the smaller boulder and then back to the right over a 3-4′ drop.

SHUTTLE: Set up easily from F.S. 76 between the Cranberry and Big Rock Campgrounds. Campsite No. 7 is a good put in.

C. Webster County Line to Gauley River—7 Miles

CLASS	GRAD.	VOL.	SCENE	TIME	LEVEL
2-4$_5$	40	215	A	3	3.5-5.0′

MAPS: USGS—Camden on Gauley
MNF
COUNTY—Nicholas

DESCRIPTION: This is a delightful stream pouring noisily through some of the state's most beautiful scenery. A put in can be made anywhere along F.S. 76 from the Woodbine Recreation Area to the Cranberry Recreation Area, but a put in at Bee Run on the county line is preferred for a run on this section. A put in at this location is zestful as one immediately is faced with slaloming through boulder passages and chutes of Class 3-4 difficulty. Particularly impressive is the entrance rapids to "Snake Hole" immediately above the bridge. The descent is rather steep, but tapers off slightly at Woodbine. Downstream from Woodbine for about 2 miles is very delightful in that the rapids are straight forward Class 2-3 that permit the paddler to appreciate the beauty of the intimate surroundings. The river has broadened out and there are few boulders and ledges in this stretch.

Soon and almost imperceptibly the river picks up speed and begins to narrow down. The paddler's attention is drawn away from the scenery to begin boulder dodging and negotiating the tricky chutes.

DIFFICULTIES: About 3 miles below Woodbine the paddler enters a 300-yard-long rapids of Class 3 rating which occupies his attention so much he may fail to see what is coming up. The main part of the river begins to turn right and then makes an S to the left out of sight. At the point where the main river turns to the right there is a large brushy island.

Just below this island where the two branches rejoin is a mean Class 4-5 boat buster, Cranberry Split. Here the river has been necked down to 10 yards, but there is a big boulder sitting right in the middle of a steep drop. At high water the river smashes furiously against it and bounces off at 75° angles to either side. At low water it is undercut and has been known to pin a paddler. The left appears unrunnable as there are smaller boulders in its channel that would certainly smash a hull. More recently a log with grabbing branches has occupied the left channel. Run to right obviously but be aware that good paddlers have had trouble putting the advice to practice. In high water there is a sneak on the far right. It is not easy at any level although it appears deceptively simple. There are several tricky rapids below this, but after having seen this hazard, they seem like child's play. Two miles below the Split, one enters the Gauley. You have gotten used to a small stream even though its rapids are difficult and now you enter a river whose volume is considerably greater. Even its small waves are very forceful and caution is urged. The Gauley is a wide powerful river at this point with long stretches of Class 2-3 water with hidden boulders and souse holes. Proceed down river for 2 miles to Curtin for an easy take out under the W.V. 20 bridge. These 2 miles of the Gauley have a 31 fpm gradient. Due to the westerly course of both rivers, the glare of the sun on the water is considered a hazard and sunglasses are recommended for afternoon paddling.

GAUGE: There is a government gauge located on the bridge leading to the Woodbine Recreation Area. Consider 3.5′ as zero and 5.0′ as high and pushy. The Craigsville gauge (529-2318, ext. 604) should be over 11.6′.

SHUTTLE: F.S. 76 leads from the outskirts of Richwood to the recreation areas. The take out is reached via W.V. 20 west of Richwood where there is a bridge over the Gauley.

NORTH FORK OF CHERRY RIVER

Hacking Run to Richwood—5 Miles

CLASS	GRAD.	VOL.	SCENE	TIME	LEVEL
3-4	66	S	B-C	2	13-14′

MAPS: USGS—Lobelia, Webster Springs SW,
Camden on Gauley, Richwood
MNF
COUNTY—Nicholas

DESCRIPTION: This little branch of the Gauley parallels W.V. 39 and can be surveyed for water level from the road. It has been paddled in flood water seasons from the second bridge above Richwood.

DIFFICULTIES: Tricky maneuvering is required to avoid boulders and fallen trees. At the east end of Richwood the dam behind the motel must be carried. The best Class 4 section of the run is immediately below the dam. There is a second dam which can be run on the left.

GAUGE: Take a look at the North Fork of Cherry when Craigsville gauge is over 13′.

SHUTTLE: From W.V. 39 bridge where the river crosses from the south to the north side of the road to the Richwood School bridge is the usual run.

LAUREL CREEK

Jetsville to Fenwick—4 Miles

CLASS	GRAD.	VOL.	SCENE	TIME	LEVEL
3	75	5	B	1	13-14′

MAPS: USGS—Richwood
MNF
COUNTY—Nicholas

DESCRIPTION: This run is a delightful little pastime of eddy hopping when other rivers are roaring to get out of their banks.

GAUGE: The Craigsville gauge is an indicator.

SHUTTLE: From Fenwick bridge go south off W.V. 39 on "39/14" paralleling the creek and railroad. Put in at the railroad bridge four miles upstream from Fenwick.

SOUTH FORK OF CHERRY

Beech Lick Run to Richwood–6 Miles

CLASS	GRAD.	VOL.	SCENE	TIME	LEVEL
$2\text{-}3_4$	52	S	B-C	2	8″-?

MAPS: USGS–Richwood and Lobelia 15′
COUNTY–of no help; inquire locally.

DESCRIPTION: A small, rocky stream with steep gradient, very short pools and almost continuous action. The rapids are rock strewn and passages often intricate. The most obvious looking choice at the head of a rapids may lead you into a cul-de-sac. The river looks like a runt-sized cross between the Williams and Cranberry with a difficulty rating somewhere between the two. It is a stream for white water boats only.

DIFFICULTIES: About one-quarter to one-half mile below the put in two trees lay across the stream. At 8″ or above the first can be run on the extreme right by riding up and over the small branches, the second offers a passage through the middle if you lay flat on the deck. A few more inches of water will close this passage. Both trees might go out during a heavy runoff. Somewhat less than halfway through the run is a light Class 4. The 4-5′ drop itself is not too bad providing you hit the narrow chute in the middle . . . too far to the right you and the current piles into a rock . . . too far to the left and you drop into a deep hole. The real difficulty is in the winding approach which makes it difficult to get in position for the chute. Below here are a few more tangled passages, but the drop soon lessens and the last half of the trip presents no real problems.

GAUGE: None; assuming zero to be the lowest runnable level the 8″ level was arbitrarily assigned by guesswork.

SHUTTLE: Put in about one-half mile above Beech Lick Run where the South Fork road ends at the washed out bridge. Take out one-quarter mile below the junction of the North and South Forks of Cherry at the bridge in front of Richwood school.

CHERRY

Dain Bridge to Mouth on the Gauley—9 Miles

CLASS	GRAD.	VOL.	SCENE	TIME	LEVEL
2-3	30	406	C-D	3	0-2′

MAPS: USGS—Richwood 15′; Camden on Gauley and Craigsville
COUNTY—Nicholas

DESCRIPTION: This raucous little sister to the nearby Cranberry is a real thriller. It passes through some pretty dreary scenery, but the paddler's attention is focused on the boiling eddies, large haystacks, and hidden hydraulics that will completely stop an unwary paddler pausing to marvel at the landscape. A small river with almost unaccountably big water at times (possibly due to its narrow, confining, steep rocky banks), it does not have the slaloming characteristics of the Cranberry. It comes up faster, but it goes down quicker, also. The action is fairly continuous with very little quiet water. The river is split at least three times below Fenwick with the best and sometimes only passage being to the left each time. This river changes drastically with different water levels.

DIFFICULTIES: About 200 yards above and in sight of the Fenwick bridge there is a steep ledge or small falls. Suitable passages exist on either side. At high water it can be run in the center by skilled paddlers *if* they know that it is there, but it is easily missed from upstream observation. Below Fenwick after a long quiet stretch and just above Holcomb, there is a long slide rapids terminating in big stoppers. There are 3 major rapids below a tipple that is about 2 miles below Holcomb. The third of these, the Trough Drop, can be a real challenge in high water. It consists of two very sharp river-wide drops in pretty heavy water. At lower levels it presents as a series of staggered ledges. Interesting rapids continue to the mouth for an easy take out on the other side of the Gauley.

GAUGE: On the Fenwick bridge, watch out if you can't see the 2! From 0-1 is suitable for intermediates in open boats although much maneuvering would be required. Decking is needed over 1′ and the water becomes very heavy over 2′.

SHUTTLE: Put in under the Dain bridge on the west side of Richwood. The Fenwick bridge is also popular. Take out under the W.V. 20 bridge on the Gauley.

MEADOW RIVER

A. East Rainelle to Russellville—15 Miles

CLASS	GRAD.	VOL.	SCENE	TIME	LEVEL
3-5	32 4@64	526	A	5	4.6-6.0

MAPS: USGS—Rainelle, Corliss, Winona
COUNTIES—Greenbrier, Nicholas, and Fayette

DESCRIPTION: The first eight miles to the railroad bridge at Burdette Creek are flat, but there is a fast current broken occasionally by shoals and riffles. The bridge marks the transition point between an easy gentle river and a furious, exciting course through a canyon.

DIFFICULTIES: The unique thing about this river is the very long, continuous rapids, *THE* Rapids. *THE* Rapids begins with a zesty Class 3 run under the bridge, quickly converts to a Class 4 and 5 boulder strewn descent, and remains that way for almost four miles. There are only two small pools throughout the length of *THE* Rapids. Only eddies offer temporary sanctuary for the pooped paddler. The difficulty rating bounces back and forth between 3 and 4 on individual segments with the 5 primarily due to the continuousness of the challenge. Diagonal ledges, high ledges up to five feet, big souse holes, stoppers, and tortuous channels characterize the run.

Two large drops are particularly dangerous. The first is 1½ miles from the start of *THE* Rapids. The river appears to be completely blocked, but there are two passages on the right. About one mile farther, below the second pool of *THE* Rapids, there is another drop that requires special care. A natural weir plunges the water into a small aerated cauldron followed by an S-shaped run out from the left over several 2-3′ ledges.

There is a falls near the end of *THE* Rapids which drops over a steep rock face into a very rocky, aerated turbulence split by a boulder. Passage and/or carrying must be done on the left. To the right is a huge undercut rock cradling a large trapping log.

Scouting is difficult due to the density of the second growth thickets lining the banks. As with many rivers of this type, a view of the rapids from upstream is difficult due to the length of the individual rapids and the bends of the river. Scouting will have to be done from the boat while harbored in eddies, hence a high degree of boat control is absolutely necessary.

As suddenly as *THE* Rapids began, it ends. The remaining three miles to the take out is a fast run over occasional class 2-3 rapids.

GAUGE: The Mount Lookout gauge is at the mouth of the Meadow. Obviously few paddlers will ever see it, but fortunately the Corps of Engineers in Huntington gets a daily reading by phone. They will tell you that reading if you phone 529-2318 ext. 604.

SHUTTLE: The put in is reached from U.S. 60 by driving north on Snake Island Road "60/1" in East Rainelle and continuing for three miles. The river runs parallel to the road, but is rather flat and uninteresting. It is an easy but unpleasant put in via the city dump. (An unfortunate and illegal practice of many small communities—an unsanitary waterfill instead of a sanitary landfill.) An alternate put in for 4-WD vehicles is at Rader Ford reached via Corliss on a two-mile rocky and muddy steep road. This shuttle requires only 30 minutes and cuts out five miles of flat water.

B. Nallen to Corridor L (U.S. 19) Bridge—5 Miles

CLASS	GRAD.	VOL.	SCENE	TIME	LEVEL
3-4	39	646	A	3	4.5-7.0

MAPS: USGS—Winona, Summersville Dam
COUNTIES—Nicholas and Fayette

DESCRIPTION: The flat section of the Meadow from above Russellville to Nallen continues for about a mile along W.V. 41. The river is befittingly named in this sector where it can be seen by the non-paddler. This sector and the name are a paradox. Above is *THE* Rapids. Below is this fun section and below that is Hell.

After an initial mile below Nallen the river begins dropping through boulder gardens between rocky, forested banks. The rapids alternate with pools. This enjoyable run continues to the take out. The gorge gets progressively deeper. The high sandstone cliffs fringed with hemlock are more spectacular than on the Gauley. The best rapids are in the mile just above and below the point where the river leaves W.V. 41.

DIFFICULTIES: None. An ideal busy intermediate run. Significant water, beautiful scenery, easy shuttle. Just don't be lured downstream from the take-out bridge.

GAUGE: See section A.

SHUTTLE: Put in about one mile below Nallen to catch the first rapids. Take out at the U.S. 19 bridge except that the bridge is 200 feet above the water. You can carry all the way up. You can drive halfway down from the south and west side if it is not too wet. You can drive all the way down on the north side with 4-WD by turning west off U.S. 19 at the first crossroad north of the bridge and taking an immediate left. Continue for a few hundred yards to another left onto a dirt road and follow to the river. At the river take a hard left and proceed to the grassy area under the bridge.

The road from take out to put in is north on U.S. 19 to the Mount Lookout road, east to W.V. 41 and south toward Nallen.

C. Corridor L to Carnifex Ferry—5 Miles

CLASS	GRAD.	VOL.	SCENE	TIME	LEVEL
4-6	94	646	A	5	4.0-5.0′

MAPS: USGS—Summersville Dam
COUNTIES—Nicholas and Fayette

DESCRIPTION: This is for the Kamikaze Kanoeing Klub only. The river changes character immediately with a winding Class 4 plus rapids just beyond the bridge and picks up from there. Rapids become boulder piles, eddies disappear into narrow chutes over high ledges and bubble up from under monstrous boulders. Scouting and carrying become the primary activity.

DIFFICULTIES: In three miles of this low section there are 17 rapids all of Class 5 and 6 variety. Almost every rapids has a death trap. Undercut rocks abound. Attempts to even see all this part of the Meadow have been difficult. Most parties reporting runs on the lower Meadow have given up on the mid-lower section, with its 250 feet in two miles drop, and carried along the railroad track on the left side for a mile. Below this mile are still many short carries and more scoutings. One group paddled the entire river with only one carry at 4.2′ in 1974. Only in the last mile does the river again ease off to a reasonable run—only 60 fpm.

GAUGE: See section A.

SHUTTLE: The take out is as nearly impossible as the river. It is from the site of Carnifex Ferry which must have closed down after General Floyd's retreat September 10, 1861. (Coincidently it was on the 110th anniversary of the Civil War battle that this river was first paddled.) The twentieth century retreat from defeat on the lower Meadow is the same as it was after the capture of Camp Gauley—by foot, carrying all equipment north one mile up to the battlefield state park, or east 1½ miles to the end of "24" which comes through Mount Lookout from U.S. 19 four miles north of the put in, or south a mile up to the trail off Sunday Road "4" coming in from Hico on U.S. 60. Instead of walking the paddler can paddle on down the Gauley. It's only 21 miles to Swiss and a riverside road.

GAULEY

A. Webster County Line to Jerryville—5 Miles

CLASS	GRAD.	VOL.	SCENE	TIME	LEVEL
3-4	70	S	A-C	1	13-15′

MAPS: USGS—Mingo 15′ and Bergoo
MNF
COUNTY—Webster

DESCRIPTION: These headwaters of the Gauley are just too small and rocky at the level they have been run. When everything is flooded it would be worth another look. The scenery is distracted by Jerryville's coal mine tipple. Generally speaking, don't bother to paddle this one. During the spring season when the water might be up there are many many better places to spend your time in this area, e.g., Williams, Cranberry, Elk. When the water is not up, there are 100 miles of excellent Gauley downstream.

DIFFICULTIES: Tight and steep particularly in the highest part. There is a low water bridge in the second mile.

GAUGE: The reading is for the Craigsville gauge at Curtin on the Gauley, not to be confused with Curtin on the Elk. This gauge is 35 miles downstream and there may be many local variables.

SHUTTLE: Go up the Gauley from Bolair which is on W.V. 20. Follow "42" until it peters out at Jerryville, just above the take out bridge. Then go on via an old railroad bed to about one mile beyond a usable old RR bridge.

B. Jerryville to Curtin—40 Miles

CLASS	GRAD.	VOL.	SCENE	TIME	LEVEL
1-2	15	572	A-B	10	11-13′

MAPS: USGS—Bergoo, Webster Springs, Cowen,
Camden on Gauley, and Craigsville
MNF
COUNTIES—Webster and Nicholas

DESCRIPTION: The first portion of this run is the smallest and steepest (257 cfs, 18 fpm). The course is obvious and easily scouted from the road. For several miles around Bolair the scenery is interrupted by ramshackle dwellings. It is a 12-mile trip to Bolair where the river gets back to W.V. 20. The highway parallels the river then for the next six miles and one mile later the Williams doubles the river's discharge.

The mouth of the Williams is an excellent place to start an open boat trip. The then much larger river leaves civilization to meander through National Forest land for nine miles. The course has boulder patches covered by irregular waves big enough to ship into an open canoe, but more characteristically it is a series of pools and low ledges. The trip could be ended when the river flows out of the forest at Camden on Gauley. Above and below Camden for about three miles the river is flat. The next 11-mile segment again leaves the road. Another quantum of water is added by the Cranberry two miles above the take out.

DIFFICULTIES: The only specific problem on this scenic open-boatable excursion is a six-foot slanting ledge in the section between the mouth of the Williams and Camden. The lower portions can get to be an awfully big river in the spring and there is enough gradient to make it a very uncomfortable long wash to the paddler clinging to a swamped open canoe.

GAUGE: The readings are for the Craigsville gauge at Curtin obtainable via Huntington Corps of Engineers (529-2318 ext. 604) or add 10.6 to the canoeist's gauge at Curtin bridge, W.V. 20.

SHUTTLE: The uppermost put in for this section is the take out for section A, see above. There is access to the river at Bolair. The next suggested segmenting point is at the "46" bridge just above the mouth of the Williams. Again in Camden there is easy access. The final take out is on the right side just beyond the W.V. 21 bridge at Curtin.

C. Curtin to Donegan Mine No. 10—5 Miles

CLASS	GRAD.	VOL.	SCENE	TIME	LEVEL
2-3	23	1202	A	1	10-12′

MAPS: USGS—Craigsville
COUNTY—Nicholas

DESCRIPTION: This is a big powerful river traversing excellent scenery. At the higher levels this is no place for beginners. The rapids are generally long sloping Class 3 runs. At lower levels the first rapids below the put in is the shallowest of the trip. The river then transcribes a huge loop, Cupperneck Bend. This can be viewed from high above on W.V. 20.

DIFFICULTIES: About two miles from the put in and after rounding the bend a ledge is encountered which is followed by a pool with a cliff on the right. The river now runs down a narrow channel to the left which looks harmless, but at the end there is a very heavy chute with a large souse hole on the right. This is probably more hazardous at medium to low water levels as it is pretty well covered in high water.

Beware of a 12,000 volt power line that you have to walk under at the take out!

GAUGE: Use the Craigsville or Curtin gauge as noted in section B.

SHUTTLE: Put in under the W.V. 20 bridge near the mouth of the Cherry. Take out can be reached by driving west to the top of the hill. Turn left beyond the American station on "14". Continue for two miles to a left turn unto a wide dirt road leading to the mine. The take out is at the mine buildings. Better ask permission to leave a car and to cross their property from the river.

D. Donegan Mine No. 10 to W.V. 39 Bridge—11 Miles

CLASS	GRAD.	VOL.	SCENE	TIME	LEVEL
A-3_4	4@20	1202	A	5	10-12′

MAPS: USGS—Craigsville and Summersville
COUNTY—Nicholas

DESCRIPTION: This section includes the best white water of the upper Gauley but it costs a lot to run it. The run starts vigorously as a Class 3, builds to Class 4 then stops when you are still nine miles from the take out. The last nine miles are flat flowing water merging imperceptibly with the Summersville reservoir. In the winter the flowing water is extended by the huge drawdown of the reservoir, but the distance is still not shortened and the silt encrusted rocks are much less scenic.

When the drawdown is enough to put the lake level at the W.V. 39 bridge, there is another mile of Class 3 water just above the take out. This is the beginning of the Gauley canyon extending to Swiss. (See sections E and F.)

DIFFICULTIES: The first mile and a half contain a good deal of Class 3, boulder strewn rapids, but beware of what happens at the point where the river gives the illusion that it has come to a dead end. A tangled array of boulders 20-60 feet across funnels the river over a ledge and down a narrow chute. The chute heads diagonally to the right, then straightens and plunges under a ship's bow rock. Wild water angrily peels off to either side. The right side is blocked by another rock which must be passed still farther to the right. The left is runnable only at the 12-foot level. This one will require scouting to determine the best available passage. (Overland?) Water levels will greatly affect this decision.

GAUGE: Use the Craigsville and Curtin gauges as described under section B.

SHUTTLE: The put in can be at the take out for section C. For an alternate put in which adds a mile of interesting water and abbreviates the shuttle take "39/15" from W.V. 39 to Marybill.

The take out is the underwater extension of old W.V. 39 on the left side near the present W.V. 39 bridge. At low water there is a bit of goo to get through, thanks to our Army friends with the hard hats.

E. Summersville Dam to Peters Creek—16 Miles

CLASS	GRAD.	VOL.	SCENE	TIME	LEVEL
4-5$_6$	28	2605	A	8	3-4.5′

MAPS: USGS—Summersville Dam, Ansted
COUNTIES—Nicholas and Fayette

DESCRIPTION: Pull out all stops on the superlatives to describe this unique wildwater river. It is the absolute swirling, pounding, crashing end. In 1961 it was rafted. The reports were frightening. It was 1968 before it was paddled in white water boats by a group of the world's most expert paddlers. The word spread and the number of paddlers has increased each subsequent year. The Gauley has become the East's qualifying cruise for the title of expert paddler. It is big, it is long, it is inaccessible, it is tough, it is dangerous, it is intoxicating.

The Gauley canyon is an alternating rapids and pool river. The rapids are complex and challenging beyond description. The pools permit rescue and repair and an opportunity to marvel at the grandeur of this remote, vernal, steep-walled canyon.

There are 100 rapids between the dam and Swiss as counted from the Corps of Engineers stereo photos of the Gauley. No river in this part of the world has so quickly picked up so many named rapids. This is evidence of the complexity and memorability of the variety of rapids.

A run down of the named rapids in the order they appear follows: INITIATION—This is a drop below the far end of the dam outflow parking area with a mean surprise hole on the right. So run to the left. Class 4. FUNNEL—No problem but distinctive with a descriptive name and a rock in the stem of the funnel that one tends to wash over. Class 3. INSIGNIFICANT—This is anything but. Spotted by seeing a high sandstone wall ahead in the distance about 45 minutes into the trip. It is a long, open rapids with some bad holes usually marked by inverted boats and bobbing helmets. Class 5. IRON CURTAIN—Named for the iron oxide stains on the high sandstone wall on the right. Rapids is significant because it warns that Pillow Rock is around the next left bend. Class 4. PILLOW ROCK—This is a 25′ falls stretched over about 50 yards of holes, piling up against a demi-dam on the left, and slithering around and over a terminal megachunk of Guyandotte Sandstone. The pillow is where the river hits the wall which extends out from the left. The Pillow puts many paddlers down for a damp rest. This rapids is visable from the Carnifex Ferry overlooks. Scout or carry on either side. Class 5. LOST PADDLE—The first rapids below the mouth of the Meadow River, Carnifex Ferry. With its downstream brother in mayhem it is known to Nicholas County natives as Mile Long Shoals. After 200 yards of rocks and holes the river channels to the right side and drops steeply onto a marginally covered rock pile. Run to left where it's steepest if you want to take the big gamble—one drop, one hole, and out. Run to the right if you want to descend more gradually but risk unseen rocks banging stern and/or head. Class 5. Scout from boat in eddy on right above last big drop. TUMBLEHOME—Ugly for the swimmer. Start left or right but end up on right or in trouble. Micro pool after big drop is usually not big enough for rescue so wash on through the six-foot middle slot to safety. Class 4+. TABLE ROCK—Second rapids below Tumblehome. This is a flat rock 10 feet high and 50 feet long extending across the center of the Gauley. The long approach should be down the left side and diagonally across to the right of the table. Running to left or straight for the table puts the paddler into the Orangejuice Squeezer. The water churns across the undercut front face of Table Rock from right to left. Give this wide berth to the right. Class 3. IRON RING—Two rapids below the Orangejuice Squeezer the river bends to the right and the current is compressed along the right shore by a point of rocks. The rapids is named for a huge eye ring set in the rocks. The ring dates from an attempt to blast a log floating passage past the point in the early 1900's. The result of this dynamiting is an irregular mid-channel obstruction. The river drops down a six-foot high slide into a hole a few feet above the obstructing boulder. The current welling up out of the hole mostly slips down the right side. Some splashes over the rough man-made block. About ¼ flushes under and around the left side of the jagged stone in a channel between it and its mother stone. The channel is crooked and turbulent without enough straightaway for a swamped boat and with enough force to fold an errant man and boat together. Class 6. Carry on the left or run tight right and upright. SWEET FALLS—One mile and six rapids below Iron Ring the Welch Sandstone, shale, and thin strata of Sewell coal rise straight up from the right side of the water. Just around the right, then left, jog the river drops over a cliff of this sandstone as a heavy steep ten-foot falls. It was named for John Sweet who ran it on the initial Gauley trip. Others try it but few make it without completely disappearing and popping up bottom first. The sheer falls can be detoured on a left side sneak channel. Class 5+. INSIGNIFICANT No. 2—This misnomer occurs after three miles of no significant water below Sweet Falls. It is a heavy, long rapids with a terminal surfing wave. Class 3. Immediately below here at the south tip of Legg Bend is the Wood's Ferry take out. ENDER WAVES—There are a series of six-foot waves at the end of the Wood's Ferry pool. FIVE BOAT HOLE—Two and one-half miles below Wood's Ferry on Koontz Bend is this rapids also known as BACKENDER. Run it on the left if you want to avoid the wide but not horrendous hole. Class 4. KOONTZ FLUME—Next below

Five Boat Hole is this baddie. Most paddlers stop halfway down to boat scout the flume but this is a mistake because it is difficult to get across the rushing current to be in position. Just run down the center right. Class 5. CANYON DOORS—Next rapids on Koontz Bend marked by tall vertical breaks in the right canyon wall. This is a fun series of long easy surfable stoppers, Class 3. JUNKYARD—Next rapids. It is at the site of a 300-foot high dump. What fun it must be to be ecologically irresponsible enough to dump your trash off a 300-foot cliff into a clear tumultuous river. Run on left to avoid being hit by a falling car. Class 3.

DIFFICULTIES: See DESCRIPTION! See the "Golley." This is no place for the sometimes roller. Be forewarned not to attempt this course without the degree of skill, confidence, and endurance that make the Cheat or New River gorges a cakewalk. And even then only undertake this trip accompanied by a party who has previously experienced the "Golley."

GAUGE: The fall is the best time for a Gauley trip not only because of the splendid colors but because after October 1 the water level is guaranteed by the let-down schedule for the Summersville Dam. The discharge can be obtained at the dam keeper's office at the put in. The exact flow for the last half of the trip is obtainable from the Huntington Corps or Weather Service as the Belva Gauge. (Values above.) This is at a discrepancy with the dam release if the Meadow is up.

SHUTTLE: The put in is easy—the only easy thing about the trip. It is at the base of the Summersville Dam and is reached by going south then west from Summersville.

The first possible take out is at the mouth of the Meadow—Carnifex Ferry. This is adjacent to a state battleground at the site of a Confederate rout. The access is one mile up a steep trail and is recommended only in an emergency. A jeep trail also gets to near this ferry pool from Mount Lookout or from Hico to the south. Again these are only for emergency use. At Woods Ferry 12 miles into the trip a ½ mile jeep trail from the Saturday Road to Leander leads to the river. It is a good take out for a shorter trip. A little used railroad parallels the river for a walk out or scouting access. At Koontz Bend it cuts through a half mile tunnel. Walking through this refrigerated trainwide dark hole on railroad ties is a thrill in itself, especially when a half mile long coal train catches you in the tunnel.

The usual take out (with serious reservation) is near Peters Creek railroad bridge. Turn off W.V. 39 at Otter Creek School west of Lockwood. After the blacktop ends take left fork up hill to a right fork along the ridge. The carry out from the water is from a right side beach one-half mile above the railroad bridge. It is a half mile steep switchback jeep trail.

A good alternative is to use this take out trail or walk along the tracks up Peters Creek without your boat. Then come back the next day to complete the run to Swiss. A better alternative is to stop the trip at the upstream end of the Koontz Bend Tunnel, hide your boat and walk out through the tunnel and up the tracks. It takes only 10 minutes longer and saves the interesting three miles of Koontz Bend water for day two.

F. Peters Creek to Swiss—8 Miles

CLASS	GRAD.	VOL.	SCENE	TIME	LEVEL
3-5	26	2605	A	3	2-4.5′

MAPS: USGS—Ansted
COUNTIES—Nicholas and Fayette

DESCRIPTION: This part of the Gauley is less strenuous than the upper run below Summersville, but is heavy and still challenging. Each rapids has an abundance of stoppers and hydraulics. There are a few 3's but you had better go prepared for 4's and 5's. Each rapids is followed by a pool, but that pool may be a quarter-mile away if you flip high in the rapids. It is great big water play.

The named rapids in order are: MASH—A U-shaped ledge followed by big waves. DIAGONAL LEDGES—Play, play, play. GATEWAY TO HEAVEN—A long approach to a ten-foot wide squeeze. It's a lot of river to thread through this needle eye. RIVERWIDE STOPPER or THE HOLE—The fifth rapids from Gateway. The river is bending left in a 100-yard approach and then it bends down and then up and then the paddler gets bent. Maybe it will help to stay to right of middle. You'll be in trouble so paddle like Hell! PLAYTIME—A surfing wave. RATTLESNAKE—Long rapids with a rattler on the end especially if you start on left. CLIFFSIDE—Easy on right. Fun on left. Recognized by its landmark on the left. PURE SCREAMING HELL—Next below Cliffside after pool with cabin on left the river cuts right. This is a long intricate curving approach to some big stoppers and troublemaking right shore rocks. Just stay in center. Right side tends to trap boats against the rocks or lure them into stoppers.

DIFFICULTIES: The Hole and PSH—See above.

GAUGE: See section E.

SHUTTLE: For put in see shuttle under section E.

The take out is one mile up the river from Swiss along "19/25". After this road parallels a railroad siding for several hundred yards it swings away from the tracks up a creek. Stop here. The take out is over the tracks on or just above a sandy peninsula. This siding is appropriately named Omega, the end of a classic trip.

G. Swiss to Gauley Bridge—10 Miles

CLASS	GRAD.	VOL.	SCENE	TIME	LEVEL
B-1	5	2605	C	3	Any

MAPS: USGS—Gauley Bridge
COUNTIES—Nicholas and Fayette

DESCRIPTION: After venting its spleen for 23 miles in the gorge as a result of being insulted by the Summersville Dam, the Gauley returns to a peaceful coexistence with open boats all the way to its junction with the New at Gauley Bridge. It is an uninteresting river with limited redeeming scenic value. Its only justification is that it is close to Charleston and a safe ice-breaker run.

GAUGE: If there is enough water spilling over the low ledge a third of a mile above the mouth, you're on.

SHUTTLE: Put in and take out at random along W.V. 39 or on down the Kanawha to the area at the hotel on the right above Kanawha Falls.

LEFT FORK OF HOLLY

Hacker Valley to Kanawha Run—17 Miles

CLASS	GRAD.	VOL.	SCENE	TIME	LEVEL
2-4	40	S	A-B	5	–

MAPS: USGS—Hacker Valley and Newville
COUNTIES—Webster and Braxton

DESCRIPTION: This is quite an exciting and attractive little stream. In addition to almost continuous white water, the pastoral scenery is very nice and is a good example of how rural areas can blend with the surroundings without devastating them.

The river itself is small with continuous and closely spaced rapids. For the first 7 miles the water is Class 2-3 until a 3′ ledge is encountered. Below this, things pick up a good bit to Class 3-4 for several miles, after which it gradually tapers off to nothing within 2 miles of the take out.

The Right Fork of Holly parallels "5" most of the way, but doesn't have the gradient as the Left Fork. It, too, can only be run when the rivers are at flood stage and *appears* to be only Class 2 (hasn't been run yet). It would be more interesting above W.V. 20, however.

SHUTTLE: Put in under the "3" bridge near Hacker Valley. To reach take out, take "3" from Hacker Valley to Replete. Follow this dirt road for 10 miles through Replete to Kanawha Run. Take out at the campground (also reachable on a better road from Diana).

GAUGE: Use the right abutment of the concrete bridge at the put in as a marker. The water should be half way up the 2′ abutment for a decent run. This stream could only be run when all of the other streams in the area are flooded.

BACK FORK OF ELK

End of Access Road to Webster Springs Bridge—5 Miles

CLASS	GRAD.	VOL.	SCENE	TIME	LEVEL
3	44	S	A-B	1-2	–

MAPS: USGS—Webster Springs, Bergoo, and Skelt
COUNTY—Webster

DESCRIPTION: This starts out below an 8-10′ waterfall as a lively little stream in a most beautiful setting. For the first three miles the scenery is wild with hemlocks lining the banks. At one point near a swinging bridge, the largest sycamore in the state may be seen on the left. This is (was) a popular trout fishing stream, but strip mining activities are threatening it with constant siltation. Soon the outskirts of Webster Springs is reached and the river comes to an ignominious end when raw sewage enters from the right just above the Rt. 20 bridge (although as of this writing, plans are about complete to install treatment facilities). The action is fairly continuous and very few pools are encountered.

DIFFICULTIES: Just a few hundred yards below the put in is a high ledge or small falls. Run this on the extreme left. Scouting may be helpful. The rapids immediately below the falls are tricky so it would be well to chute the ledge precisely. The next ledge opposite a charming cabin forms a tricky, but idyllic setting. Be sure to have a camera ready for this one.

SHUTTLE: Follow the road from the bridge up the left (facing upstream) side of the river. Ignore the first hard road veering off to the right. Continue straight ahead until the road seems to come to an end, but in reality drops out of sight straight over the top of the hill. Hang on—it's Class 6 from here to the end of the "road." Drive slowly.

GAUGE: None at present, but inspection is easily made from riverside in Wester Springs. A good dessert run when in the area running the Elk.

ELK

A. Bergoo to Webster Springs—11 Miles

CLASS	GRAD.	VOL.	SCENE	TIME	LEVEL
1-4_5	31	639	B	3	5.5-6.5′

MAPS: USGS—Bergoo, Skelt, and Webster Springs
COUNTY—Webster

DESCRIPTION: This interesting stream has more variety possibly than any other stream in the state. It begins as a small hell-bent-for-leather, steep ripsnorter with hardly any quiet water. These rapids are all straight forward over rock gardens or shallow ledges. Soon the gradient lets up, but the rapids become heavier and interspersed with some longer pools. Then it finishes up by bouncing downhill over a wild staircase until the outskirts of Webster Springs are reached. Rapids continue all the way through town.

DIFFICULTIES: No real difficulties are reached until you start hitting the ledges below Curtin. At Parcoal one encounters what is essentially a falls, but acts like a long slide rapids terminating in big stoppers and/or hydraulics. This will be a 5 in high water and may require scouting depending on water levels. In low water begin in the middle and work hard to get to the left. In high water avoid the right like the plague. The area known as Cherry Falls is a most interesting series of 4 rather high ledges (2-4′) that are very close together. None of these are easily read from upstream. If the water is high enough, it wouldn't make too much difference where you went over, but you would have to maintain some semblance of alignment between each pair.

GAUGE: See next section for phone. Consider 5.5′ as "zero" for this section. Water ought to be at the top of the concrete footing of the Bergoo bridge abutment for a decent run.

SHUTTLE: To reach put in, take W.V. 15 east out of Webster Springs. Turn right at the third road towards Bergoo. The roads are well marked. Take out at the bridge on either side of the island in Webster Springs although the left side is a shade easier and neither are very.

B. Webster Springs to Centralia—26 Miles

CLASS	GRAD.	VOL.	SCENE	TIME	LEVEL
3-A, B	7@30 12@18	639	A-C	5-6	5.0-6.0′

MAPS: USGS—Webster Springs, Diana, and Erbacon
COUNTIES—Webster and Braxton

DESCRIPTION: This is a long section of the Elk that can be conveniently divided into two parts: the fast upper part of 16 miles containing 14 miles of Class 3 water and the flat lower part of 10 miles down to Centralia. Most of this last section has little gradient and would make a good open boat trip, especially if combined with camping, fishing, or hunting. The two sections are conveniently marked by where "7" fords the river. There are occasional riffles and waves in the flat part and these might possibly increase during periods of drawdown although this hasn't been determined. Open boaters should proceed accordingly.

The upper section below Webster Springs is good intermediate water and resembles a big river. The gradient doesn't give a good idea of the steepness of the rapids because there are several long pools interspersed amongst the action. The rapids are for the most part unobstructed descents through big waves and curlers. Occasionally the river necks down in a curve creating more complexity, but in general it is a fast moving river with straightforward rapids. When the water is high, your time is apt to be very fast. It is the best intermediate run in central West Virginia.

The scenery presents unbelievable contrasts. On one hand is the remote, rugged mountains with few signs of civilization apparent, yet on the other is the overly littered condition of the riverbanks and trash eddies emanating from Webster Springs. Occasionally one passes a farm or country home and again these are either very well kept or horribly trashy. In general, however, there is much, much more of the better scenery.

SHUTTLE: If you only want to run the upper part, you can easily reach the take out by taking "7" from the edge of Webster Springs (turn downstream across the bridge over Back Fork) and drive anywhere from 8 miles to the ford (14 miles) to leave the car off. The first 8 miles by road (10 by river) is several hundred feet above the river, but after that it travels at river side offering many take out possibilities. Put in at any of 3 bridges in Webster Springs (the 2 on the Elk on either side of the island or the Back Fork bridge). The ford is uncrossable if the Elk is runnable and the road below the ford is impassable anyway, hence a trip to Centralia is a real project. Starting at Centralia, take "19" west to U.S. 19, south to Birch River, east on "1" and "30" to Cowen, and northeast on W.V. 20 to Webster Springs. This takes 1½ hours alone!

GAUGE: Call for the Webster Springs reading on the Elk. Consider 4.8′ as "zero." Tremendous waves and Class 4 conditions will probably be encountered at about 6.5′. There is also a canoeing gauge on the left side of the right bridge.

C. Sutton Dam to Kanawha River—97 Miles

CLASS	GRAD.	VOL.	SCENE
A, B-1	3	M-B	B-D

MAPS: State Road Map
COUNTIES—Braxton, Clay, and Kanawha

DESCRIPTION: The whole gradient in the 97-mile stretch between Sutton Dam and its mouth on the Kanawha is such that the Elk is a rather peaceful, at times meandering river. Although there are many riffles, they seldom exceed a Class 1 rating, at least at ordinary water levels. During times of heavy runoff the river can be wide and powerful.

In general, W.V. 4-U.S. 119 parallels the river almost the entire way, except for one section between Clay Junction and Procious. This allows one to set up many different trips easily. Due to its proximity to Charleston, its easy rapids, and the good fishing provided, it is popular with canoeists. The river from Ivydale to Procious is fairly well known and mostly attractive except at Clay. Two roadside parks (Mary Chilton and Evans) and Coonskin Park at the edge of Charleston are located near nice wide rapids and thus offer excellent sites for holding instructional sessions for beginners. Below Clendenin the scenery begins to get cluttered and junky. Near Charleston, major shipping and dredging operations are even encountered.

SEASON: Can be run at almost any time except when frozen or in periods of extreme dryness. Excellent river for float fishing trips (bass and muskie).

CHAPTER VII

BIG WATER FROM THE SOUTH THE NEW AND BLUESTONE

The New River begins high in the Blue Ridge Mountains, in North Carolina, crosses Virginia, enters West Virginia near its southernmost tip, and heads straight north to meet the Gauley to become the Kanawha. In so doing it manages to transect every ridge in the Allegheniies. Its name is actually a misnomer in that geologically, it is one of America's oldest rivers. Prior to the time of glaciation the river, known as Teays, flowed even farther north to the vicinity of the present Great Lakes. Actually, the Ohio which didn't exist then should be called the New, and the New should be called the Old. Where it cuts across the place called the Narrows in Virginia, near the state line, some of the oldest rocks in the east have been exposed.

The river flows in a comparatively straight line through our state and drains a tremendous watershed. It has scores of small tributaries, but only two significant ones, the Bluestone and Greenbrier. It has long been a major route of exploration and travel and one of the major RR lines in the state follows it closely. The river flows through a rugged canyon most of the way through the state breaking out into a broad valley only as it forms the Kanawha at Gauley Bridge. As such, most of the route is unsettled, there is little industry other than coal mining, and no agriculture. Mostly it is a recreation attraction, one of the state's major ones.

The Bluestone Reservoir is a major broadwater recreation area with several private and public campgrounds developed around it. Some of the backwaters extend up the Bluestone River to a state park bearing the same name. The Bluestone itself is a small river tumbling through largely inaccessible country. Another state park, Pipestem, is situated high above the Bluestone River. Both have camping facilities, the former right on the river. Below the Bluestone Dam is one of the most fantastically productive warm water fishing areas in the United States. The river here is extremely broad and flows over shallow shoals creating ideal wading conditions for bass, redeye, bluegill, catfish, and suckers. Farther down, large muskies may be taken. The river is fished hard, but still large catches may be made even by the inexpert angler. This fishing activity continues for many miles. Other riverside recreational developments continue through Sandstone Falls, another popular fishing spot.

From here on, one finds only occasional fishermen who somehow find ways into the rugged canyon to fish in real isolation. A new recreational venture, unique in West Virginia, is being developed at Thurmond. The state's only commercial white water firm is located there specializing in raft trips in the New River Gorge. This sort of development is a welcome one that will certainly bolster the economy of such forgotten places. Finally, three other state parks, Grandview, Babcock, and Hawk's Nest are perched hundreds of feet above the river on the canyon rim, but will not even be seen by the paddler. Only Babcock has camping facilities, but they are a 4-mile walk from the river.

The New in its entire West Virginia length passes through only one major city, that of Hinton, a former lumber and RR center. This in itself is remarkable. Other cities such as Beckley, Oak Hill, and Fayetteville are nearby, but cannot be considered river cities. There are very few towns or access points of any kind on the New, so the twentieth century anachronism of Thurmond stands out like a sore thumb. It began as a coal and RR center at the turn of the century in an area fabulously wealthy in natural resources. The only way in and out of the town of then 500 hardy souls was via the RR as there were no roads in those days. As such, it was a lawless town somewhat akin to the Dodge City of the Old West. Its infamous 100-room Dunglen Hotel was host to the longest continuous poker game in history, some 14 years! Women, booze, dice, and cards were brought in fresh every day while unlucky losers of arguments over same were quietly disposed of in the New. Two old sayings survive that describe the town colorfully: "No Sunday west of Clifton Forge and no God west of Hinton" and "the only difference between Hell and Thurmond was in that a river ran through Thurmond."

But the most noted thing about the New River that would shame even Thurmond were the events surrounding construction of the Hawk's Nest bypass tunnel near the mouth of the river. This 4-mile tunnel was built for the New Kanawha Power Company, a subsidiary of Union Carbide, for the purpose of diverting the New's water through a conduit for power production. The tunnel was drilled through solid silica rock under conditions resembling the Dark Ages. The men who were "employed" on the project were practically slaves. At least 476 men were known to have died from contracting silicosis and many were quietly buried in unmarked graves. Attempts to investigate or report on this matter were suppressed for many years. What is most amazing about this heartless chapter in American river history is that these events didn't happen prior to the Civil War, but as recently as during the Depression!

There are only two dams on the New at the moment and none on the Bluestone. The Corps has a huge flood control dam on the New above Hinton which doesn't have many of the undesirable ecologic features as do the huge drawdown reservoirs. The Bluestone Reservoir seems to be one worthwhile project that brings real benefits to the state. The second dam is below Hawk's Nest and is run by Union

Carbide in conjunction with the tunnel bypass. As of this writing, a reservoir two states away threatens the New River. A power company is being forced by the federal government to construct a huge pumped storage project on the North Carolina-Virginia border (Blue Ridge Project). The daily releases from this reservoir would be greatly increased bringing about two very undesirable West Virginia effects. Most importantly it would ruin the fishing below the Bluestone Dam by decreasing fish productivity and making wading impossible. It would also make white water sport very dangerous or even impossible at such high flows. Another design on the New occurs perennially. A well-known Wheeling empire builder wants to connect Virginia's James River with the New by means of canals for purposes of establishing navigation commerce with the Atlantic, presumably to make Wheeling a seaport! The distressing thing about this is that he successfully gets a senator or a congressman to introduce a bill into Congress each year asking for study money for the Corps. We understand they even do it with a straight face. There is another plan to dam all 25 miles of the Bluestone.

Appalachian naturalist Maurice Brooks has written of the New River as a means of introducing plant species into the state from more southerly regions—the Catawba rhododendron, Carolina silverbell, sweet gum, Spanish oak, and others. Many other streamside plants attract the naturalist-paddler. Water willow fills the shallow waters near the shore in great profusion during the summer. Many other plants not common to other parts of the state may also be seen. Waterfowl are common on the upper reaches.

The New, then, is one of the state's most magnificent treasures, but only the white water paddler can see it all. There are not many paddlers native to the area, most come from the Charleston area, although the unlikely town of Thurmond is rapidly becoming the mecca for such in summer months. Maybe the old grandeur and rowdy days will once again return to this hamlet.

BIBLIOGRAPHY

Anon. 1973. U.S. House of Representatives Hearings on Hawk's Nest Tunnel Construction, will be in Vol. 7 of the *West Virginia Heritage* series. Richwood, W.Va.: Bronson McClung, publisher.

Brooks, M. 1970. The Very Old New River. *Wonderful West Virginia.* Vol. 34, no. 1.

Miller, J. H. 1908 (reprint 1970). *History of Summers County.* Parsons, W.Va.: McClain Printing Co.

Scott, E. *THURMOND: Dodge City of West Virginia. Believe It or Not City.* This interesting and cheaply produced little book of uncertain publishing origin and vintage may be purchased from stores in southern West Virginia.

Skidmore, H. 1970. Hawk's Nest. *West Virginia Heritage* series, vol. 4. Richwood, W.Va.: Bronson McClung, publisher.

BLUESTONE

Spanishburg to Bluestone State Park—25 Miles

CLASS	GRAD.	VOL.	SCENE	TIME	LEVEL
2-4	16@31 9@17	432	A	8	5-9

MAPS: USGS—Athens, Flat Top, and Pipestem
COUNTIES: Mercer and Summers

DESCRIPTION: If ever paddling gets to the commercial status of skiing this will be the Stowe of white water. It is just off the interstate system connecting it to all points of the country. The run is continuous intermediate water through a spectacular narrow gorge. The flow is fed by 200-foot tiered waterfalls regularly spaced along the gorge sides. The flora is a mixture of evergreens and hardwoods. Ducks, deer, and beaver are prominent habitants of the narrow undeveloped defile.

The Indian name for this stream was "Momongoseneka" meaning big stone. The river tumbles continuously along a rocky bottom for the first 20 miles before it reaches a pool of any size and if that does not cause a paddling freak to be "big stoned" he had better go back to TV football.

The river meanders a bit as a continuation of its highlands watershed collecting role, but in a few miles it starts down its chasm to the New. The roughest water, Class 4, is in the six miles bracketing Eads Mill situated hundreds of feet below the W.V. Turnpike span over the Bluestone. Eads Mill can be reached by road to scout the nature of the river, but this is essentially the only place the river can be seen except by boat.

After the 16-mile run from Spanishburg or nine miles from Eads Mill, a mirage suddenly looms—a luxurious lodge and restaurant in the middle of this wilderness. The state of West Virginia built this Mountain Creek Lodge in conjunction with the large Pipestem recreational complex on the plateau above the Bluestone. Generally the lodge can be reached only via tramway. It is currently open only from May to September. They should open it in March and April as a white water lodge. The lodge would be a good overnight stop for the full 25-mile run or a warm lunch break for those starting at Eads Mill. On the overnight trip, campers could leave their boats at the river and ride the tramway out to their cars.

The run beyond the Mountain Creek Lodge is continuous Class 2 water for about four miles. At five miles beyond the lodge there is a long pool transected by a gas pipeline. It is three miles of flowing water from there to the take out which is at the head of the large Bluestone Reservoir of the New.

DIFFICULTIES: The beauty of this run is that it is challenging without penalties. At about one mile above the turnpike bridge a half dozen long series of sloping river wide ledges begins. These are usually good for a flip by someone who gets broached before he slides into the bottom stopper. Without a roll this will result in washing over a number of subsequent ledges before being rescued.

Beyond these ledges and under the turnpike bridge the river channels down and centrifuges around multiple curves with big standing waves and a few holes. This section continues past the bridge near Eads Mill, past the campground, past the Eads Mill take out, and to below the mouth of Brush Creek. This is two miles of the best (worst) the Bluestone offers. The judicious paddler can sample the Eads Mill bridge to Eads Mill take out before committing himself to the long run.

GAUGE: There is a USGS gauge 1.2 miles downstream from Mountain Creek which is reported via telemeter daily to the Hydraulics Section of the Corps of Engineers in Huntington (529-2318 ext. 604). This gauge can also be read by the paddler. A canoeist gauge which has a five-foot differential is painted on the Eads Mill bridge.

The rub with this white water dream run is that the watershed is small and the upper part is denuded of forest. One must be there when the rain falls. The proximity of the turnpike and the availability of the gauge reading by phone makes this possible. The Bluestone should be runnable about 50 days per year, mostly in February, March, and April.

SHUTTLE: Take out at the Bluestone State Park Campground near Hinton. If that is closed in the winter season one can take out at the boat dock in front of the park headquarters one mile down the reservoir. The put in is reached via W.V. 20 passing Pipestem State Park and on into Princeton then north on U.S. 19-21 through Spanishburg. Turn right just before the new Spanishburg Church on the right onto "19/10." This goes to the riverbank at the site of a breached dam. The Eads Mill bridge and put in can be reached via Camp Creek, on 19-21 north of Spanishburg, or via Speedway on W.V. 20 from the south (see map).

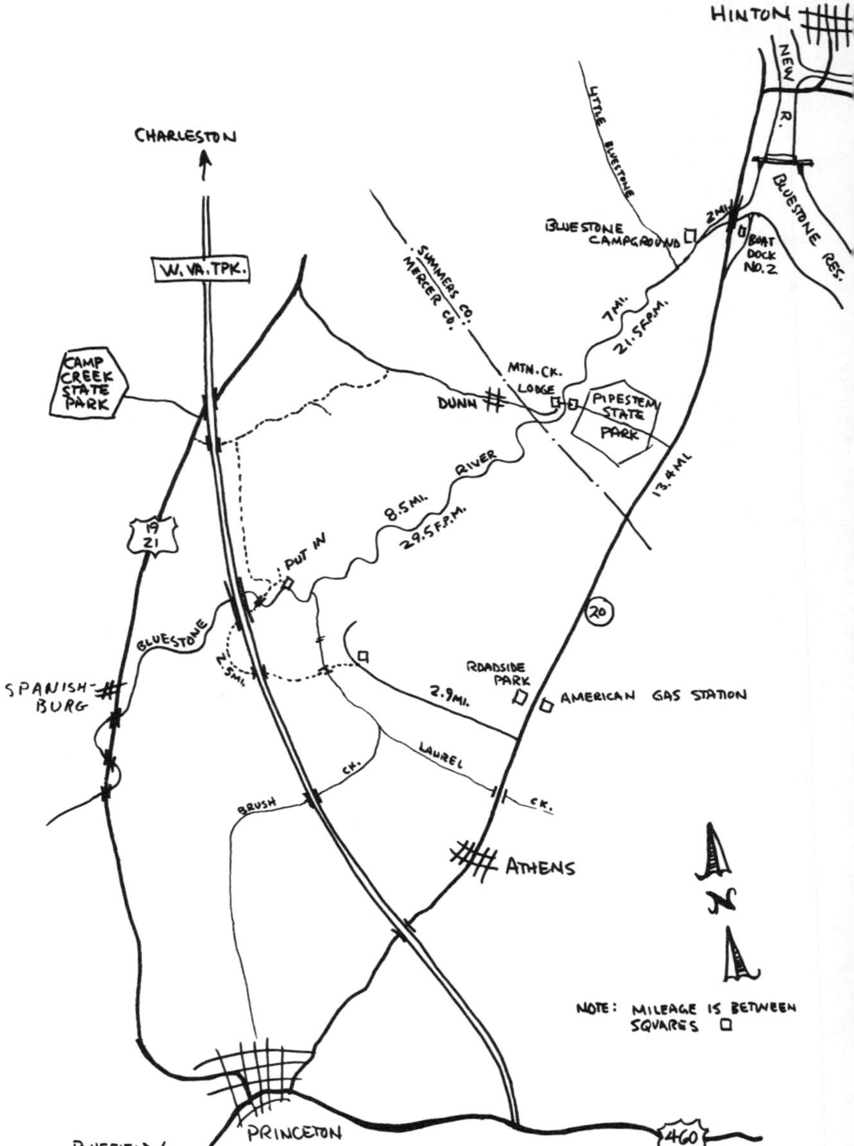
HINTON
NEW R.
BLUESTONE RES.
LITTLE BLUESTONE
BLUESTONE CAMPGROUND
2MI.
BOAT DOCK NO. 2
CHARLESTON
W. VA. TPK.
SUMMERS CO.
MERCER CO.
7MI.
21.5F.P.M.
MTN. CK. LODGE
CAMP CREEK STATE PARK
DUNN
PIPESTEM STATE PARK
RIVER
8.5MI.
29.5F.P.M.
13.4MI.
19
21
PUT IN
20
BLUESTONE
2.5MI.
ROADSIDE PARK
2.9MI.
AMERICAN GAS STATION
SPANISH-BURG
LAUREL
CK.
BRUSH
CK.
ATHENS
N
NOTE: MILEAGE IS BETWEEN SQUARES
PRINCETON
460
BLUEFIELD

—J. Wartluft

NEW

A. Glen Lyn, Va., to Bull Falls Campgrounds—20 Miles

CLASS	GRAD.	VOL.	SCENE	TIME	LEVEL
1-3	8	5059	A-B	7	–

MAPS: USGS—Narrows, Peterstown, Forest Hill, and Pipestem
Virginia state road map
COUNTIES—Summers and Mercer

DESCRIPTION: This is a long stretch of predominantly flat water interspersed by a few ledges that is occasionally run as an overnighter. There is little to recommend it due to the sparse rapids, the brutal shuttles, the outrageous trash and litter, and the widely fluctuating river levels which detract from whatever fishing qualities this river might have. Every rapids in this part of the country is called a "falls," but all are really low ledges. They do demand respect, however, due to the volume of the river. Wylie Falls is right at the state line so if you plan on a fishing trip, you will need two licenses. The reservoir flat water begins near the campgrounds. Do not expect to see Bull Falls unless you are a SCUBA diver.

DIFFICULTIES: Shumate Falls, about 2 miles below Glen Lyn, is the most difficult rapids on the whole run. It can be mean in high water and should be scouted by first timers. Run on the left. Four miles below here is Wylie Falls, easily run on the right. The names of the next "falls" which you might not even see if the water is high, are Sand Bar Falls, Anderson Falls, Harvey Falls, and then Harmon's Rapids near the mouth of Indian Creek. Since Wylie Falls is somewhat of a landmark, it may be easily recognized by an abandoned car in the middle of the river. What a welcome to West Virginia! Other than for Shumate, all of the falls may be run on the right.

GAUGE: Meaningless due to the extreme daily fluctuation from a power dam upstream. Remember this when your favorite power company announces designs for your special river.

SHUTTLE: Brutal and 2 hours one way. From Princeton take U.S. 460 and 219 to Glen Lyn, Va. Put in at the bridge. Bull Falls Campgrounds, a Department of Natural Resources area, may be reached by taking the very steep road towards the river from W.V. 20 near Pipestem.

B. Bluestone Dam to Sandstone—11 Miles

CLASS	GRAD.	VOL.	SCENE	TIME	LEVEL
1-3_4	10	7531	B	3-4	2.0-3.0

MAPS: USGS—Meadow Creek 15′ and Hinton
COUNTY—Summers

DESCRIPTION: This section begins immediately below the Bluestone Dam and flows through a very scenic valley. The mouth of the Greenbrier River joins the New from the right just below the dam. Gentle, easily negotiated rapids are encountered between flat stretches. About a mile after passing the bridge in Hinton a very long Class 2-3 rapids is encountered which makes excellent canoeing. After this there is a rather long flat stretch with intermittent riffles where the river has broadened out to almost a half a mile.

DIFFICULTIES: At the end of this flat stretch a very loud rumble and appearance of spray warn the paddler of something special. This is the impressive Brooks Falls which is a vigorous drop over the complete width of the river. This should be scouted although the river is so wide it doesn't help much. Several low, but powerful ledges are first encountered as the water picks up speed and then within a few yards drops about 6′ at places over the wide reef. Several passages exist—one on the extreme right, one about one-third of the way from the left, and the most dangerous, the extreme left against the bank, are a few. At higher water levels, one can go over at almost any place, but the turbulence may be greater. It is probably more difficult at lower water levels. These falls would have a Class 3-4 rating, but may be run in an open boat.

Between Brooks and the mighty Sandstone Falls there are only three rapids in 3½ miles. The first two, within ¼ mile of each other, are river-wide ledges. The first of these is fairly high and does not offer many safe passages. The second is lower and more easily negotiated. Each of these may most safely be run on the extreme left if in doubt. The third rapids is wide and minor, but an upset on such a wide powerful river would make rescue very difficult so proceed with caution. Carefully land on the right bank well above the fast water above the falls (the worst part of the falls is also on the right) and portage along the RR tracks. It is a strenuous carry, but it is easier than the left. If one wants to put in immediately below the falls, he can play in the Class 4 rapids and turbulence over quite an area. There are no rapids between the falls and the village of Sandstone.

SHUTTLE: Put in just below the dam on either side of the river at the Corps of Engineers' parks. This is located at Bellepoint on W.V. 3 and 12. An alternate put in is on the mouth of the Greenbrier at the end of the bridge. Take outs can be made most anywhere from a dirt road following the left side of the river or along W.V. 20 on the right. The property immediately below Brooks Falls is private (on the right) so permission would have to be obtained first. Rt. 20 leaves the river near this point and doesn't come back until the village of Sandstone is reached. There is no good take out in Sandstone. The riverbank is fouled with sewage and litter, but one tries to take out behind the general store-post office-filling station. The folks in Sandstone are pretty cooperative about letting you use a little right-of-way down to the river, which allows one to drive most of the way to the bank.

C. Sandstone to McCreery—15 Miles

CLASS	GRAD.	VOL.	SCENE	TIME	LEVEL
1-3	8	7531	A	4-5	1.75-2.5

MAPS: USGS—Meadow Creek and Beckley 15′
COUNTIES—Summers, Fayette, and Raleigh

DESCRIPTION: This is a very long run consisting of several nice impressive rapids, but, as with much of the New, these are interrupted by long expanses of flat water. It is a big powerful river, but very beautiful, always up in the summer, and it provides excellent fishing. Numerous campsites abound and it is perfect for overnight trips. The rapids are mainly long chutes dropping gently over ledges. Although the waves are large not much maneuvering is required.

DIFFICULTIES: Open boats and novices will encounter only two places that may cause trouble. The first of these occurs at the top of Horseshoe Bend seen from Grandview State Park. The entire river is necked down creating essentially heavy water which will swamp open canoes immediately. This is located about a half mile downstream from the obsolete concrete bridge piers at Glade. It is the second rapids from there. The river heads to the left and turns sharply back to the right. In this curve there is some very heavy water including a Class 3 stopper. After the rapids have pushed their way to the right, they straighten out and more very heavy turbulence may be seen in midstream. There is a mean hole in this turbulence large enough to fit the whole canoe. In order to get through this one, a lot of drive is required. Open boats or novices may avoid all of the heavy water by maintaining control and staying to the far right.

The second potential trouble spot is a delightfully long Class 3 rapids at Quinnimont just before reaching the RR station. Not difficult, but open canoes might swamp due to the length of it. Such canoes might consider dumping halfway down. Near the bottom, a huge drainpipe enters from the right. Just before this there is a powerful hydraulic in the middle of the river followed by 20 yards of flat water and then another very deceptive wave that camouflages a hole deep enough to set a C-2 in. Fun, but surprising!

SHUTTLE: Put in at the Sandstone site mentioned in Section A. Take out is easiest at a very large sandy beach located on the left two rapids beyond the U.S. 19 bridge. This may be reached by car by turning right off U.S. 19 onto a dirt road where 19 turns left to go up the mountain. This is McCreery. The trip can be shortened in two ways. Move the put in 3 miles downstream to Meadow Creek, but this still leaves a 35-mile shuttle. A put in at Glade just above the Grandview Rapids makes for a 7-mile trip and a 7-mile shuttle, along the left-hand side of the river. Drive up the river from the U.S. 19 bridge for 7 miles and turn left just before the road crosses Glade Creek and drive to the water.

D. McCreery to Thurmond—15 Miles

CLASS	GRAD.	VOL.	SCENE	TIME	LEVEL
2-3$_4$	10	7531	A	4	1.75-2.5

MAPS: USGS—Beckley 15′
COUNTIES—Fayette and Raleigh

DESCRIPTION: The stretch from Prince to Thurmond is characterized by fewer rapids and longer flat water pools, but in general the individual rapids are heavier than those in the upper river. The river is wide and powerful at 2.5′ on the Hinton gauge and it would be unwise for novices or open boats to proceed at this or higher levels. Each rapids is a river-wide long stretch of big waves with very little obstruction. Occasionally a ledge is encountered at one side or the other, but it is always eroded in the heaviest current. Consequently, although large stopper waves and an occasional hydraulic are encountered, very little maneuvering is required.

DIFFICULTIES: Intermediates with heavy water experience should encounter no difficulties or unexpected surprises, but this is no place for beginners. More than halfway and after a particularly long flat stretch, four coal silos appear on the right bank of a left-hand turn. Just below this, very heavy water is encountered near the right bank. Very large Class 4-sized waves are present, but are avoidable if desired. Another long flat stretch, two minor rapids, and a zesty chute over a ledge brings the paddler to the take out.

SHUTTLE: Put in below the U.S. 19 bridge on the left bank mentioned in Section C. The easiest take out is on the sandy beach 200 yards above the bridge located a mile above Thurmond (the first bridge you will encounter). This take out, located on the left side of the river may be reached by a dirt road. It is pretty flat from this bridge to Thurmond itself although there is a nice Class 2 rapids right under the Thurmond bridge. Although there is a dirt road connecting Prince with Thurmond, it is not recommended to use it in setting up the shuttle. Take Rt. 19

from Prince toward Beckley, turn right on W.V. 61 to Mount Hope, turn right onto U.S. 21 for about a mile and then make one more right turn at a secondary road leading to Glen Jean and Thurmond.

GAUGE: For the first 3 sections below the Bluestone Dam, call the dam at 466-1234 and ask for the Hinton gauge reading which takes into account the output of the Greenbrier. The river seldom drops below 1.75′ and is often at this level in the summer. Approach the entire river with great caution if over 2.5′.

E. Thurmond to Fayette Station—14 Miles

CLASS	GRAD.	VOL.	SCENE	TIME	LEVEL
3-5	12	7531	A	6	0.5-2′

MAPS: USGS—Beckley and Fayetteville 15′
COUNTY—Fayette

DESCRIPTION: This is the biggest white water river in West Virginia. The long flat pools in the first half of this run are the admission price for entrance, but once the gorge starts below the RR bridge at 8 miles the surging waters are repayment with foaming dividends. The challenge in this type of water is remaining upright while bobbing among the 6-8′ waves, dodging souse holes, stoppers, and whirlpools. The entire river flows through an immense gorge with extremely rugged mountains and cliffs in view all of the way.

DIFFICULTIES: Your first clue as to what is in store for you occurs when you hit a small wave and discover how forceful it is. Look out for the first major rapids (Surprise). From the top it looks like an ordinary riffle, but halfway through the paddler realizes he is in a funnel and all of the water is converging towards a huge mountain of a double wave. There is a hole between the first regular wave and the second curler wave. This is too much at the higher levels and should be snuck on the left.

Look for a RR trestle 3 miles below Surprise. Upper Railroad Rapids just above the trestle is a steep drop over a shelf and is best run just right of a dry rock in the center of the river. The next rapids, Lower Railroad, is a formidable cascade of water through a complicated barrage of boulders. It can be snuck on the far right with a good deal of maneuvering or run at one-third of the way over from the left with some scouting and bravado. There then follows a set of 5 rapids which offers no special problems and at high water provides a roller coaster ride over the large waves.

You are now ready to enter the big stuff, the Keeney Brothers. Regardless of how these rapids look, the best way is through the center no matter what the size of the waves. Upper Keeney is recognized by a huge boulder the size and shape of a whale. The current will take you to the right edge of the rock behind which is a fine place to eddy out and gather your spirits for Middle Keeney. At higher levels these two rapids merge, hence a roll-less flip in the Upper makes for a long day. Middle Keeney has three large holes in the center channel, but this is the safest route. The paddler should head just to the left of a dry camelback rock in mid-channel. These are difficult and flip many a paddler. At levels of 4′, waves here are 12′ high and merge with the granddaddy of them all, Lower Keeney. Larger holes exist to the right and left, so don't try to sneak it.

After this it is a good idea to get out and scout the next rapids. Lower Keeney is scouted everytime even by those very familiar with the river. It cannot be snuck, it cannot be lined, and it is one hell of a carry over the house-sized boulders so you may as well make up your mind how to run it. In general the river has necked way down to the size of our small trout streams thus concentrating the action enormously. The current surges from the right to the left side bombarding a huge boulder on the left. If you are following someone closely, do not be disheartened when he drops suddenly from view into the first hole because you will look the same to the paddlers behind you. It is a short 50-yard rapids, but a flip (usually in the first hole) is long remembered.

The two rapids below here are uncomplicated, but powerful. Next is Sunset, or the Double Z, a long rapids that is marked by a chain of rocks extending halfway across the river from the right. Enter the rapids and eddy out behind this chain in order to reach the safe extreme right channel and avoid a nasty complex V ledge and hydraulic in the center. The right channel will take you diagonally to the left, but tumbles steeply through a field of holes and boulders. An honest Class 5. Avoid the huge boulder on the bottom left which is undercut and has a powerful current under it. There then follows about three more rapids which anywhere else would be regarded as difficult, but here they are a welcome breather (Old 99 Hook, Greyhound Bus Stopper, and Tipple Rapids).

Next is *THE* Undercut Rock, a right-hand turn out of a pool into another undercut rock. Avoid the temptation to begin at the far right, but begin just right of center and paddle towards the big rock on the right staying to the left of the chute and thinking left, left all of the way! You will encounter some enormous waves, but they are fun to ride. Do not begin on the far left as it is not only too shallow usually, but also there is a 4′ falls at the bottom.

This is it if you are taking out at the Fayette Station bridge. But one of the best rapids is just below the bridge and should not be missed. Run on mid-right side. Since you have come this far, you might as well dig into it. It is a multiholed roller coaster with some deceptively vigorous drops in it hidden by the big waves. Other than for 1 or 2 minor rapids, there is mostly flat water in the next 4 miles to the Hawk's Nest Dam and hence is seldom run.

SHUTTLE: The shuttle amazingly enough is all on hard surface roads. Fayette Station can be reached from U.S. 19 west of the New River Gorge bridge on W.V. 82. Put in is Thurmond reached by "25" from Glen Jean exit off U.S. 19. An alternate put in is just above upper railroad rapids. It is reached by following signs out of Fayetteville to the sanitary land fill. The trip takes ½ hour to reach the river for a six-mile 2-3 hour run, but do not try it unless you can handle bad roads.

GAUGE: Gauge is located just under the Fayette Station bridge. The gauge can be estimated from the Hinton gauge by multiplying Hinton reading by three and subtracting six. Honest it works.

F. Hawks Nest Dam to Gauley Bridge—6 Miles

CLASS	GRAD.	VOL.	SCENE	TIME	LEVEL
3-5	18	—	A	3	3.5-4.0′

MAPS: USGS—Beckwith, Gauley Bridge
COUNTY—Fayette

DESCRIPTION: Hawks Nest Dam and the associated infamous tunnel divert the New River five miles to a power plant owned by Union Carbide. When there is more water than the reservoir or tunnel can handle the excess is released back into the old riverbed. The section is referred to by paddlers as the DRIES. The tunnel has a voracious thirst so the river is empty until the New's flow exceeds 10,000 cfs (3.5′) at Hinton or 4′ at Fayette.

The Cotton Hill Bridge Rapids consists of long smooth slides terminating in stoppers. Below Cotton Hill the river is very rocky, the rapids closely spaced, and there are many 2-3′ drops. Scouting is difficult due to the huge boulders. Some rapids may have to be carried in low water because the river appears completely blocked with only small keyholes allowing the water to pass. The largest boulders on the Cheat or Gauley are a dime a dozen here. There is a mile long continuous Class 3+ rapids that ends in a pool dammed behind a massive landslide. It is runnable although finding the passage is difficult. Remember that the last rapids above the railroad bridge again has the full volume of the New. It is below the diverting power station tunnel.

DIFFICULTIES: The Landslide Rapids chokes the river into five or six shoots between house sized boulders. The second from the left is unrunnable. The next two to the right are OK. A carry can be made on the left.

GAUGE: These readings are for the Corps gauge at Hinton. 3.5′ is the level that exceeds the capacity of the tube. Four feet is a 4,000 cfs excess at Hinton 60 miles upstream. A lot can happen between Hinton and Hawks Nest Dam so this gauge range is only an approximation. The section has been run at 6.5′ on the Hinton gauge or about 26,000 cfs in the Dries. It was mind-shattering. (Not to say what it could do to bodies.)

SHUTTLE: Put in on Hawks Nest Reservoir which can be reached via "60/2" from Ansted. This put in is 0.6 mile above the dam. As an alternate miss the first mile and put in from the south end of the Cotton Hill Bridge on W.V. 16. Take out along U.S. 60 above Gauley Bridge.

PINEY CREEK

Beckley to McCreery—12 Miles

CLASS	GRAD.	VOL.	SCENE	TIME	LEVEL
3-5	79	S	A	4	—

MAPS: USGS—Beckley, Prince
COUNTY—Raleigh

DESCRIPTION: This tiny tributary of the New falls off the plateau near Beckley. After passing the Beckley sewage plant, which adds more than volume to the river, only the railroad tracks are an indication of civilization. The river is anything but civil. The stream is in a very deep and intimate gorge—the intimacy of a grizzly bear hug. The stream bed becomes multiple three to five-foot ledges with irregular broken ledge rubble. It then gets worse. Finally as it nears the take out it levels off to a Class 2-3.

DIFFICULTIES: In one memorable stretch with a gradient of 160 fpm the river disappears over five steep, intricate cascades in a narrow, twisting riverbed with four-foot high drops three feet wide. One shoots out between an overhanging house-sized boulder and a meat cleaver rock. Later a succession of three to four-foot ledges ends on the brink of an eight-foot water fall.

GAUGE: If there is a lot of water at the take out the gorge will probably be too high. This run is too unknown to have hard facts on suitable levels. Just be sure you are good and humble enough to scout.

SHUTTLE: Take out at U.S. 19 bridge at McCreery. Put in via Raleigh Motor's parking lot off U.S. 19 in Beckley.

CHAPTER VIII

TROUBLED WATERS DRAINING THE WEST

Most everything bad you have ever heard about West Virginia and almost every picture showing Appalachian poverty or desolate land abuse you have ever seen has come from the southwest portion of the state. This section of the state is very rugged and historically has always been isolated. Coal is the unquestioned king and nothing else counts. Since the days of the ridiculous Hatfield-McCoy feud (folk heroes down there), the southwest corner of the state has been associated with lawlessness and stupidity that continue into the present day although some may choose to call it mountaineer independence and honor. The area has traditionally been poorly represented in the legislative halls and the countryside looks it.

Its watersheds are in terrible shape and uncontrolled strip mining has ruined vast areas. The resulting erosion and siltation have fouled every stream. Flooding is common and spring forest fires a way of life (purposely set to drive out the snakes!). Such an environment leads to an apathetic populace and streamside littering is atrocious. The area is drained into three main rivers: the Guyandotte, the lower Kanawha, and the Tug Fork-Big Sandy, our western border. When a dam is built, no one cares. The R. D. Bailey Dam is being constructed on the Guyandotte to control flooding and "improve" water quality. The lower Kanawha has three sets of locks and dams for commercial navigation. There is a spectacular Kanawha Falls located just downstream from the New-Gauley junction.

Being so isolated (roads didn't enter the area until the late twenties), conventional history and progress have bypassed the area entirely. No famous Civil War battles or Indian skirmishes are associated with the region, but that doesn't mean it hasn't seen its share of war and bloodshed. Some of the bloodiest encounters in American labor history were waged in this area between company hired thugs and labor hooligans. Cabin Creek and Paint Creek both of which drain into the Kanawha only one ridge apart were the scenes of strike murders 60 years ago. Matewan and Welch were witness to mass murders in broad daylight in the twenties, while a pitched battle of thousands of men took place over a coal strike in 1921 on the Guyandotte and Coal River valleys.

War doesn't seem so glamorous when you are that close to it temporally as well as spatially.

As this book was being prepared for press, a tributary of the ugly Guyandotte, Buffalo Creek, made national headlines when a coal slag dam burst during a period of high runoff causing a tragic flood that took at least 130 lives and left hundreds homeless. The land abuse that led up to this tragedy unfortunately seems typical of this area and as of this writing, everyone concerned is trying to pin the blame on someone else, even on God.

BIBLIOGRAPHY

Crawford, H. 1969. An American Vendetta in Vol. 3 of *West Virginia Heritage* series. Richwood, W. Va.: Bronson McClung, publisher.

Lee, Howard B. 1969. *Bloodletting in Appalachia.* Parsons, W. Va.: McClain Printing Co.

ARMSTRONG CREEK

MacDunn to Kimberly—8 Miles

CLASS	GRAD.	VOL.	SCENE	TIME	LEVEL
3-4	60	S	D	2	(–)

MAPS: USGS—Powellton and Montgomery
COUNTY—Fayette

DESCRIPTION: When everything else is too flooded and you need an hour of mud and chills, try this honey. At medium flood the Armstrong and both its forks are amusing streams. It is narrow (5-30′) and drains a lot. At high flood it has lots of yummy flotsam including outhouses, Christmas trees, dead chickens, and dying paddlers.

DIFFICULTIES: The MacDunn Fork has several good rapids and a hairy bridge near the junction. The Elkridge Fork is quieter, but has a nasty three-foot backwave at a pipe within eyesight of the junction.

From the junction to Kimberly take out numerous undercut banks and trees are hazards. A fallen footbridge, three miles from the junction can be snuck on the right. Less than one mile farther a wooden bridge cannot. Since it comes immediately after a severe right-hand bend, eddy out immediately as it wants to smash your skull with two low eight-inch posts. Current is incredible from here on.

GAUGE: Flooding.

SHUTTLE: Turn off W.V. 61 at Kimberly up "6." Since the road runs beside and sometimes under the stream at a runnable water level, getting there may be half the fun. The take out is a grassy bank between the railroad bridge and the W.V. 61 bridge.

COAL

MAPS: COUNTIES—Boone and Kanawha

A. Marsh Fork, Naoma to Whitesville—12 Miles

This tiny trash-laden stream drops continually as a Class 2-3 stream according to scouting reports.

B. Whitesville to Seth—13 Miles

This section has less gradient and more volume. It continues to move along rapidly with Class 1 rapids according to scouting reports from the road.

C. Seth to Ashford—12 Miles

The only portion of the Coal which has been paddled is fast flowing silted water banked by mud and only very occasionally whipping up to a Class 1 rating. The average discharge is 496 cfs. This section is bordered by roads, rails, and buildings throughout its length. It is suitable for an open boat winter trip by beginners and can be segmented at several bridges along the distance.

D. Ashford to Mouth of Kanawha River—30 Miles

Reportedly and not surprisingly this section is flat and flowing. Despite the river's name and the acid streams usually associated with mining this is an excellent section for bass and cat fishing. At 12 miles the volume is almost doubled by the discharge from the Little Coal. At Tornado is the only significant obstruction on this section, High Falls. This is a four-foot dam above a 10-foot crumbled ledge. Low Falls is a misnomer six miles below High Falls for a Class 1 gravel bar.

LITTLE COAL

MAPS: COUNTIES—Boone and Lincoln

A. Above McCorkle

This section has been partially scouted. In the upper reaches it is a continuous Class 2 run in a small trash-laden bed. By the time it reaches Madison it has flattened to only occasional easy rapids with an average discharge of 334 cfs.

B. McCorkle to Alum Creek—10 Miles

This is the only part of the Little Coal that has been paddled. It is A to Class 1 water winding through relatively remote country. A roadhead meets the river at midpoint and parallels it on the left for an early take out. The junction with the Coal is one mile upstream from Alum Creek.

GUYANDOTTE

Simon to Justice—13½ Miles

CLASS	GRAD.	VOL.	SCENE	TIME	LEVEL
1-3	17	736	C-D	4	5-7′

MAPS: USGS—Baileysville and Gilbert
COUNTIES—Wyoming and Mingo

DESCRIPTION: This section of the Guyandotte, the only part with significant rapids, winds through what should be a very picturesque cliff-lined watercourse, but unfortunately the entire run is also lined with discarded car bodies, old tires, garbage and trash piles, etc. The side opposite the cliffs is marred by old logging operations and eroded skid roads.

The rapids begin where the first cliff appears and at medium levels are of Class 2 difficulty. They remain this way until halfway through the run when the rapids begin picking up to a Class 3 as some interesting hydraulics, holes, and surfing waves appear. Less flat water is found in this lower part, also. The rapids continue until a mile from Justice.

A Corps of Engineers dam is scheduled to go in at Justice in the near future. This is one Corps project that will probably improve the appearance of the area. Due to the tragic land abuse in this part of the state, there is frequent flooding of the Guyandotte, which has a fairly large watershed. It is easier to build a flood control dam than to correct land abuse practices which are the earmark of this part of the state.

DIFFICULTIES: This river can come up a great deal at which time the rapids would take on a Class 4-5 character. Since the favorite local pastime seems to be bouncing discarded automobiles over the cliffs, the paddler conceivably could get hit by one.

SHUTTLE: To reach the put in, take "7" south out of Oceana on W.V. 10 for about 7 miles through Clear Fork. Turn right on "6" to Simon. Follow "6/2" from Simon to W.V. 9 and then right on U.S. 52 to Justice. Take out is near Justice at the U.S. 52 bridge.

GAUGE: Call the Huntington River District office and ask for the Branchland reading.

PAINT CREEK

Plum Orchard to Burnwell—15 Miles

CLASS	GRAD.	VOL.	SCENE	TIME	LEVEL
2-4	35	S	A,D	5	0-1.5′

MAPS: USGS—Pax, Powellton, and Eskdale
COUNTIES—Fayette and Kanawha

DESCRIPTION: The upper part of the run down to Westerly is isolated and scenic. In the first one-half mile a power pole and transformer on the right indicates Stone House Rapids. There are remains of two old houses on the right. The rapids consists of a series of many intricate ledges and hydraulics with a long rock garden swimway. Another similarly complex rapids among the many is named Dreaded Drop. It is about two miles from the low water bridge below Mossy.

Below Westerly Paint Creek ambles on down to Burnwell in a Class 1-3 manner through the most depressing scenery. Coal tipples, slag piles, junkyards, garbage dumps, red dog heaps, etc., create Type D scenery throughout the run. About all that can be said about it is that it provides interesting sport very close to Charleston when other rivers are too high.

DIFFICULTIES: There are culverts at Westerly that look inviting but the water gushes onto rocks at the lower ends. One-quarter mile beyond the railroad bridge below Westerly there is an unrunnable falls. The second bridge below the falls is impassable as the culverts have been filled with concrete. Other hazards are strata of undercut rocks protruding over the main channel. These are at sites where they can be avoided. Keep a careful watch for ties, logs, and metal trash in this desecrated stream.

SHUTTLE: Take the Mossy exit from the W.V. turnpike. The put in is upstream toward Plum Orchard Public Fishing Area and one mile beyond at a large white church. Take out where you become psyched-out by the river, upper half, or the trash, lower half.

GAUGE: There is a low water bridge one-quarter mile downstream from the Mossy exit along "15". The top of the bridge is zero but the lower section can be run to -0.3′. A Ms. Wriston, phone 304-469-9933, is willing to give a reading in relation to this low water bridge.

TUG

"The Mighty Tug." West Virginia's answer to the Cuyahoga. The sewer of the "Billion Dollar Coal Field."

Do not waste your paddling time on this shameful desecration. It has no redeeming cultural value. It should be stamped with an XXX rating. At one time it may have been a river. Now it is a big ditch and depository for the refuse of the southwestern border area of the state.

In McDowell County, where it has a gradient indicative that it once was a white water river, it has been dredged straight to make room for railroad yards and depressed company towns along the narrow river benches. The towns are populated by persons that have been forced into generations of serfdom by an inhumane, extractive, absentee-controlled industry. The riverbanks serve as open dumps which are smeared along the valley each spring by the flooding, leaving plastic-bag festooned riverbank shrubs. The banks are silt stabilized by cans, glass, and brightly colored plastic bottles. If one were able to overcome his nausea long enough to paddle this water his primary problem would be to avoid being pinned across the broken out windshields of the mid-stream abandoned cars.

After the Tug leaves McDowell County it flows with minimal gradient 100 miles as the border between West Virginia and Kentucky. It merges with Kentucky's Levisa Fork to form the flat Big Sandy River. The latter is not to be confused with the white water gem, Big Sandy Creek, in the Cheat Basin. It is along this flat section that the senseless backwoods gangsterism of the Hatfields and McCoys was conducted for over 50 years to be replaced by the lawless violence of the labor union wars. It is along this section that the spring rains run off the denuded strip mines and smoldering slag dumps to annually flood. The locals predict the crest of the flood when the bleach bottles are no longer floating down the center of the river.

The Ugh River!

CHAPTER IX

AND A COUPLE FROM NEIGHBORING STATES

Although this is supposed to be a comprehensive guide for the rivers of West Virginia, it doesn't seem right not to include two outstanding rivers from nearby states for several reasons. First of all, white water sport knows no political boundaries and secondly the two rivers in question, the Youghiogheny and the Savage, are paddled extensively by West Virginia paddlers. And what the heck—they are West Virginia rivers anyway what with the headwaters of the Yough arising in our Preston County and it being a part of the Monongahela Basin and with the Savage being right on the state line and being a part of the Potomac system and all.

The Yough is probably the most often paddled river in the East being supplied from a large reservoir through the dry summer months and also close to large population centers. It has at least four commercial firms sponsoring raft or float trips on it and it has long been the site of racing events and slalom training camps. It can be mean and brutal in high water and has taken the lives of several non-paddlers in recent years. It is one of the prime recreational meccas of the state of Pennsylvania and is known nationwide among paddlers. The Yough is right in the midst of George Washington country. In fact George was probably the first white paddler on the Yough having explored the Confluence to Ohiopyle run in 1754. The word has come down that George didn't want to tackle the Loop.

The Savage is a river comparatively new to the paddling game, probably having first been paddled responsibly by Joe Monahan and Phil Allender as recently as 1968. It too is a dam controlled river, but the reservoir is not large enough to accommodate summer-round paddling. The river has become famous as a site of national races and the first Olympic tryouts were attracted there in July of 1972. It is a river characterized by very big water in a very small stream bed and has been the single most responsible reason that the quality of serious white water paddling has improved so much in the East in recent years.

YOUGHIOGHENY

A. Sang Run to Friendsville—10.5 Miles

CLASS	GRAD.	VOL.	SCENE	TIME	LEVEL
	48				
4-5	3.5@116	632	A	5	1.9-2.8

MAPS: USGS—Sang Run and Friendsville
COUNTY—Garrett, Maryland

DESCRIPTION: Where do the Yough guides go on their days off? To the Upper Yough if they've got the bravado. Most other paddlers don't have to go to the Upper Yough cause it rarely runs on weekends. This section of river is fed by the hydroelectric dam at Deep Creek Lake which is used for power only on weekdays. The water gets to the Sang Run bridge at about noon. Because of the temporal inaccessibility for most paddlers the Upper Yough remains one of the dragons of white water tilting. When you do get around to running it there are two approaches. 1) Go with your usual paddling buddies and be prepared to spend hours scouting, lose a boat, walk out through prime rattlesnake country in the dark, and wish you'd taken up hang gliding instead of insanity; or 2) Get one of the Demaree brothers to go with you. Dave and Dan Demaree live nearby and have run the Yough enough to have tamed it and named it—rock by rock, hole by hole.

Below Sang Run bridge there are three miles of flat water to warm-up riffle and then Gap Falls which is run on the left. One mile of Class 3 water follows and then the Bastard—start in the middle and get to the right avoiding a left terminal hole. Next is a complex three part rapids called Charlie's Choice. Followed by another Triple Drop—Snaggle Tooth, Middle Drop, and National Falls (run left). Stay right to avoid Tommy's Hole, then run a left diagonal stopper with a house size boulder in the center requiring a quick right turn. The latter is called Zinger. After a series of ledges stay away from the right to run the heavy four-foot Hinzerling Falls. A choice bit of mayhem awaits the paddle downstream called Meat Cleaver and featuring in mid-channel Shark's Tooth. Run this from the right and turn to the left. Three big boulders are studded right to left across the channel next. Slip between one and two and see, or electively experience, Powerful Popper between two and three. After a few playful sideways surfing holes comes Lost and Found. There is a tombstone midstream. Lost is on left, Found is on right. Cheeseburger Falls should be run on the left. Dosido is the right side of Cheeseburger. After a series of moderate hydraulics follows Wright's Hole. Sneak it on right middle or plan to spend a week in it on the left or swim through Double Pencil Sharpener next downstream.

The paddler has now come 3.5 miles from Gap Falls. Ahead is four miles of anticlimax.

DIFFICULTIES: Are you kidding?

GAUGE: The above readings refer to a gauge painted on the bridge at Sang Run. There is a USGS gauge in Friendsville reported daily by Pittsburgh National Weather Service. It might prove useful for setting up a weekend trip in high water season. Try for something around three feet on the Friendsville gauge.

SHUTTLE: Leave take out car at Friendsville. Drive south on Maryland 42 for 5 miles. Turn right at green trailer on left then take next turn to right to Sang Run.

B. Confluence to Ohiopyle—10 Miles

CLASS	GRAD.	VOL.	SCENE	TIME	LEVEL
1-2	10	1899	A	3½	1.7-4′

MAPS: USGS—Confluence 15′
A state road map would be helpful

DESCRIPTION: This is a good run for novices or intermediates that passes through a beautiful winding gorge. If there is not enough discharge from the dam, put in downstream beyond the mouth of the Casselman. For about 2 miles below the dam, there are only occasional riffles with flat water predominating. About a mile below the outskirts of town, the river turns away from the broad valley and heads left into narrow confines. The first of several Class 2 rapids begins here. These are all easily read and delightful to run when the water is adequate. Soon the rapids recede and the river broadens out considerably for 3 or 4 miles. If it is a windy day, this section can be painfully arduous (the wind *always* blows upstream for some reason).

Soon, however, the canyon walls begin to squeeze the river in and rapids reform for the last 3 miles of the trip. Aside from the RR tracks on either side, the river flows through a roadless, peopleless setting.

DIFFICULTIES: As one sees the first signs of Ohiopyle in the distance on the right bank, he should begin to plan his approach. The more conservative paddlers will want to hang to the left of the island above the Ohiopyle bridge and land on the rocky "beach" just below it. More experienced paddlers will want to run the more difficult passages to the right and take out at either side of the bridge. An upset at this point in the water under 2 is not serious as all one has to do is stand up and walk to shore. Nonetheless, a take out in Ohiopyle should always be made with caution and respect for the inexperienced members of the group due to the falls immediately below. Do not paddle beyond the railroad bridge.

SHUTTLE: Put in on the left side of the river in Confluence anywhere from the Corps of Engineers recreation area on downstream for 2 miles. Heading back to Ohiopyle, take the first right beyond the cemetery.

C. Ohiopyle to Stewarton—7 Miles

CLASS	GRAD.	VOL.	SCENE	TIME	LEVEL
	1@100				
2-4	6@13	2494	A	3	1.7-4′

MAPS: USGS—Confluence 15′
A state road map would be helpful

DESCRIPTION: The first mile of this section, known as the Loop, is the most popular and contains a great deal of action. The paddler has everything thrown at him, but the kitchen sink. For openers, the paddler, after putting in below the falls, must face the series of ledges known as Entrance Rapids without any warm-up. It is a long tortuous course into twisted currents. For indiscretions, a huge rock (Sugarloaf) stands in mid-river as a sentinel to broach paddlerless boats or even paddled boats. Half of the upsets on the Loop take place here. Most paddlers stick to the left and regroup in an eddy below Entrance to mend boats, bandage bodies, retrieve paddles, and gather courage for the next rapids—Cucumber.

A long rock garden precedes an extremely vigorous drop through a narrow passage. Usually you should stick to the far left carefully avoiding anything resembling a broaching situation, and gradually move to the right where huge boulders have forced the course of the river. The best advice from here is to hang on and keep your reflexive and anticipatory braces ready. Going through Cucumber with or without a boat is what it must be like to be flushed down the john.

The next rapids is merely a minor surfing hydraulic divided in midstream by a boulder. Next is an interesting drop into an S-shaped curler. After this there is a long steep rock garden which can be run in a variety of ways. The far right is the most direct except for an extremely sharp left-hand turn that must be made precisely to avoid running your boat several yards up on shore. Another vigorous, but straight forward rock garden known as Dartmouth Slalom Rapids follows.

The final Loop rapids, Railroad, is another infamous boat chewer. Several passages exist over the steep drop, the most vigorous of which is slightly left of center, but you won't recognize it until you are right on it. If you wind up too far to the right you will be in a particularly juicy hydraulic known as Charlie's Washing Machine and it will be over very quick. A flip will take a boat or paddler a considerable distance in high water, perhaps as far as well below the bridge and the next rapids. Immediately after dropping over the ledge, several options may transpire depending on water level. If the water is low, you will have to immediately make a sharp left to avoid the next set of boulders. In high water, you can paddle straight ahead over them. If you have had enough you can take out up a very steep bank on the right, take a long trail up to the picnic area which it ain't.

Generally, paddlers spend a lot of time playing around on the Loop and then keep going on to Stewarton. For those not up on handling such rough water, a put in can be made below Railroad Rapids and with a few judicious carries, the trip can be made to Stewarton in comparative safety. The first 2 miles below the Loop are open and easily read Class 2 descents with only one dropping sharply.

Soon the river narrows and appears to end, but a loud roar coming from the left warns the paddler of a special treat. The first-time paddler may want to scout this—the Dimple—considered by some to be the most difficult on the lower Yough. The current is choked down into a bulging filament, smashes directly into a large boulder, and veers off to the right. Immediately below this is a dazzling combination of reefs and boulders and below these are a long field of haystacks and a river-wide, gaping hydraulic (Swimmers' Rapids) followed by more haystacks, hence goofing the Dimple can make a long day for the paddler. Do not try to miss the big boulder at the top, but ride right with the current and bounce off the pillow with the appropriate lean and brace.

Other gems before reaching the take out are: Bottle of Wine, next below Swimmers, the Double Hydraulic, which is just what it says and if you don't drive through the first, forget about the second, River's End, where huge boulders seemingly dam up the river, but actually funnel it through a sharp left and steep drop, and Schoolhouse Rock, possibly so named because of the expensive tuitions it has collected in broached boats.

Be sure you know where the Stewarton take out is because it is a long way to the next one. Interesting rapids continue for four miles to the mouth of Indian Creek, but as of this writing there is no vehicular way in here except for a Class 6 tank trap leading down to Indian Creek on the right or its counterpart Camp Carmel on the left. From there to Connellsville is about 8 miles of fairly flat water.

SHUTTLE: Put in at the raft loading area just below the falls. Leave upstream cars in one of the regular parking lots and not along the road. To reach the take out drive out of Ohiopyle north on Pa. 381 and drive about 6 miles to a crossroads at the top of a hill where a church sits on the left. Turn left and then left again at the cemetery. Drive down the steep hard road to the bottom where it forks. Take a left as far as you can go, but do not block any driveways. Leave your car where it won't get snookered by buses or trucks during the rafting season. The take out from the river has got to be the worst anywhere. It is a climb of several hundred feet straight up over a billy goat trail that is sure to unmask any latent sign of a slipped disc, a budding inguinal hernia, or a narrowed coronary artery.

GAUGE: As of this writing all bets are off for gauge readings at Ohiopyle thanks to bridge construction. At the put in beach is a boulder. It should be wet but not drowned. The gauge levels above are for the Confluence gauge available from Pittsburgh National Weather Service. In this range it runs about 0.8′ higher than the old Ohiopyle USGS gauge.

SAVAGE

Savage River Dam to Mouth on the North Branch—5.5 Miles

CLASS	GRAD.	VOL.	SCENE	TIME	LEVEL
	1@100				
2-4 $_5$	63	S	A-B	1½	800-1400 cfs

MAPS: USGS—Westernport and Barton
A Maryland state road map would be helpful.

DESCRIPTION: This is the most well-named river you will ever run. The Savage is small, but fierce and horrendous. It might be considered as one 5½-mile long rapids, completely white except for two very small pools (one just above the old Piedmont Dam, the other 400 yards from the mouth). The water is going downhill all of the way and is in a big hurry to get there. Running the river is dependent on getting releases from the Savage River Dam through the cooperation of the Upper Potomac River Commission. Joe Monahan has popularized running this river and obtaining the releases. Generally the water is released for sporting events at from 800 to 1200 cfs which is a lot of water for a stream you can almost spit across. Occasionally, it is up in the winter months.

At 800 cfs, the water is mostly continuous Class 3. The waves are fairly high and a little maneuvering is required around a few exposed or slightly covered boulders. It is just one haystack after another and gives the impression you are riding a rocking horse instead of a white water craft.

At 1200 cfs the river is something else and extremely challenging. Most of the rocks are completely covered and well padded, but the force of the current and the power of the waves are greatly increased. The hydraulics are almost keeper sized and several waves are absolute stoppers. The paddler will find his attention glued to the action and many demands made on his paddling ability. The river is mainly Class 4 at this level due to the very continuous heavy water without let up. Other than for avoiding the larger holes, there is not much maneuvering required. Above 1200 cfs, the river can get very nasty and the hydraulics very dangerous. Consider this 5.

DIFFICULTIES: The whole river. The chief difficulty is that there are hardly any rescue spots. Upon flipping, a hapless, boatless paddler can usually make it to shore in the narrow river without losing too much skin, but don't bet on it. It is extremely difficult to rescue the boat and other equipment, so the paddler should exert all effort to stay with his boat to help. There are no really dangerous spots until one reaches the old Piedmont Dam about a mile downstream from the first bridge. It is broken out on the left and can be run, but you tend to submarine into a mean hydraulic at 1000 cfs or more. It is also broken out on the far right bank and is occasionally run by the "suicide squad" types.

A half mile below the dam, the water becomes heavier and begins a steeper descent around a long right-hand bend where the river runs against the high roadbank. Where the river abruptly swings to the right leaving the road is a terrific drop through a heavy corkscrew set of violent waves called Criss-cross opposite a boulder fittingly named Monument Rock. Below here are some mean hydraulics and a severe stopper, followed by a boulder on the left side of the river. Run this one as close to the right side of the boulder as possible being careful not to get sucked into the vicious hole behind Memorial Rock on the right. At 1200 cfs you can sneak to the left of the dry boulder. In this section the river is dropping the 100 fpm. It should be remembered that in addition to the hazards mentioned, there is also plenty of other continuously heavy white water.

One more warning. At every 1200 cfs release, there always seem to be at least one or two jokers who think they can run this in open boat. Usually the canoes look like some monster had chewed them up (which in fact it has) when they are salvaged after the water gets turned off. An *expert* can handle this solo in an open boat at 800 cfs, but he is very defensive about it. A pinned open boat is a hazard to navigation. Having to help rescue one is a hazard to life and limb.

SEASON: Usually a timed release situation. If water is sufficient, there are usually at least 4 releases—late March, May, Labor Day Weekend, and November. The middle two releases are for racing events and part of the river may be restricted for these purposes at such times. Heavy rains or snows permit additional releases.

SHUTTLE: A road out of Bloomington follows the river closely to the Savage River Dam and offers several steep put in-take out possibilities. To run all of the river, put in below the big dam (reached from a dirt road forking up on the river left just before the second bridge). At the take out, paddle up the North Branch to the bridge for a steep take out. If in doubt as to whether your ability can handle the river, it is suggested to put in at the steel bridge one mile above the mouth. If you have trouble with this part (the easy portion), it wouldn't be advisable to run the rest.

CASSELMAN

Markleton to Harnedsville—11 Miles

CLASS	GRAD.	VOL.	SCENE	TIME	LEVEL
1-3	25	649	A-B	4	2-4′

MAPS: USGS—Confluence 15′
Pennsylvania road map

DESCRIPTION: This is a very pleasant run for intermediates at medium water levels or for advanced paddlers at high water. It is up during most of the winter and it comes up fast after rainy weather. This is an excellent second choice if you find the Yough too high. The water is acidic and polluted, but the action is pretty constant and varied. Many of the rapids in the upper part of the course are very long, but in most you can usually find sneak routes if you prefer, that avoid the big stuff. The lower course below Fort Hill becomes easier and interspaced with more flat water, but the scenery is good giving way to more settled farm land. Most of the rapids occur at wide places in the river and many are straight forward, open descents. A few more are like larger rock gardens, but not requiring too much maneuvering and there are only two or three potential trouble spots.

DIFFICULTIES: The rapids immediately after the easy opening rapids below the put in bridge is a rather sharp left hand turn. At the outside of the curve there is a large boulder always awash and creating a mean hydraulic downstream.

About 3 miles into the top run, the river appears to be dammed up by boulders. This is a complex drop and could be tricky to the inexperienced. Stay to the far left in doubt, but remember that it will still be a double drop. In very high water, a girl scout route exists on the far right. At any level, the more entertaining descent is through the center and requires a sharp right hand turn.

As you approach the second RR bridge, avoid the extreme left as there are some keeper sized hydraulics there in very high water. In low water, it is a sharp, dry drop.

No really difficult spots below Fort Hill unless you choose to make it so. About midway there is a nice rapids that turns sharply to the right against a fantastically beautiful waterfall entering the stream from the left. The river is divided by a large boulder at this point. An easy, but wavy run to the right, a very interesting fandango on the left!

GAUGE: The Markleton gauge is available via the National Weather Service in Pittsburgh. No good riverside gauge except by inspection at take out bridges (and this is reliable).

SHUTTLE: The take out is the bridge right below Harnedsville which is only 1 mile south of Confluence on Pa. Route 53. This road goes on out to U.S. 40 only a few miles away. To reach the put in, go north on Pa. 53 through Ursina and turn right. The river you cross is the Laurel Hill. In about 5 miles the first right takes you down to the midpoint for a short take out at Fort Hill. The next right (4 more miles) takes you to Markleton.

INDEX

Abram Creek, 6
Anthony Creek, 100
Armstrong Creek, 145
Back Creek, 33
Back Fork of Elk, 125
Big Sandy Creek, 66-68
Black Fork of Cheat, 57
Blackwater, 56
Bluestone, 132-34
Buckhannon, 73-75, 80
Buffalo Creek, 57
Cacapon, 27-29
Casselman, 159-60
Cheat
  Cheat Valley, 60
  Narrows, 60-62
  Canyon, 62-65
Cherry, 112
  North Fork, 110
  South Fork, 111
Coal, 146
Cranberry, 107-9
Decker's Creek, 88-89
Dry Fork of Cheat, 51-53
Dunkard Creek, 86
Elk, 126-28
Gandy Creek, 49
Gauley
  Upper, 116
  Above Curtin, 116-17
  Curtin to Reservoir, 117-19
  Below Summersville, 119-22
  Below Swiss, 123
Glady Fork of Cheat, 45
Greenbrier, 95-99
  Forks of, 95
Guyandotte, 148
Horseshoe Run, 59
Hughes, 86
Knapp Creek, 100
Laurel Creek, 110
Laurel Fork of Cheat, 46-47
Laurel Run, 67
Left Fork of Holly, 124
Little Cacapon, 34
Little Coal, 147
Little Kanawha, 90
Little Sandy, 67
Little Wheeling Creek, 86-87
Lost, 26
Lunice Creek, 34
Meadow, 113-15
Middle Fork, 71-72
Middle Island Creek, 86
Moorefield, 18-19
Muddy Creek, 58
New Creek, 34
New River
  Above Bluestone Dam, 135
  To Sandstone, 136-37
  To McCreery, 137-38
  To Thurmond, 138-39
  Gorge, 139-41
  Dries, 141-42
North River, 29, 33
Otter Creek, 38
Paint Creek, 149
Patterson Creek, 33-34
Piney Creek, 142
Potomac
  North Branch, 9-12
  North Fork, S. Branch, 14-17
  Main Stem, 32-33
  South Branch, 20-25
    Smokehole, 20-22
    Trough, 23-24
  South Fork, S. Branch, 18-19
Red Creek, 50
Right Fork of Holly, 124
Saltlick Creek, 57
Savage, 157-58
Second Creek, 101
Seneca Creek, 13
Shavers Fork of Cheat
  Spruce, 39
  McGee Run, 40
  High Falls, 41-42
  Bemis to Bowden, 42-44
  Bowden to Parsons, 44
Shenandoah, 30-31
Sleepy Creek, 34
Stony Creek, 101

Stony River, 7-8
Swago Creek, 101
Tearcoat Creek, 34
Thorn Creek, 34
Three Fork Creek, 84-85
Tug, 150
Tygart
  Above Elkins, 76
  Loop, 76-77
  Gorge, 77-79
  To Philippi, 80
  Arden Run, 80-82
  Valley Falls, 82-83
  Hammond to Colfax, 83
Wheeling Creek, 86-87
Whiteday Creek, 91
Williams, 105-6
Youghiogheny
  Upper, 152-53
  Middle, 153-54
  Loop and Stewarton, 154-56